The Complete Guide to
Growing and Using
Wheatgrass

**EVERYTHING YOU NEED TO KNOW
EXPLAINED SIMPLY
INCLUDING EASY-TO-MAKE RECIPES**

LORAINE R. DÉGRAFF

THE COMPLETE GUIDE TO GROWING AND USING WHEATGRASS: EVERYTHING YOU NEED TO KNOW EXPLAINED SIMPLY — INCLUDING EASY-TO-MAKE RECIPES

Copyright © 2011 Atlantic Publishing Group, Inc.
1405 SW 6th Avenue • Ocala, Florida 34471 • Phone 800-814-1132 • Fax 352-622-1875
Web site: www.atlantic-pub.com • E-mail: sales@atlantic-pub.com
SAN Number: 268-1250

Dégraff, Loraine R.
  The complete guide to growing and using wheatgrass : everything you need to know explained simply-- including easy-to-make recipes / by: Loraine R. Dégraff.
     p. cm.
  Includes bibliographical references and index.
  ISBN-13: 978-1-60138-339-6 (alk. paper)
  ISBN-10: 1-60138-339-8 (alk. paper)
  1. Wheatgrass (Wheat)--Therapeutic use. 2. Wheatgrass (Wheat) I. Title.
  RM666.W45.D44 2011
  641.5'63--dc22

                          2010045755

Printed in the United States

PROJECT MANAGER: Melissa Peterson • mpeterson@atlantic-pub.com
INTERIOR LAYOUT: Antoinette D'Amore • addesign@videotron.ca
PROOFREADER: Crystal McKenna • crystalmckenna@me.com
COVER DESIGN: Meg Buchner • megadesn@mchsi.com0
BACK COVER DESIGN: Jackie Miller • millerjackiej@gmail.com

Printed on Recycled Paper

We recently lost our beloved pet "Bear," who was not only our best and dearest friend but also the "Vice President of Sunshine" here at Atlantic Publishing. He did not receive a salary but worked tirelessly 24 hours a day to please his parents. Bear was a rescue dog that turned around and showered myself, my wife, Sherri, his grandparents Jean, Bob, and Nancy, and every person and animal he met (maybe not rabbits) with friendship and love. He made a lot of people smile every day.

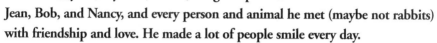

We wanted you to know that a portion of the profits of this book will be donated to The Humane Society of the United States. —*Douglas & Sherri Brown*

The human-animal bond is as old as human history. We cherish our animal companions for their unconditional affection and acceptance. We feel a thrill when we glimpse wild creatures in their natural habitat or in our own backyard.

Unfortunately, the human-animal bond has at times been weakened. Humans have exploited some animal species to the point of extinction.

The Humane Society of the United States makes a difference in the lives of animals here at home and worldwide. The HSUS is dedicated to creating a world where our relationship with animals is guided by compassion. We seek a truly humane society in which animals are respected for their intrinsic value, and where the human-animal bond is strong.

Want to help animals? We have plenty of suggestions. Adopt a pet from a local shelter, join The Humane Society and be a part of our work to help companion animals and wildlife. You will be funding our educational, legislative, investigative and outreach projects in the U.S. and across the globe.

Or perhaps you'd like to make a memorial donation in honor of a pet, friend or relative? You can through our Kindred Spirits program. And if you'd like to contribute in a more structured way, our Planned Giving Office has suggestions about estate planning, annuities, and even gifts of stock that avoid capital gains taxes.

Maybe you have land that you would like to preserve as a lasting habitat for wildlife. Our Wildlife Land Trust can help you. Perhaps the land you want to share is a backyard— that's enough. Our Urban Wildlife Sanctuary Program will show you how to create a habitat for your wild neighbors.

So you see, it's easy to help animals. And The HSUS is here to help.

THE HUMANE SOCIETY
OF THE UNITED STATES®

2100 L Street NW • Washington, DC 20037 • 202-452-1100
www.hsus.org

DEDICATION

"To God Be the Glory"

Much love and thanks to Mom and Dad. You taught me to appreciate life and the beauty of the earth for its ability to bring forth life. Thanks also to my husband and children for your love, support, patience, and help. Abundant hugs, Wylecia ... you are a real big sister. In spite of your own colossal project, you were right there with me through mine. Thanks and more thanks to the members of Arverne Church of God. Your prayers and encouragement were just what I needed. Thanks to you, also, Suraj. You helped me keep the garden growing, even when there was no time.

TABLE OF CONTENTS

Chapter 5: What to Know Before You Grow ..129

Chapter 10: Growing Wheatgrass for Profit **255**

Chapter 11: Moving Beyond Home..................**287**

INTRODUCTION

I attribute my love for growing to my father. Many Saturdays while growing up, we watched as he worked. I cannot say that I enjoyed gardening back then; there were too many bugs and that Carolina sun was definitely a scorcher. I would much rather have been inside in an air-conditioned room reading a good book. Saturday afternoon in the yard was not fun.

Today, I value time spent outdoors. I get great satisfaction from growing my own fruits and vegetables and cultivating my own flowers. Now it is my children who wonder what is so exciting about seeing the first tulip buds burst through the winter-hardened ground or why I must make multiple rounds of our yard each day to see what new thing is growing. And they definitely do not understand how I can keep company with the mosquitoes. Perhaps one day they too will discover how invigorating, yet relaxing, the gardening experience can be.

Although I enjoy planting things and watching them grow, I never gave much thought to growing grass — at least, not since I planted grass seed in my backyard and my long-awaited lawn began to sprout. Grass was for cutting. Grass was for watering and maintaining a beautiful lawn. Grass was for picnics and lounging. Grass was good for a number of things. But, for growing and eating?

When one of my husband's friends began to expound upon the benefits of sprouting, juicing, eating raw foods, and consuming wheatgrass, I thought, "Good for him." I was also interested in being healthy, eating well-balanced meals, and providing nutritious food for my family, but I had never considered consuming *grass*. The day that my husband decided that he too would begin the wheatgrass regimen, I again thought, "Good for him, but this has nothing to do with me." And it did not — until he wanted to try growing wheatgrass in our home. Well, who do you think got that job? You guessed it — yours truly. After all, I am the farmer; I had grown tomatoes, peppers, peas, and collards ... but *wheatgrass*?

I know a lot more about wheatgrass now than I knew then. I have even begun to consume it myself. If wheatgrass is as good as they say it is, I might as well take advantage of the fact that it is being juiced in my own home. If fact, I began to do my own research about the product. The contents of this book will elaborate on all aspects of this powerful super food. If you are interested in learning all about wheatgrass and how it can benefit you and your family, continue reading. Perhaps you have heard of its nutritional properties and would like to learn more. Those seeking natural treatments to health ailments might find this book especially beneficial. Individuals looking for a profitable business venture might also find solutions within these pages. This book will show you how to grow, use, and even sell wheatgrass. You will learn what wheatgrass can do for you and your body. The nutritional benefits are discussed in detail, including the vitamin content and how wheatgrass compares to other super foods. If you want help overcoming slothfulness, sluggishness, and maybe even sickness, continue reading. With the help of this book, you can expand your knowledge of wheatgrass and learn more about its benefits.

CHAPTER 1

What is Wheatgrass?

*"The humble grass is more than food for man and beast.
It hides its glory beneath a lowly aspect."*
~ The Essene Gospel of Peace

It is always best to start with the basics. The following is a simple explanation of what wheatgrass is — and what it is not:

> Wheat is a grain in the cereal grass family gramineae, and wheatgrass is the young blades of the common cereal wheat plant. It is often called "green blood" or "green gold" because of its high nutritional content. It grows outdoors as a perennial plant, but it is often cultivated indoors for therapeutic purposes. Wheatgrass has increased in popularity over the years, and today, it is a vital part of the green health movement.

There you have it. Wheatgrass is not a magical potion. It is not an overnight cure-all, and it is not a replacement for a nutritionally balanced diet. It is a live food that, when woven into a program of exercise and other life-giving foods, can help the body to rejuvenate and overcome sickness and disease.

At this point, it would be good to note the difference between wheatgrass and "wheat grass." Although many tend to use both spellings to mean the same thing, the latter spelling refers to a variety of cereal grasses such as oats, barley, and rye that are grown in open fields. In many cases, these grasses are grown for animal fodder, but in some cases, they are grown, dehydrated, and prepared for a number of wheat grass products or dietary supplements. Wheatgrass — as one word — generally refers to the wheat product that is cultivated indoors for therapeutic purposes.

Wheatgrass is a health food made from young wheat shoots. It is grown in the United States as well as in several countries worldwide. Once wheatgrass reaches an approximate height of seven inches, it is cut and squeezed to produce a highly nutritious liquid that can be consumed in small quantities in various forms. Wheatgrass can be freshly juiced or dried into a powder for human and animal consumption. It is available in many local, national, and online health food stores and can be purchased as fresh produce, frozen juice, powder, and tablets. Wheatgrass is mostly known for its health benefits and is a popular health and diet food in America. The tender grass is ready for harvest when it reaches its nutritional peak, also called the jointing stage. During this stage, the grain ovule has left the root and moved up into the shaft of the plant. The plant has now accumulated a large amount of energy, which will fuel a tremendous growth spurt in the plant. At this point, the plant is compressed and the potent energy is captured in the dark green liquid that is expressed called wheatgrass juice. This juice contains vitamins, minerals, enzymes, and amino acids. These energy producers bathe the cells of the body, refreshing them and helping them to perform effectively. The juice also helps purge toxins that can accumulate in the body's cells. These toxins are a hindrance to the performance of the cells. Wheatgrass is a nutritional green, along with alfalfa, chlorella algae, aloe vera leaf, barley, and kelp.

History of Grasses

The foundational food for most land-based life is grass. There are more than 9,000 edible grass seeds found in various parts of the world, and these seeds have been gathered and used as a primary food source for centuries. The cultivation of seeds became a driving force of survival for early civilizations. The dwindling supply of game for hunting and an increase in human populations prompted a systematic harvesting of the grains that grew in the wild. Cereal grasses — grasses that produce a starchy, edible grain — that were once gathered from the wild and consumed, were now cultivated on a regular basis and used to support the increasing population.

Grasses have always been nutritious. They can be found in cultures all around the world and in a number of forms. All cereal crops produce a grain that, when planted, produces grass. Grasses have long been a major source of human food, as well as food for domesticated and wild grazing animals. Societies, as well as individual groups of people, throughout history have valued grasses and touted their healing properties.

Origination of wheatgrass

Wheatgrass is one of several cereal grasses. In terms of nutritional value, it is similar in content to both barley and alfalfa. The nutritional value is dependent on where the grass is grown and at what stage it is harvested. In terms of taste, wheatgrass is generally sweeter than other cereal grasses.

Wheatgrass is the most popular of the cereal grasses because of its availability and health benefits. It originated with the cultivation of wheat, one of the most important agricultural crops in human history. Modern wheat originated in Southwest Asia and evolved from two forms of wild wheat — emmer and einkorn — used in Mesopotamian civilizations.

The ancient Egyptians are also affiliated with wheat and are noted for regarding the young wheat plant as a sacred item, treasuring the positive effect it had on their health and vitality. Many claim that King Nebuchadnezzar in the Old Testament's book of Daniel was restored to mental health after his seven-year grass diet. For centuries, farmers recognized the improvement of livestock when they fed on the young grasses of early spring. Based upon these observations, early 20th century scientists began to study grasses in an effort to disclose its nutritional mysteries and include it in animal feed.

Wheatgrass is the first blades of grass that develop from the plant after the wheat grain has germinated. It has been a source of study since the early 1900s.

Hungarian philosopher Edmond Bordeaux Szekely discovered and translated an ancient biblical manuscript that he found near the Dead Sea in the 1900s. This manuscript is said to have revealed a unique and healthy way of eating as taught by Jesus of Nazareth. Szekely published and began distributing his translation called *The Essene Gospel of Peace* in 1928 in an effort to share this supposedly "new" diet with those around him. "All grasses are good for man and wheatgrass is the perfect food for man," is a main theme of the Essene Book IV cited by many sources.

The following notable people were instrumental in the popularization of wheatgrass.

The work of Dr. Charles Schnabel

Wheatgrass consumption in the Western world began after a series of intensive research studies in agriculture conducted in Kansas in the early 1900s by agricultural chemist Dr. Charles Schnabel and his colleagues. Dr. Schnabel experimented with various feed mixtures in an attempt to increase chicken health and egg production during winter months. Initially, he found no differences in chicken health or egg production, but he did notice that hens sought out and consumed young cereal grasses when they were let out to feed. He then included dehydrated wheatgrass and oat grass in the feed and noticed that ailing hens recovered quickly, grew faster, and had an increase in fertility.

Dr. Schnabel continued his studies and enlisted the help of a few colleagues. These men identified wheatgrass as a valuable grass food when they discovered that animals could survive on wheatgrass alone when they could not survive solely on other healthy vegetables such as broccoli, alfalfa, or spinach. Further research revealed that wheatgrass contained a vast assortment of vitamins, minerals, antioxidants, enzymes, amino acids, and essential fatty acids. Their research also identified benefits unrelated to any of these recognized nutrients. These additional strengths, unique to grasses alone, are termed the "grass juice factor," which will be discussed in detail later in the chapter.

Dr. Schnabel was so fascinated with the discovery of the nutritional benefits of wheatgrass that he fed his family with dehydrated grass. Dr. Schnabel and his family included the grass in their diet for eleven years. He reported that his children remained healthy and did not even suffer from tooth decay.

Dr. Schnabel then began promoting his discovery to other chemists as well as to feed mills and the food industry by stating, "15 pounds of wheatgrass is equal in overall nutritional value to over 350 pounds of ordinary vegetables." Although this statement has since been proven inaccurate, American Dairies, Inc. and Quaker Oats accepted these promotions and invested millions of dollars to further research, develop, and produce nutritional products for humans and animals. By 1940, cans of Dr. Schnabel's powdered grass were selling in pharmacies throughout the United States and Canada. Wheatgrass and other cereal grass tablets were the nation's No. 1 mineral supplement of the decade.

Dr. Schnabel also patented the jointing theory. He emphasized that the timing of plant harvests must coincide with the nutritional peak of the plant and that the grass must be cut at the jointing stage to be most nutritionally beneficial.

The work of Ann Wigmore

Although Dr. Schnabel is attributed with the early consumption of wheatgrass in a dehydrated form, credit for popularizing the use of freshly squeezed wheatgrass juice goes, almost singly, to Ann Wigmore. As a child in Lithuania, Wigmore learned the power of natural healing from her grandmother, who helped heal wounded World War I soldiers with herbs, grasses, and plants. Wigmore was able to apply this valuable knowledge to her own life when she migrated to America and contracted gangrene in the 1940s after a terrible automobile accident. She successfully treated her own gangrenous legs with grass treatments, saving them from amputation.

She then began an in-depth study of natural healing and, with the assistance of her friend Dr. George H. Earp-Thomas, discovered 4,700 varieties of grass, all beneficial to humans. From a series of experiments conducted on her pets, she concluded that wheatgrass was a premium grass. In the 1950s when Wigmore contracted colitis and then colon cancer, she claimed she was able to cure herself through a diet of seeds, grains, raw greens, and wheatgrass. She was disease-free within a year and began researching the beneficial uses of grasses, focusing on the healing properties of wheatgrass. She discovered that the grass could be consumed easier by juicing and began to share her wheatgrass juice with a number of ailing friends and neighbors. In 1956, she established the Hippocrates Health Institute in Boston, adopting the principle of Hippocrates, the Greek father of modern medicine. According to her book, this philosophy surrounded the popular saying from Hippocrates, "The body heals itself. The physician is only nature's assistant."

Wigmore claimed that her wheatgrass diet could cure disease, and she treated countless individuals with serious health ailments. She believed cell toxemia, resulting from nutritional deficiency, to be the only disease in existence among Western man and that all degenerative ailments stemmed from this one malfunction. Basic deficiencies, according to Wigmore, came from cooked and over-processed food as well as the chemicals consumed when these foods were eaten. Fevers, swellings, and frequent colds were warnings of the onslaught of a more serious complication. If these warnings could be properly addressed when present, there would be no need for the body to develop any serious disease. Living by the principle "let food be your medicine," Wigmore taught individuals worldwide about the health benefits of grasses and a living food healing program.

How wheatgrass use has evolved

Dr. Charles Schnabel and Ann Wigmore were pioneers in the wheatgrass movement. They began a collection of scientific research that was duplicated and enhanced by a number of other physicians and scientists. Key milestones in wheatgrass development and evolution include:

- Japanese pharmacist Dr. Yoshihide Hagiwara confirmed wheatgrass to be of major therapeutic significance by analyzing edible greens and comparing their active medicinal ingredients. He established the *Hagiwara Institute of Health* in 1980, which is dedicated to supplying information on the medicinal properties of grasses.

- In the 1940s, Charles Kettering, researcher and former Chairman of the Board of General Motors, learned of the healing properties of plant chlorophyll and good health and donated large sums of money to support the escalating research done by medical doctors.

- New York internist Dr. F. Howard Westcott reported that obnoxious odors such as perspiration and bad breath were effectively neutralized when chlorophyll, the green pigment found in plants, was ingested in adequate quantities.

- Dr. Earp-Thomas of Bloomfield Laboratories in New Jersey discovered that adding wheatgrass to fluoridated water could change the chemical element fluorine into a harmless calcium-phosphate-fluoride compound. The fluoridation of public water has been a controversy since the 1940s. Opposers of fluoridated water have argued that fluoride in water can cause health problems in children and those of a weak constitution. Dr. Earp-Thomas also found that chemically contaminated fruits and vegetables were thoroughly cleansed when washed in wheatgrass water.

- A 1950 U.S. Army report revealed that guinea pigs exposed to lethal doses of radiation had a higher survival rate if they were fed a chlorophyll-rich diet. Wheatgrass, which has high chlorophyll content, was then used as an absorber of radiation from such devices as X-rays and televisions.

- Swiss scientist Dr. Max Bircher called chlorophyll "concentrated sun power" and attested that its stimulating properties were effective in increasing the function of the heart and other bodily organs.

Wheatgrass was identified for its ability to transfuse the body's organs through its many nutritive components, including chlorophyll.

- Dr. Chiu-nan Lai, of the University of Texas M.D. Anderson Cancer Center, reported that chlorophyll found in wheat-sprout extracts, which can be obtained from freshly cut wheatgrass, can reduce the metabolic activity of carcinogens, which are cancer-causing agents.

- Nobel Prize winner Dr. Otto Warburg observed that a lack of oxygen in the cells was a major cause of cancer and that chlorophyll, which is a major component of wheatgrass, could supply needed oxygen to the cells due to its high iron content.

Chlorophyll, the green substance in plants, absorbs sunlight into plants and converts it into energy. Chlorophyll works to nourish the cells and increases the function of body parts. Studies concerning chlorophyll date back to the 1700s to the chemist Joseph Priestley who observed, through his candle and mice experiments, that life was sustained in the presence of green plants. Additional chlorophyll studies were conducted in the 1800s by Zurich University medical graduate Dr. Max Bircher and several other physicians using the standard of double-blind studies required by the U.S. Food and Drug Administration (FDA). In a double-blind study, certain aspects of the experiment are withheld from all parties involved in the test to guard against a biased outcome. Dr. Bircher and his colleagues concluded that chlorophyll had significant healing properties and used it as a healing aid for several years. Subsequently, the use of chlorophyll as a healing aid rapidly declined with the modern development of steroid drugs and antibiotics.

Dr. Bircher and fellow researchers also noted the ability of wheatgrass to absorb concentrated nutrients from the soil, which made the plant a valuable food source. As grasses cover more of the earth's land surface than any other flowering plant family, wheatgrass and other grasses have added significantly to the world's food supply. Many species of grass have adapted to different climate conditions and soil types. Intermediate wheatgrass, introduced to the United States from Asia due to its beneficial properties, is one type of wheatgrass species that has adapted well to a different environment. Its extensive, deep roots are capable of absorbing nutrients from a wide land area. It outperformed other grass species as a pasture crop. In an act of self-preservation, intermediate wheatgrass and other grasses developed their "jointing" characteristics. As the blades began to mature, they would divide at the joint. Large amounts of nutrients and enzymes are stored in the young blades in the early growth stages. If these young blades are left intact, the plant will mature and produce seeds. If the blades are pulled off or bitten by grazing animals, they will grow again. Emphasis was placed on the increased nutritional level of the plant at the jointing stage, causing further research to take place that demonstrated the dynamic potency of wheatgrass and other grass foods. This research was conducted by George Kohler and colleagues in the 1930s. The work that was begun by Schnabel and Wigmore has left its mark in history, as many health-conscious individuals today embrace the beneficial properties of the potent plant. Currently, a number of healing centers use wheatgrass as a major part of their healing plan. Classes and seminars throughout the world teach the benefits of consuming wheatgrass and raw, living foods.

Using Wheatgrass

Wheatgrass is a complete food, meaning that it provides a balanced proportion of every vitamin, mineral, enzyme, and amino acid that the body needs for physical and mental health. The uses of wheatgrass have been tested extensively in the United States for the past 60 years, and wheatgrass has been claimed to be used successfully in the following ways:

- Wheatgrass juice has been used to eliminate scars in the lungs formed from inhaling acid gasses. The chlorophyll increases hemoglobin production, minimizing the effect of carbon monoxide. Dr. Benjamin Gruskin, former director of experimental pathology and oncology at Temple University School of Medicine, experimented with chlorophyll as an antiseptic in the 1940s. He found that chlorophyll not only stopped infections and eliminated bleeding in wounds, but it also sped up the healing of wounds and reduced the scarring of tissues.

- Wheatgrass juice is an effective internal body cleanser and has been used to protect the body from air and water pollution. It does this by strengthening body cells and detoxifying the blood and major body organs.

- Dr. Yoshihide Hagiwara and other Japanese scientists discovered that certain amino acids and enzymes in young cereal grasses were effective in deactivating cancer-causing pollutants and eliminating toxins from the body.

- Ann Wigmore and other wheatgrass users suggest using wheatgrass to help eliminate dandruff and clean excess sebum (an oily substance secreted by the skin) from the scalp. Wigmore also recommended wheatgrass for preventing and correcting pre-mature graying.

- In his book *Survival into the 21st Century*, holistic health practitioner Viktoras Kulvinskas advocates the use of wheatgrass juice to effectively relieve toothaches and help prevent tooth decay. Dentist Homer Judkin of the Paris Hospital in Paris, Illinois, treated the gums of his patients with chlorophyll and reported the elimination of gum disorders. Because of its chlorophyll content, wheatgrass can be used as a mouthwash. Dr. F. Howard Wescott, a New York City internist, reported chlorophyll to be effective in eliminating offensive breath and body odors when taken internally.

- According to holistic nutritionist Dr. Bernard Jensen, wheatgrass is a superior blood builder. He mentions several cases in his book *Chlorophyll Magic From Living Plant Life* where he raised the blood count of patients by having them soak in a chlorophyll bath. From these results, he determined chlorophyll-enriched wheatgrass to be an effective help for anemia.

- Wheatgrass can be used as a beauty treatment for the skin. Radiant skin results from good blood circulation as well as exercise and diet. Chlorophyll baths and drinking wheatgrass can enhance the appearance of the skin. This beauty treatment can be attributed to the work of Dr. Bernard Jensen.

- Wheatgrass helps the body to combat aging. Research performed by Dr. Peter Rothschild at Smith-Kline Bio-Science in Honolulu revealed wheatgrass and other young grasses to be an excellent source of superoxide dismutase (SOD), which is a powerful anti-aging enzyme.

- Wheatgrass energizes the sex hormones. San Diego biologist Dr. Yasuo Hotta scientifically confirmed that P4D1, a compound found in young cereal grasses, is able to stimulate the production and repair of DNA of human sperm cells.

- The chlorophyll in wheatgrass helps protect the body from radiation from X-rays and security metal detection devices. Body cells and tissues continuously exposed to radiation can lead to serious health conditions. Studies concerning radiation and vegetable matter began in the 1930s. Although beta-carotene, also found in wheatgrass, was also thought to be an active ingredient in vegetables for eliminating radiation, studies in the 1960s conducted by Doris Calloway and colleagues attributed this radioactive property to the grass juice factor.

- Wheatgrass has been used as a vitamin supplement. As early as the 1930s, young cereal grasses have been recognized as a complete food. They contain all of the nutrients the body needs for survival — all known vitamins, minerals, proteins, enzymes, antioxidants, and fatty acids. In 1939, dehydrated wheatgrass was accepted as a natural vitamin food by the American Medical Association. Wheatgrass has been used as a disinfectant and water purifier by Dr. Earp Thomas and others.

Health use

There are many claims of health benefits from consuming wheatgrass, some of which are unproven scientifically. Ann Wigmore used wheatgrass and other raw greens to treat her own case of ulcerative colitis, which is an inflammation of the large intestine and rectum. A 2002 double-blind scientific study, published in the *Scandinavian Journal of Gastroenterology*, found that wheatgrass can, indeed, reduce the symptoms of ulcerative colitis. In addition to treating ulcers, it is believed that wheatgrass can treat constipation and diarrhea as well as other gastrointestinal issues. Chlorophyll has been linked to a strengthened immune system and used to detoxify blood. Based on the work of Bernard Jenson, many holistic health practitioners believe that wheatgrass and other cereal grasses can increase red blood cell count, neutralize toxins and carcinogens, and repair cells. Because of this belief, wheatgrass is often used to aid in the treatment of both AIDS and cancer. The following are additional claims of the health benefits of wheatgrass:

- German scientist Ehrenfried Pfeiffer reported dehydrated wheatgrass to have a protein composition of 47.7 percent, which is three times as much protein concentration as beef.

- According to Dr. Earp Thomas and Dr. Bernard Jensen, when combined with an organically grown living food diet, wheatgrass juice can increase white blood cell counts. The body needs white blood cells to fight off infection.

- Because of the results of hair mineral analyses of guests at the Hippocrates Health Institute in Boston, Ann Wigmore concluded that wheatgrass juice can be successfully used to remove toxic metals from the body.

- As wheatgrass is a good source of calcium, it is helpful in strengthening the teeth. According to Dr. Homer Judkin of the Paris Hospital in Illinois, wheatgrass is also helpful for eliminating toxins from the gums due to its chlorophyll content.

- According to Ann Wigmore, wheatgrass can disinfect the body, eliminating bacteria and viruses. It can also be used as a douche for vaginal infections.

- According to Dr. Benjamin Gruskin, wheatgrass can alleviate sore throats and heal mouth sores.

- According to Ann Wigmore, wheatgrass juice implants used after an enema are great for detoxifying and healing the colon walls and cleaning all internal organs.

- Dr. Arthur Robinson, co-founder of the Linus Pauling Institute at Oregon State University, concurred that wheatgrass juice helps blood circulation and, thus, helps to stabilize blood pressure.

- Wheatgrass increases red blood cells, helping to eliminate anemia. Research for this claim was conducted in 1913 when Dr. Richard Willstatter noticed the similarity between chlorophyll and hemoglobin. In 1933, Dr. Arthur Patek of Harvard Medical School reported positive results when anemia-deficient patients were given chlorophyll along with their iron treatments. He concluded that the chlorophyll worked along with the iron to bring faster and more effective results to the patients.

The nutrient profile of wheatgrass juice can be found in the following table. Daily recommended intake (DRI) of the various nutrients is based on a 2,000-calorie diet.

Wheatgrass juice	1 fluid oz.	100 grams	DRI
Calories	5.95 cal	21.0 cal	2,000 cal
Carbohydrates	0.567 g	2.0 g	300 g
Chlorophyll	11.96 mg	42.2 mg	n/a
Dietary Fiber	< 28.35 mg	< 0.1 g	25 g
Fat	0.017 g	0.06 g	25 g
Moisture	26.93 g	95 g	2 liters
Protein	0.55 g	7.49 g	50 g

Wheatgrass juice	1 fluid oz.	100 grams	DRI
Vitamins			
Biotin	3 mcg		30 mcg
Choline	26.20 mg	92.4 mg	550 mg
Folic Acid / Folacin	8.22 mcg	29 mcg	400 mcg*
Vitamin A	121 IU	427 IU	3,000 IU
Vitamin B1 (Thiamine)	22.68 mcg	0.08 mg	1,4 mg
Vitamin B2 (Riboflavin)	36.86 mcg	0.13 mg	1,6 mg
Vitamin B3 (Niacinamide)	31.19 mcg	0.11 mg	18 mg
Vitamin B5 (Pantothenic Acid)	1.701 mg	6.0 mg	6.0 mg
Vitamin B6 (Pyridoxine HCl)	56.7 mcg	0.2 mg	2.0 mg
Vitamin C (Ascorbic Acid)	1.0 mg	3.65 mg	75 mg
Vitamin E	880 mcg	15.2 IU	10 mg
Minerals			
Calcium	7.2 mg	24.2 mg	1,000 mg
Iron	0.66 mg	0.61 mg	18 mg
Magnesium	6.80 mg	24 mg	350 mg
Phosphorus	21.31 mg	75.2 mg	1,000 mg
Potassium	42.0 mg	147 mg	3,500 mg
Selenium	< 0.284	< 1.0 ppm	55 mcg
Sodium	2.92 mg	10.3 mg	2,400 mg
Zinc	0.094 mg	0.33 mg	15 mg
Amino Acids			
Alanine	86.75 mg	0.295 g	Unknown
Aspartic Acid	74.0 mg	0.453 g	Unknown
Cysteine	8.84 mg	0.134 g	Unknown
Isoleucine	16.0 mg	0.287 g	12 mg
L-Arginine	38.0 mg	0.425 g	Unknown
L-Lysine	10.49 mg	0.245 g	32 mg
Leucine	30.0 mg	0.507 g	26 mg

Wheatgrass juice	1 fluid oz.	100 grams	DRI
Methionine	26.54 mg	0.116 g	13 mg
Phenylalanine	29.31 mg	0.350 g	16 mg
Proline	67.19 mg	0.674 g	Unknown
Threonine	79.38 mg	0.254 g	10 mg
Tyrosine	18.0 mg	0.674 g	Unknown
Valine	12.72 mg	0.361 g	14 mg

The nutrient content of wheatgrass varies according to its source, which includes timing of harvest, method of growing, and method of production. Laboratory reports also vary. This table is compiled from a variety of sources and should be considered an approximation. These values are not meant for diagnosis and are for informational purposes only. *Pregnant women should aim for 600 mcg of folic acid.

Growing Wheatgrass

Wheatgrass has adapted to a variety of growing conditions. Wheatgrass users can take advantage of the versatility of this grass and set up a wheatgrass garden in their home. Many users enjoy the growing process because it offers them the opportunity to control the entire process — from soaking the wheatberries to harvesting and juicing the tender blades of grass. Growing wheatgrass at home is also economical; one ounce of fresh wheatgrass juice can cost about $2 to $3 from your local juice bar, and this is assuming that you *have* a neighborhood juice bar. Driving out of your neighborhood every day to purchase a shot of wheatgrass juice can quickly become costly. Many wheatgrass drinkers save money and time by growing and juicing at home.

Although growing wheatgrass is not a complicated process, it can be somewhat tricky in the beginning. It is important that the wheatberries are sufficiently sprouted. Creating the proper sprouting environment and recognizing the appropriate time for sprouting is essential to the successful outcome of the process. Planting the wheatberries correctly can also take some practice. Overlapping the berries can cause uneven blade growth and might even encourage mold growth. Knowing how to prepare the soil, how often to water, and how much light to give is also important. Too much water can drown the wheatberries and cause mold growth. Not enough light can hinder the chlorophyll from developing within the grass blades.

A good amount of wheatgrass is needed to make one ounce of juice, so growers must be prepared to produce a significant amount of wheatgrass for the project to be worthwhile. Six to eight ounces of juice can be generally obtained from each tray of grass, depending on the size of the tray. Many online and health food stores sell wheatgrass growing kits that include seed and soil. These kits range in price from about $15 to $100 or more, depending on what else is included in the kit. Some of the more expensive kits include a wheatgrass juicer. When growing wheatgrass for the first time, you might want to use one of these kits, as it makes the process a bit easier. When using a kit, you will not have to worry about mixing the soil or finding the right seed. For example, wheatberries for making flour are not the ones to use for sprouting, and you might not know this when first beginning to grow. As you continue, it will become more economical to purchase seed and soil separately and create your own "kit." Health food stores can supply you with seed, and soil can be purchased cheaply at your local gardening shop. *More about growing wheatgrass at home can be found in Chapters 5 and 6.*

Wheatgrass products

Because wheatgrass has so many beneficial properties, it has been incorporated into many products that are sold commercially. Wheatgrass tablets and powders are popular. It must be pointed out, however, that the preservation of the many enzymes in wheatgrass is paramount to getting maximum nutrition. Manufacturers looking to make a profit might not put forth the time and expense needed to use good drying techniques, thus producing an inferior product. Fresh is best. Optimal health benefits are achieved by juicing at home from live wheatgrass. If you must purchase tablets and powders, however, be certain to purchase from a reputable distributor. Considerable nutritional benefits can be gained from frozen or freeze-dried wheatgrass juice, and for the purpose of travel, freeze-dried powder can provide a good solution.

Manufacturers in the health and beauty industry have tried to capture the essence of wheatgrass in their hair and skin products. Emulsified and non-emulsified cosmetics use wheatgrass as a main ingredient, distinguishing them from ordinary cosmetics. Emulsified cosmetics include ingredients that do not blend with each other, while non-emulsified cosmetics include blending ingredients. Cosmetics and other beauty products with wheatgrass additives are being offered as a natural tonic for skin and hair rejuvenation and regeneration. Manufacturers are capitalizing on a "miracle product with no side effects" theme to market these products. While all of these products can offer some benefits, the best way to take advantage of the rejuvenating properties of wheatgrass is to consume freshly squeezed juice. It is also possible to make your own rejuvenating products. *This will be discussed in Chapter 7.*

The food industry is also taking part in the wheatgrass phenomenon. Functional food products using wheatgrass include flours, pastas, breads, cakes, powdered beverages, jellies, fruit bars, yogurts, candies, and even ice cream. Many of these foods can be purchased at your local health food store. Of course, as always, it is best to make your own to ensure the wheatgrass is as fresh as possible. *You can find recipes for creating your own wheatgrass products in Chapter 7.*

The Mysteries of Wheatgrass

Wheatgrass is not a drug or a magic potion, but there is a certain enigma surrounding it. As with life in general, it has properties that are easy to understand as well as those that are a little more difficult to understand. Wheatgrass, like most plants, undergoes photosynthesis. Photosynthesis is the process of turning light energy into chemical energy, and it is not a simple process. Even so, a variety of scientists — beginning with Flemish chemist Jan Baptista van Helmont in the 1600s — have worked to bring us the understanding that we have of photosynthesis today.

Research chemists, beginning with Dr. Charles Schnabel, have worked to unravel another plant mystery. Dr. Schnabel and colleagues identified all the known biologically active substances found in wheatgrass and claimed it to be a perfectly balanced source of nutrition; it contained the perfect assortment of all the vitamins, minerals, enzymes, and amino acids needed for human health. Continued studies, conducted by George O. Kohler and a team of other Wisconsin scientists, revealed that guinea pigs tremendously prospered when grass powder was added to their feed. These men concluded that the "growth stimulating factor" of the grass could not be categorized with any of the other identified nutritional substances known to be in wheatgrass. Hence, they referred to this unidentified property as the "Grass Juice Factor." Explaining the Grass Juice Factor still presents a challenge to researchers today.

Although the exact nature of the Grass Juice Factor remains a mystery, some of its properties are said to be linked to the precise timing of the wheatgrass sprout growth. This timing is called the jointing theory and was identified and patented by Dr. Charles Schnabel and later confirmed by George Kohler in the 1930s. Early in its growth cycle, and for only a short time, wheatgrass develops an abundance of nutrients and stores it in its blades. This development coincides with the time the young wheatgrass blade divides into two blades to begin the formation of the wheat seed. At this precise moment, a heightened concentration of vitamins, minerals, amino acids, and the mysterious Grass Juice Factor exists. This is the ideal time to harvest the wheatgrass, as the nutritional content can be beneficial to the body. Kohler did significant research on the Grass Juice Factor and discovered that it was a unique element of grasses and had a major effect on normal and reproductive growth in animals. His findings were confirmed by Dr. Mott Cannon and others at the University of California at Berkeley in 1939.

The healing power of wheatgrass

Ann Wigmore's belief in the healing power of grasses was based on the Biblical account of Nebuchadnezzar, King of Babylon. He spent seven years of his life insane, and during this time, he lived as a wild animal, eating the grass of the fields. Because he recovered from his insanity, Wigmore attributed his healing to the grasses he consumed. The common observation that cats and dogs chew grass when not well strengthened Wigmore's belief in the healing power of grasses.

Since Wigmore's observations in the 1940s, wheatgrass has been intensively studied on a healing level by several scientists. Researchers, testing a variety of disorders, have reported success with wheatgrass treatments and, in most cases, improvement was recorded with no side effects. Wheatgrass, in itself, is not a cure for illness, but it can help establish an atmosphere that is conducive for healing to take place. It does this by strengthening and rejuvenating body cells and body parts. According to the philosophy of the Greek physician Hippocrates, the human body was designed to heal itself, and wheatgrass is a powerful tool that can aid in the self-healing process.

How wheatgrass works

Humans and animals depend on plants for survival, and plants use the carbon dioxide from humans and animals to sustain themselves. Green plants are the only life endowed with the ability to create their own food. During the photosynthetic process, they remove carbon dioxide from the air and convert it into energy. This energy can be used immediately or stored in the form of sugar for future use. Chlorophyll helps with this energy conversion by absorbing the sunlight that is also needed for the conversion. Chlorophyll is a pigment in plants that gives them their rich, green color. Grass is one of the richest sources of chlorophyll.

The concentrated chlorophyll in wheatgrass translates to enzymes, which help control the metabolic processes of the body, giving the body the ability to grow and reproduce, maintain its structures, and respond to its environment. The enzymes in wheatgrass juice help the body to cleanse itself by detoxifying the liver and bloodstream. Detoxifying means getting rid of toxins or pollutants from the body. Once detoxification takes place, the strengthened cells can better fight disease, and new, disease-free cells can form. According to Wigmore's belief, these new cells will replace the old, diseased cells, and the body will experience a period of rejuvenation that will lead to healing.

Chlorophyll is often referred to as the "blood" of the plant because its chemical makeup resembles that of the hemoglobin of human blood. The most apparent difference is that the fundamental element in hemoglobin is iron, while in chlorophyll it is magnesium. This chemical similarity between chlorophyll and hemoglobin was explored in 1913 by Dr. Willstatter. During the following 20 years, considerable research was done by Dr. Arthur Patek and others to determine if the two substances were mutually convertible in the body. What was derived from the comparison was the understanding that once wheatgrass is consumed, the chlorophyll is rapidly assimilated into the bloodstream. Although iron and magnesium were not found to be interchangeable, the magnesium molecule was found to enhance the production of globin — a blood protein — in the body. Thus, it is not difficult to understand how a "green blood transfusion" can energize the body and give new life in the same way that blood transfusions commonly performed in medical settings today can.

The other side of the story

There are usually two sides to every story, and wheatgrass is no exception. Although several studies reveal similarities between chlorophyll and hemoglobin, wheatgrass critics point out that the best purifier the body will ever need is the liver, followed by the lungs and kidneys. These organs were designed to work together to cleanse and detoxify the body through their natural functions. Although critics insist most wheatgrass findings are unsubstantiated and, therefore, false, this book presents testimonials and case studies from wheatgrass users who attest to the healing properties of the grass. It is up to you to determine for yourself how you view wheatgrass.

CHAPTER 2

The Composition of Wheatgrass

"Nature heals; the physician is only nature's assistant."

~ Hippocrates

A lthough wheatgrass is grown from grain, once sprouted, it completely transforms into a vegetable. Sprouts are formed when seeds begin to grow into vegetables. Because wheatgrass is harvested while still a sprout and not a grain, it is compatible even for individuals with gluten allergies. There are more than 3,800 nutrients identified in food groups — and wheatgrass is esteemed because of the balance of nutrients it possesses. This nutrient balance makes wheatgrass a complete food. We will now take a look at the composition of this versatile food and how its nutrients can benefit the body.

Fiber

Since the 1970s, scientists have realized the importance of fiber in the daily diet as a means of disease prevention and health maintenance. Insoluble fiber — fiber that is not water soluble — is recognized for its ability to restore and maintain bowel regularity. It can also be an important source of food energy.

High-fat, low-fiber diets, which are generally maintained by individuals of Western industrialized countries, seem to greatly contribute to widespread illnesses such as coronary heart diseases and cancer. According to a 2008 report from *Circulation*, the journal of the American Heart Association, "The typical Western diet — fried foods, salty snacks, and meat — accounts for about 30 percent of heart attack risks across the world." The typical American diet provides only about 12 grams of the recommended daily intake of 20 to 35 grams of fiber. Most dietary fiber comes from fruit and vegetables, dried peas, beans, and other legumes and grains. The outer layer of the grain contains the most fiber, and unfortunately, this layer is removed during the refining process. Five grams of dehydrated wheatgrass contains about 2 grams of insoluble vegetable fiber, which is helpful for cleansing the digestive tract and promoting good colon health. Beans, fruit, and dark, leafy vegetables are examples of other foods that contain fiber.

Protein

The human body is composed of about 60 percent water, and of the remaining 40 percent, protein accounts for the greatest percentage. Protein, made up of amino acids, is a part of every cell, muscle, tissue, and bone. Protein builds the body and is important for all body functions. It strengthens the immune system and helps the body to prevent and overcome diseases. It provides the enzymes needed for digestion and metabolism. It helps with the production of healthy hair and skin. Proteins can be complete, and derived from animal foods such as chicken and fish, or incomplete, and derived from beans and peas. Incomplete protein can be made complete when paired with plant foods such as grains, seeds, nuts, and vegetables. There are about 25 grams of protein per 100 grams of wheatgrass powder. This compares to 2.86 grams of protein in 100 grams of spinach and 2.98 grams for every 100 grams of broccoli. Appropriate amounts of wheatgrass can provide the body with about 25 percent of the daily recommended amount of protein.

Vitamins

Vitamins are organic molecules that play various roles within the body, mainly working as cofactors for enzymatic reactions. Because they cannot be created by the body, vitamins must be supplied by an outside source. According to the FDA, there are currently 13 vitamins essential for preventing nutrient deficiency and maintaining good health. Other nutrients, such as choline (a nutrient in the B vitamin family), have also been identified as beneficial to human health but whose dietary allowance has not yet been established. As there are possibly more unknown vitamins, researchers and health practitioners recommend eating a variety of foods to gain optimal nutrition.

Vitamins alone cannot cure a disease. They cannot sustain life or restore potency. They benefit the body through their ability to make the carbohydrates, fats, and proteins in the food available for use as energy. Although vitamins can be purchased as supplements through pharmaceutical companies, the most beneficial vitamins for our bodies are the ones found in high-quality foods. Wheatgrass contains each of the essential vitamins that the body needs, and these vitamins can be easily absorbed into the system through the consumption of wheatgrass juice. The following vitamins are found naturally in wheatgrass.

Vitamin A – beta-carotene

Beta-carotene is an antioxidant compound in plants that protects DNA from cancer-causing substances. It is also a processor of vitamin A. Vitamin A is an important nutrient for vision, cell division and differentiation, bone growth, and reproduction. Vitamin A also benefits the urinary and intestinal tracts, the respiratory system, and the surface linings of the eyes. One hundred grams of whole leaf dehydrated wheatgrass contain 513 IUs of beta-carotene compared to the 178 IUs of beta-carotene in chicken.

Vitamin B group

The B group vitamins are known as a complex family because they occur together in natural sources and work best when they are together. These vitamins are water soluble — able to be dissolved in water or another solvent — and can be easily eliminated from the body or destroyed through meal preparation or food storage. Because they are not stored in the body, they must be added daily. The B group vitamins convert carbohydrates, help metabolize protein and fats, and help the nervous system to function properly. All eight of the B group vitamins can be found in wheatgrass. The following are the individual vitamins within the B group:

Vitamin B1 – thiamine

Vitamin B1, or thiamine, encourages growth and strengthens the heart muscle. It also helps with the conversion of carbohydrates into glucose, providing energy. It aids digestion, helping to overcome constipation, and helps with the manufacturing of urine. B1 works to assist the functioning of the nervous system. It helps the body to maintain its normal blood cell count, promotes healthy skin, and improves circulation. It helps reduce fatigue, increase stamina, and increase mental alertness. Wheatgrass contains 0.350 mg of thiamine per 100 grams of dehydrated grass.

Vitamin B2 – riboflavin

Vitamin B2, or riboflavin, is important for proper cell growth and general body health. It works with the enzymes that are responsible for the metabolism of proteins, fats, and carbohydrates. It helps with digestion, keeps the nervous system functioning, and maintains body tissues. B2 helps prevent constipation and promotes healthy nails, hair, and skin. B2 is important for cell respiration and red blood cell formation. It is also important for good eye health and helps the body to use oxygen properly. Wheatgrass has a high riboflavin content — 16.9 mg per 100 grams compared to the 0.119 mg in broccoli and 0.189 mg in spinach. Because riboflavin is light sensitive, it is best to keep wheatgrass products in opaque containers, and you should drink wheatgrass immediately upon juicing to benefit from the riboflavin content.

Vitamin B3 – niacin

Vitamin B3, or niacin, plays a key role in cell restoration and also works to release energy and metabolize carbohydrates, proteins, and fats. It helps with the maintenance of the gastrointestinal tract and is important for healthy skin, as it promotes good blood circulation. B3 is also important for the synthesis of estrogen, testosterone, progesterone, and insulin. It also helps the nervous system. There is 8.35 mg of niacin per 100 grams of wheatgrass compared to the 0.638 mg in broccoli and the 0.724 mg in spinach. The recommended daily allowance (RDA) of niacin is 14 mg for adult women and 16 mg for adult men.

Vitamin B5 – pantothenic acid

Vitamin B5, or pantothenic acid, works with the enzymes responsible for the metabolism of proteins, fat, and carbohydrates and the synthesis of fatty acids and amino acids. It also helps with forming porphyrin, the pigment structure of hemoglobin. B5 helps produce the adrenal hormones and protects against toxins and physical and mental stress. It also helps the body ward off infection and decreases recovery time from illnesses. B5 helps with the development and maintenance of the central nervous system and protects against radiation and premature aging. There are 0.750 mg of pantothenic per 100 grams of wheatgrass compared to the 0.535 mg in broccoli and 0.065 mg in spinach. Consuming wheatgrass can aid blood circulation and help with sicknesses.

Vitamin B6 – pyridoxine

Vitamin B6, or pyridoxine, is needed for proper food assimilation as well as the metabolism of protein and fat. It is involved in the production of antibodies, which protect the body from bacterial diseases. It activates enzyme systems and aids in the proper function of the brain and nervous system. B6 prevents skin and nerve disorders and guards against high cholesterol levels, diabetes, and heart disease. B6 plays a key role in the reproductive process and is important for healthy pregnancies. Vitamin B6 regulates the balance between potassium and sodium and is needed for the production of magnesium. B6 also helps the body absorb vitamin

B12. Vitamin B6 is good for the treatment of hemorrhoids, convulsions, insomnia, diabetes, stress, pregnancy-induced morning sickness, and tooth decay. Although plants are not a major source of pyridoxine, dehydrated wheatgrass contains 1.4 mg per 100 grams of wheatgrass compared to the 0.159 grams in broccoli and 0.195 grams in spinach.

Biotin

Biotin, another member of the vitamin B complex, is needed for the metabolism of protein, fats, and carbohydrates. It is also needed to transfer carbon dioxide. Biotin is essential for the production of niacin (Vitamin B3), antibodies, digestive enzymes, fatty acids, and the maintenance of the immune system. It is helpful for the treatment of muscle pain and depression. It is helpful for good hair growth and prevents premature graying. It helps control color pigment distribution and maintains the skin and nervous system. One teaspoon of dehydrated wheatgrass, which is about 3.5 grams, contains 4 mcg (micrograms) of biotin.

Vitamin B9 – folic acid

Folic acid and folate are paired together. Folic acid (along with vitamin B12) helps with the manufacturing of nerve transmitters and the formation and division of all body cells. It produces RNA and DNA, which are important for establishing hereditary patterns, and helps with protein metabolism. Folic acid helps with the production of antibodies and is important for the hair and skin. Folic acid is essential for a healthy pregnancy and infancy. Folate helps produce and maintain body cells and helps protect against cancer. There are 29 mcg of folic acid per 100 grams of wheatgrass juice. Dehydrated wheatgrass contains 1,110 mcg of folate per 100 grams compared to the 71 mcg in broccoli and 194.4 mcg in spinach.

Exposing the B12 claim

Many reports claim that wheatgrass contains all of the B vitamins, including the important, but sometimes-difficult-to-obtain, vitamin B12. Vitamin B12 is an essential nutrient. It works with vitamin B6 and B9 to control homocysteine (an amino acid) levels in the blood. According to the American Heart Association, excessive amounts of homocysteine in the blood can increase the risk of stroke and coronary heart disease. Vitamin B12 also aids the central nervous system, improves memory, and helps with irritability. It helps the body to properly use carbohydrates, fats, and proteins. Additionally, it helps with the metabolism of folic acid, encourages growth, and increases the appetite in children. B12 is not actually synthesized within wheatgrass, however, as so many reports claim. Vitamin B12 cannot be produced by plants or animals. A bacterial microorganism living on the plant is what actually produces the water-soluble B12 vitamin. Most nutrient analyses report a one mcg or less reading for B12 in wheatgrass, but if the plants are washed prior to consumption, they might not contain B12 at all.

Vitamin B17 – laetrile/amygdalin

Laetrile is the trade name for a substance allegedly synthesized and patented by Dr. Ernest Krebs, Jr., a California biochemist, for treating "disorders of intestinal fermentation." Laetrile is chemically related to amygdalin, a water-soluble compound naturally found in whole foods, fruit seeds, beans, and grass. B17 has been claimed by Dr. Krebs and other proponents to nullify cancer cells while strengthening the immune system. This topic has brought about much debate in the United States and has not been approved as a cancer treatment by the FDA. Wheatgrass is a natural source of B17.

Choline – lecithin

Choline is not officially a B vitamin, but it is often placed in the category because of the role it performs in the body. Choline controls the build-up of fat and cholesterol, especially in the liver. It is an essential vitamin, responsible for the manufacturing of acetylcholine, an essential neurotransmitter in the nervous system. Wheatgrass juice contains 92.4 mg of choline per 100 grams of juice. It is a useful cleansing aid for the body.

Vitamin C

Vitamin C is an essential antioxidant that aids wound healing and strengthens the body's resistance to infection. Adequate intake can effectively lower the risk of developing various cancers by discharging free radicals before they destroy DNA in cells and initiate tumor growth. Dehydrated wheatgrass contains 214.5 mg of vitamin C per 100 grams of wheatgrass compared to the 93.2 mg in broccoli and 28.1 mg in spinach.

Vitamin E

There are eight different forms of vitamin E, each having its own specific function in the body. Alphatocopherol, the most active form, is highly present in wheatgrass. As an antioxidant, vitamin E effectively guards the cells from free radicals. Free radicals, by-products of metabolism, could be potentially damaging. Vitamin E also keeps vitamin A and essential fatty acids from oxidation. Oxidation is a chemical reaction that occurs when a substance interacts with oxygen. It can cause a loss of vitamins in food and the food to look and taste bad. Oxidation can also produce toxins that cause food poisoning. Vitamin E keeps body tissues intact. Dehydrated wheatgrass contains 9.1 mg of vitamin E per 100 grams compared to the 1.66 mg of broccoli and 1.89 mg of spinach.

Vitamin K

The body uses vitamin K to produce thrombin and liver proteins responsible for blood clotting. Vitamin K is also involved in the formation and repair of bone marrow. It is claimed that wheatgrass supplies the body with 60 percent of the RDA of vitamin K. If so, then wheatgrass treatment can be successfully applied to nosebleeds, hemorrhaging, and osteoporosis.

Minerals and Trace Minerals

Sixteen minerals, compounds found in the soil, have been identified by nutrition scientists as necessary for life. Minerals are essential for good health, playing a major role in several metabolic functions. Minerals needed in vast quantities, such as calcium and magnesium, are classified as macro minerals. Other minerals, only needed in small amounts, are classified as trace minerals. Minerals are needed to generate electrical impulses, transport nerve messages, and maintain the proper balance of fluids and body chemicals. Mineral supplements are not generally recommended due to the toxins that can accumulate if too many are consumed over long periods of time. The Expert Group of Vitamins and Minerals — an independent advisory group in the United Kingdom — was created in 1998 to determine the safety of long-term use of vitamin and mineral supplements sold under food law. In their 2003 report "Safe Upper Levels for Vitamins and Minerals," they recommended Safe Upper Levels (safe maximum dosage levels) for eight of the 34 substances assessed and issued usage guidance for 22 substances. In addition, herbal supplements are not regulated by the FDA, as are conventional medicines and foods. Therefore, it is important to use precaution when considering usage of these substances. A properly balanced diet can provide all of the essential minerals that the body needs. Many of the minerals found in wheatgrass are significant parts of enzymes, responsible for chemical reactions in the body. Wheatgrass also contains mineral salts that can be used to help guard the body of insufficiencies and keep the teeth and bones strong. The macro minerals and trace minerals in wheatgrass are as follows:

- **Boron:** The trace mineral boron plays an important role in brain activity, especially in cognitive function, hand-eye coordination, and memory enhancement. Clinical studies reveal that boron can significantly delay the onset of calcium deficiency and reduce or alleviate the symptoms of arthritis.

- **Calcium:** Calcium works in the body to aid enzyme activity. It helps with blood clotting, speeding the amount of time it takes to heal wounds, and it is important for muscle contraction. Calcium works with phosphorus to aid the prevention of osteoporosis. There are 321 mg of calcium per 100 grams of dehydrated wheatgrass compared to the 48 mg of broccoli and 99 mg of spinach.

- **Chromium:** Chromium can prevent diabetes, as it works with insulin in the metabolism of blood sugar. It also helps to stabilize blood pressure. Chromium in wheatgrass works to distribute protein to various parts of the body. There are about 210 mg of chromium per 100 grams of dehydrated wheatgrass.

- **Cobalt:** Cobalt is an essential mineral that helps the body to produce vitamin B12. Cobalt and vitamin B12 work together to build red blood cells, aiding in the repair of pernicious anemia and the myelin sheath — the membrane surrounding a nerve fiber. Pernicious anemia occurs when there is a decrease in red blood cells due to a lack of vitamin B12. One teaspoon of dehydrated wheatgrass (3.5 grams) contains about 1.7 mcg of cobalt.

- **Copper:** Copper helps with iron absorption, increasing energy levels in the body. Copper is also necessary for the assimilation of vitamin C and for converting iron into hemoglobin. There are about 0.375 mg of copper in 100 grams of dehydrated wheatgrass.

- **Iodine:** Iodine, connected with thyroid hormones, is important for healthy reproduction. Adequate amounts of iodine will help the body to burn fat, providing greater energy. Iodine is also important for healthy skin, hair, nails, and teeth. One dry teaspoon of wheatgrass contains about 8 mcg of iodine.

- **Iron:** Iron is essential for the metabolism of the B group vitamins. It aids growth and helps the body to resist infection. It also helps eliminate fatigue and is essential for the production of myoglobin, the red pigment in muscle and blood cells. Iron also has the important role of transporting oxygen through the blood to the various cells throughout the body. Copper, cobalt, manganese, and vitamin C are necessary for iron to metabolize in the body. One fluid ounce of wheatgrass contains about 0.1729 mg of iron.

- **Magnesium:** Magnesium aids in muscle contraction and the building of bone and is needed by the body for the transfer of nerve impulses. It is also essential for the conversion of stored blood sugar into energy, helping the body to better deal with emotional and physical stress. One fluid ounce of wheatgrass contains about 6.804 mg of magnesium.

- **Manganese:** Manganese helps with the building of bone and is needed to manufacture thyroxine, the main hormone of the thyroid gland. Manganese also aids muscle reflexes, improves memory, and reduces nervous irritability. One hundred dry grams of wheatgrass contains about 2.45 mg of manganese.

- **Molybdenum:** Molybdenum helps with the assimilation of iron. It also protects against cancers of the stomach and esophagus by detoxifying harmful chemicals in the body. Molybedum works with the metabolism of carbohydrates and fats and is effective in preventing tooth decay. One hundred dry grams of wheatgrass contains about 73 mcg of molybdenum.

- **Phosphorus:** Phosphorus works with the B group vitamins, helping the body to use energy from starches and fats. Phosphorus also helps to regulate the heart and allows the kidneys to function. Phosphorus is effective in reducing the pain associated with arthritis. One fluid ounce of wheatgrass contains about 21.3192 mg of phosphorus.

- **Potassium:** Potassium balances body acids and water and helps with the function of muscles and nerves. It works with sodium to regulate blood pressure and heartbeat. One fluid ounce of wheatgrass juice contains about 41.6745 mg of potassium.

- **Selenium:** Selenium works as an antioxidant enzyme in the body. It protects the cells from the negative effects of free radicals formed during the metabolism of oxygen. Dehydrated wheatgrass contains 2.5 mcg of selenium per 100 grams of wheatgrass. This compares to the 3 mcg of selenium in broccoli and the 1 mcg of selenium found in spinach.

- **Sodium:** Sodium is the major moderator of the body's water and mineral balance. It strengthens the heartbeat and helps with the functioning of all nerves and muscles. One fluid ounce of wheatgrass contains 2.9201 mg of sodium.

- **Sulfur:** Sulfur helps regulates oxygen, which is important for proper brain function. It also helps fight off bacterial infections and is essential for building collagen, protein, and certain amino acids. There are 445 mg of sulfur per 100 grams of dried wheatgrass.

- **Zinc:** Zinc helps the immune system to function properly. It exists in every cell and is essential for the healing of wounds. Zinc promotes the activity of enzymes and is also needed for the synthesis of DNA. One fluid ounce of wheatgrass contains about 0.0936 mg of zinc.

Amino Acids

Amino acids are essential for life and perform many roles in the process of metabolism. They are, essentially, the building blocks of protein and can be joined together to form a variety of proteins. Each protein is a distinct linear chain of amino acids. Amino acids are a part of the enzyme and hormonal system. Due to their vital role in biochemistry, amino acids are essential for proper nutrition.

Apart from water, protein is the most plentiful nutrient in the body, making up more than 50 percent of the body's dry cellular weight. The key function of protein is to build and maintain tissues in the body. Amino acids work together with enzymes to renew cells and produce blood, muscles, and organs. The eight essential amino acids are isoleucine, leucine, lysine, methionine, phenylalanine, threonine, tryptophan, and valine. Additionally, arginine and histidine are necessary for infants. The body actually needs 20 different amino acids, but it is able to produce the others from the essential eight. Amino acids must be obtained from food and play an important role in digestion and the assimilation of food. Amino acids help the body to build a strong immunity against disease and aid in the healing of wounds. Amino acids also help with liver function and regulate mental awareness. It is important for the body to have all eight essential amino acids for it to function optimally. Wheatgrass contains the eight essential amino acids as well as several others. There are 25 grams of protein per 100 grams of dehydrated wheatgrass compared to the 2.98 grams of protein in broccoli and the 2.86 grams of protein in spinach.

Antioxidants

Antioxidants are a collection of vitamins, minerals, amino acids, essential fatty acids, and enzymes. The body produces waste products during normal metabolism that have active atoms attached. These "free radicals" can create major problems in the body if left unchecked. Antioxidants work to offset the effects of free radicals by reducing cell mutations, artery damage, and other degenerative changes. Vitamin A, vitamin B1, vitamin C, and vitamin E are antioxidants found in wheatgrass. Other antioxidants in wheatgrass are described in the following sections.

Chlorophyll

Chlorophyll is a blood-cleansing agent. It also detoxifies and regenerates the liver. It can be used as an effective antibody and acts to strengthen the cells. Wheatgrass contains many active compounds of chlorophyll effective in blood cleansing by digesting toxins in blood cells.

Scientists have discovered chlorophyll to be an effective catalyst in the detoxification, deodorizing, and healing of wounds. Although it is strong enough to detox the wounds by acting as an antiseptic, or germ-killer, it is also gentle enough to stimulate the repair of damaged tissues. Chlorophyll reduces swelling and has been found effective in healing peptic ulcers. Chlorophyll deodorizes wounds by eliminating any odors associated with them. Chlorophyll also promotes bowel regularity.

In the 1950s, a variety of products were designed using chlorophyll as an active ingredient. Not only were food products produced, but items such as shoe liners, toilet paper, napkins, and chewing gum could also be purchased to benefit from chlorophyll.

In 1980, Dr. Chiu-Nan Lai, of the University of Texas Medical Center, discovered that extracts of wheatgrass and other green vegetables nullified the damaging effects of two carcinogens, methylcholanthrene and benzopyrene. He observed that the amount of protection increased with the amount of chlorophyll present in the vegetables.

Debunking the Myth

Contrary to the popular belief of the 1970s, wheatgrass does not contain 70 percent chlorophyll. This would be impossible as wheatgrass, like other living plants, contains 90 percent water. Wheatgrass is actually less than 1 percent chlorophyll. Within the 1 percent, however, exists more than 100 other nutrients, plant hormones, and growth factors. This puts wheatgrass, along with alfalfa and algae, among the greatest sources of chlorophyll on the earth.

Bioflavonoids

Bioflavonoids are a group of antioxidants found naturally in plants. These compounds work with other antioxidants to provide protection for the body. Several clinical studies have revealed the ability of bioflavonoids to protect the supply of vitamin C in the body. They are also noted for their anticarcinogenic, antimutagenic, and anti-aging properties. Wheatgrass is a good source of bioflavonoids and works to help strengthen blood vessels and tissues.

Linoleic acid

Conjugated linoleic acid (CLA) is a polyunsaturated fatty acid with close chemical make-up to linolenic acid. This antioxidant potentially possesses tremendous anticarcinogenic and anti-diabetic properties. It benefits the immune system and encourages lean muscle mass. There are 0.45 grams of linoleic acid per 100 grams of wheatgrass.

Lysine

Lysine, a genetically coded amino acid, is vital for good nutrition. Lysine is necessary for body growth and is helpful for balancing nitrogen in the body. It also helps with anti-aging. There are about 10.4 mg of lysine per fluid ounce of wheatgrass.

P4D1

P4D1 performs two important functions in the human body: It works to repair DNA molecules, creating the reproduction of disease-free cells, and it also strips the protein sheath off cancer cells so that white blood cells can attack and destroy them. Because of its P4D1 content, using wheatgrass can be helpful for inflammation reduction.

Peroxidase

Peroxidase is an antioxidant that detoxifies the body by eliminating hydrogen peroxide. Hydrogen peroxide is a natural by-product of oxygen metabolism. Peroxidase also provides protection for the aqueous membrane of cells. Adding wheatgrass to the diet helps boost the detoxifying effects of peroxidase.

Superoxide dismutase

Young grasses, such as wheatgrass, are an excellent source of the powerful antioxidant, superoxide dismutase (SOD). SOD presents a defense against the free radical damage of red blood cells and works to eliminate radiation damage in cells. SOD has been useful in the treatment of bladder inflammation and osteoarthritis (joint arthritis). It is also an anti-aging enzyme. Consuming wheatgrass juice will increase the blood levels of SOD, which is helpful for the treatment of arthritis and useful for cancer prevention. One gram of wheatgrass contains about 1,420 units of SOD.

Essential Fatty Acids

Essential fatty acids are fats or organic acids that the body needs but cannot produce itself. These fats are retrieved from the diet and perform as fuel for energy production. Essential fatty acids are needed to produce and repair cell membranes. They also support the immune system as well as the nervous system and reproductive and cardiovascular systems. Two essential fatty acids are found in wheatgrass. Linoleic acid performs as an antioxidant and was described in the previous section. Linolenic acid, the other fatty acid, is described in the following section.

Linolenic acid

Linolenic acid (ALA) is an omega-3 fatty acid, an essential fatty acid vital to human health. ALA is not produced physically, so it must be obtained from food sources. Once ALA is ingested, it is converted into DHA and EPA, two forms of omega-3 that are more readily assimilated by the body. These essential fatty acids exist in high concentrations in the brain and are essential for cognitive and behavioral function. Omega-3 fatty acids help reduce inflammation and swelling and are useful in the prevention of arthritis and heart disease. Wheatgrass juice is a natural source of omega-3, containing about 3.17 grams of linolenic acid per 100 grams of wheatgrass.

The Grass Juice Factor

The Grass Juice Factor is found in all cereal grasses. It has its own identity and cannot be grouped with any other nutrient. It has had powerful growth and fertility effects in experiments on animals through the years. Clinical and research evidence relayed by Dr. Chris Reynolds, of the University of Western Australia, and George Kohler has revealed the Grass Juice Factor to have a powerful effect on the body. It can stimulate growth, correct nutritional deficiencies, regenerate damaged skin, and prevent early death in plant-eating animals.

Wheatgrass: An Acquired Taste

The typical diet of today consists of an abundance of overcooked, over-seasoned, and over-processed foods. These foods also contain excessive amounts of sugars, corn syrup, or artificial sweeteners. We are not accustomed to eating cereal grasses, and for the most part, our taste buds do not find them palatable. Not many people actually care for the taste of grass. Wheatgrass, in particular, delivers a super-sweet taste that many individuals find quite odious.

Some avid wheatgrass users never get used to the taste of wheatgrass. Perhaps you fall into this category, or perhaps you enjoy the taste. If you want to consume wheatgrass and cannot seem to acquire a taste for it, you are not alone. The following are some suggestions for how to get the nutritious, but dreaded, dosage down:

- Guzzle it down with a nose clamp pinning your nostrils tightly shut.
- Wash it down with a few ounces of lemon juice.
- Suck on a lemon or tart candy immediately after consuming.
- Munch on a slice of apple or other favorite fruit after consuming.
- While drinking, meditate on how good it is for you.
- Hold your breath.
- Sip it slowly and allow the saliva to mix with the juice to dilute it. This is actually recommended by many wheatgrass growers for lightening the taste.
- Gulp it quickly.
- Have a quick drink of cold water immediately following.
- Start with a small amount and build your way up to a larger dose.
- Freeze the juice with a little lemon and have a wheatgrass ice pop.
- Mix it with other green vegetable juice to balance the flavor. Celery is a good match.
- Add a pinch of garlic powder or ginger powder to the dose to subdue the taste. Cayenne pepper also helps and is good for circulation.
- Have a bit of honey after consuming.
- Grow your own so you can experiment with the taste.

Ways to consume wheatgrass

Shot of wheatgrass with fruit to disguise the taste.

The best way to obtain the full nutritional benefits of wheatgrass, especially the live enzymes, is to juice it yourself and drink the juice within minutes of juicing. You can also purchase wheatgrass juice from an organic juice bar where they will juice the wheatgrass for you. Some people enjoy chewing the raw grass as opposed to juicing it. This is convenient and requires no equipment. Because only a small amount of the juice is being extracted per mouthful and is mixed with the saliva, the taste may not be as strong as drinking the fresh squeezed juice. It takes about eight mouthfuls of grass to accumulate two ounces of juice. As wheatgrass is a fibrous plant, chewing enough of the grass to significantly benefit the body can be a challenge.

For those who still find it difficult to down the potent juice, consuming wheatgrass tablets and capsules is a convenient alternative. Wheatgrass tablets and capsules are usually easy to swallow and do have some nutritional benefits; although, depending on the manufacturing process, the beneficial enzymes are not likely to remain completely intact. Remember to purchase tablets from a reputable source that sells the product as a nutritious whole food and not as an inclusion in a synthetic multi-vitamin. Inquire before you purchase. Tablets should be green vegetable nutrition that assimilates easily into the bloodstream. Also, check the package to determine which ingredients are contained in the product. Wheatgrass added in small amounts to ordinary vitamin tablets is of little value.

Another way to consume wheatgrass is to purchase wheatgrass powder. The popularity of grass cereal powders can be attributed to the work of Japanese physician Yoshihide Hagiwara. His goal in the 1900s was to make green foods easily accessible. Today, dried wheatgrass juice can be purchased as a concentrate. Often, the manufacturing process retains most of the nutrients and, depending on the method of extraction, some of the enzymes. There are a variety of ways to dehydrate wheatgrass such as spray-dried, drum-dried, or freeze-dried. There is also a difference between whole leaf powders (the grass was dried and then powdered) and juice powders (the grass is juiced and the juice is dried). The nutrient content of the powder depends on the drying method. A good quality powder has had minimum exposure to water, light, heat, and oxygen in the dehydration process. If enzyme presence (such as SOD) is included in the product, chances are the product has undergone a high-quality extraction. The powder can be mixed with water or other raw juices, such as celery or parsley juice, and conveniently consumed.

Frozen wheatgrass juice can also be purchased in local health food stores or online. Ask your juice retailer whether the juice has been treated with ultraviolet radiation or whether it was pasteurized. Both of these processes would be harmful to the nutrients. Otherwise, the nutrients are protected by the freezing. Frozen juice can be thawed and quickly consumed by adding water or orange juice. Keep in mind, however, that in order to gain the maximum benefit from wheatgrass, it is best to consume the liquid juice alone, freshly squeezed, and on an empty stomach. According to Wigmore and other wheatgrass experts, this is the best way for the nutrients of the wheatgrass to assimilate into the bloodstream.

Improving the flavor

Although wheatgrass has numerous good qualities, many would agree that taste is not one of them. The juice may be consumed in small doses, but many individuals still find the taste unappealing and the juice a chore to consume. If this is a problem for you, it might be helpful to add an additional flavor, such as lemon, to the wheatgrass to improve its taste. A touch of lemon — or other natural flavor — will not diminish the benefits of the grass.

There are a number of nutritional drink companies that offer wheatgrass as a main ingredient in their line of smoothies. As the taste of wheatgrass juice can be overpowering, you might have an easier time ingesting the wheatgrass if you cannot see it, smell it, or taste it.

You can also add the wheatgrass to a homemade fruit smoothie. Blend your favorite fruit with plain yogurt, wheatgrass juice, and a few ice cubes. You can also combat the sweetness of the wheatgrass juice by adding other juices to the dosage. Celery juice makes a good addition, as the sodium in the celery will balance the sweetness of the wheatgrass. Garlic can also be grated and added to the juice. If you do not care for celery or garlic, add your favorite fruit juice. Combining wheatgrass with other drinks, especially fruit-filled smoothies, can retard the assimilation of the grass nutrients into the bloodstream. This may diminish the benefits of the nutrients. Some would argue that it is better to take wheatgrass disguised than not to take it at all. If you are taking wheatgrass for therapeutic purposes, however, it is best to consume the wheatgrass by itself.

Other taste concerns

The taste of wheatgrass can be affected by a variety of factors. Different soil conditions can alter the taste of the grass. Location can also be a factor, as can the time of harvest. The following are some conditions that could potentially affect the taste:

- The taste of wheatgrass is often most unbearable when the grass is grown indoors. Sometimes indoor-grown grass breeds mold, and the mold affects the flavor of the wheatgrass. Wheatgrass with mold can taste bitter. *Wheatgrass and mold will be discussed further in Chapter 5.*

- The roots of indoor trays have limited space and the narrow blades provide less surface for photosynthesis to take place. This can account for the concentrated sweet taste of the indoor-grown tray grass. Wheatgrass grown hydroponically (without soil) or outdoors has a milder taste. *Chapter 5 will discuss hydroponic growing. Chapters 5 and 6 will discuss growing outdoors.*

- Different soil types have different nutrients. Wheatgrass grown in acidic soil can have a sharper taste than that grown in alkaline soil.

- The time of the harvest can affect the taste of the wheatgrass. After the jointing stage, the wheatgrass begins to mature and the nutrients transfer from the grass blades to the developing seed. If the wheatgrass is harvested after it begins to mature, it might taste bitter. The time to harvest the wheatgrass is right at the jointing stage, when the second blade grows out of the shaft. The entire tray should be cut at the same time. Harvested wheatgrass can be stored in the refrigerator for up to one week without losing its taste or value. If you are purchasing a tray of wheatgrass from a health-food store and the blades are yellow or not green, chances are the grass has been sitting in the store too long. The taste of this grass will be bitter.

- If you have purchased a shot of wheatgrass from a local juice bar and the juice tastes bitter, the grass may have been harvested too late. Wheatgrass juice should not taste old or bitter. It should have a fresh, sweet taste.

A word to the wise

A myriad claims exist on the health food front about wheatgrass and its amazing benefits. There are also several claims that wheatgrass has no side effects. This claim seems a bit ironic, because so many complain of headaches and dizziness when they consume wheatgrass juice. There have been cases of yeast infection flair-ups, possibly relating to the concentrated simple sugars in the wheatgrass juice. Some wheatgrass users have attributed cases of hives to wheatgrass consumption, as well. Some advocates claim these ailments are the result of toxins being expelled from the body, while others say it is a reaction to mold growth on the plant. For every claim about wheatgrass and its powerful benefits, there seems to be a complaint about how nauseating it is. It is also claimed that wheatgrass has no gluten (nutritional protein found in some cereal grains) and, thus, should have no negative effects on individuals with wheat allergies. But, if you have any allergies at all, you should consult with your physician before consuming the product.'

Manufacturers of dietary supplements, such as wheatgrass, are not required to prove their safety or effectiveness to the FDA as long as they do not claim that the product can prevent or cure a specific disease. According to the American Cancer Society, such supplements could have inaccurate nutritional labels or contain contaminants unbeknownst to the consumer. Consumers should proceed with caution when trying wheatgrass or any other dietary supplement as a health enhancer.

Dosages

Wheatgrass is a balanced food and its nutrients cannot be separated. Therefore, wheatgrass is not toxic at any dosage. As a potent detoxifier, however, it can cause a slight physical reaction, such as headache or nausea, in some individuals. Nausea might also be caused by the high sugar content of the grass. Therefore, wheatgrass should not be consumed in great quantities initially. If drinking cereal grasses is new to you, you should begin by consuming a small amount and build up to a larger quantity over time. As the grass could have a cleansing reaction on the body (loose bowels), it is best to make a gentle start.

Individuals new to the world of wheatgrass drinking should start by consuming one to two tablespoons a day. After a week, one ounce of juice per day can be consumed. After two weeks, this dosage can be increased to two ounces per day. You should aim to consume two one-ounce servings per day, with each taken at different times during the day. A typical dosage of wheatgrass is about 3.5 grams of wheatgrass powder (one teaspoon) or a one-ounce shot of wheatgrass juice.

This dosage can be safely consumed by all adults, no matter their weight or blood type. Children can also benefit from drinking wheatgrass and can begin as early as six months depending on their eating level, according to Pam Nees, program director of Optimum Health Institute (**www .optimumhealth.org**). Wheatgrass juice given to children should be mixed with water or fruit juices. Breastfed babies can also benefit from wheatgrass through their mother's consumption. *More about wheatgrass and children can be found in Chapter 8. Those interested in wheatgrass consumption during pregnancy can find information in Chapter 3.* Remember to consult with an appropriate health professional if you wish to try wheatgrass but have specific physical conditions.

Two shots of organic wheatgrass.

Ideally, wheatgrass juice should be consumed on an empty stomach and digested for 20 to 30 minutes before eating to give the nutrients a chance to assimilate into the bloodstream and begin working. Consuming it on an empty stomach will also prevent the wheatgrass from clashing with undigested foods. Feelings of nausea, however, can be assuaged by sipping a fruit juice — preferably raw — immediately after consuming the wheatgrass juice.

For most people, one to two ounces of wheatgrass per day is sufficient for maintaining good health. Individuals taking wheatgrass to treat a disease will often ingest larger doses. Four to eight ounces or more can be taken orally or as a wheatgrass implant. An implant refers to several ounces of fresh wheatgrass juice inserted and retained in the rectum for a period of time. *This is done in conjunction with colon cleansing and will be discussed further in Chapter 3.*

When consuming wheatgrass regularly, your body will eventually adjust to the properties and you will be able to consume it without feelings of nausea or light-headedness. As with any herb or supplement, taking wheatgrass continuously, day after day, without a break, can diminish its effectiveness as a healing agent. Be certain to abstain from ingesting for a day or two every few days if you are consuming wheatgrass on a long-term basis.

CASE STUDY: WHEATGRASS CONTROVERSY — "GRASS IS FOR COWS"

Stephen Barrett, M.D., board member
National Council Against
Health Fraud (NCAHF)
www.ncahf.org

Wheatgrass Therapy

The notion that wheatgrass can benefit serious disease sufferers was conceived by Ann Wigmore, a Boston-area resident. Wigmore (1909-1994) was born in Lithuania and raised by her grandmother who, according to Wigmore, gave her an unwavering confidence in the healing power of nature. Wigmore believed in astrology and described herself (a Pisces) as a dreamer who saw life from the spiritual viewpoint to the neglect of the physical. Wigmore's theory on the healing power of grasses was predicated upon the biblical story of Babylonian king Nebuchadnezzar who spent seven insane years living like a wild animal eating the grass of the fields. Because he recovered, Wigmore presumed that the grasses had cured his insanity.

Wigmore wrote at least 15 books and established the Hippocrates Health Institute in 1963, which later was renamed the Ann Wigmore Institute (AWI). Wigmore claimed to have a doctor of divinity (DD) from the College of Divine Metaphysics in Indianapolis. She also listed a doctorate of philosophy (Ph.D.) and a doctor of naturopathy (ND) degree at different times, none of which appear to have been from accredited schools. Among other things, Wigmore also promoted "natural hygiene," spiritual healing, zone therapy, hydrotherapy, acupuncture, color therapy, and spot therapy. A number of "living foods" groups around the world espouse Wigmore's teachings.

The fact that grass-eating animals are not spared from cancer, despite their large intake of fresh chlorophyll, seems to have been lost on Wigmore. In fact, chlorophyll cannot "detoxify the body" because it is not absorbed. Although it is conceivable that enzymes present in rectally administered wheatgrass juice could have chemical activity, there is no evidence that this is beneficial. In fact, when challenged legally, Wigmore backed away from healing claims stating that she merely had an "educational program" to teach people how to "cleanse" their bodies and make vegetable juices, as she also offered for sale a variety of juicers and other "health" paraphernalia. In 1988, the Massachusetts Attorney General sued Wigmore for claiming that her "energy enzyme soup" could cure AIDS. Suffolk County Judge Robert A. Mulligan ruled that Wigmore's views on how to combat AIDS were protected by the First Amendment, but he ordered her to stop representing herself as a physician or person licensed in any way to treat disease. This was not the first time Wigmore had run afoul of the law. In 1982, the Massachusetts Attorney General sued Wigmore for claiming that her program could reduce or eliminate the need for insulin in diabetics and could obviate the need for routine immunization in children. She abandoned those claims after losing in court.

Answers to Questions about Wheatgrass Therapy

Question: What is responsible for the reported "rush" that users report?

NCAHF: There is no pharmacological reason why a user should experience a "rush." Possible explanations include the placebo effect (i.e., enthusiasm for the therapy) and route of administration (i.e., rectal applications may produce a "goosing" effect).

Question: Why do people report that they are better following use of wheatgrass therapy?

NCAHF: Because there is no scientific evidence that the therapy is effective, such reports could either be due to:

- Natural changes in the symptoms people experience

- The placebo effect mentioned above

- Wishful thinking on the part of the desperate

- Lying by people who have a financial interest

- Something else that the patient is doing — especially if her or she is using psychoactive drugs, such as herbal uppers or downers

Question: Is wheatgrass therapy intrinsically dangerous?

NCAHF: Not in the wheatgrass itself, but attendant risks include:

- It can result in perforation of the bowel during enema tube insertion. This can introduce infectious agents into the bloodstream.

- It is possible that "organically grown" wheatgrass plants could become contaminated by soil constituents.

Question: Does NCAHF oppose the use of wheatgrass therapy? If so, why?

NCAHF: NCAHF opposes the use of all false or unproven remedies. This is because:

- We object to cheating people for money.

- It can divert patients from more responsible care.

- It can create false hope that eventually leads to greater despair.

- It exposes patients to charlatans and cranks who traditionally foster dependency relationships that permit further exploitation.

NCAHF representatives are sympathetic toward desperate sufferers of disease. We never blame the victims of quackery. We understand that people who are frightened will try anything that offers promise with little perceived risk. We regret having to be cast in the role of "doing away with Santa Claus" when it comes to fad remedies. However, NCAHF's dedication to providing reliable information on health and disease makes it impossible for us to do other than to tell the truth as we perceive it at the time. Furthermore ... grass is for cows.

© 1998, National Council Against Health Fraud.

Portions of this article are reprinted courtesy of the National Council Against Health Fraud.

The full article can be read at the NCAHF website: **www.ncahf.org/articles/s-z/wheatgrass.html.**

CHAPTER 3

Wheatgrass and Your Health

*"Every human being is the author
of his own health or disease."*

~ Buddha

All plants are living organisms of the kingdom plantae, and they exist in every culture of the world. Of the 350,000 species estimated to be in existence, about 287,655 species have been identified. The existence of plants is essential for the existence of human and animal life. Plants provide oxygen, food, clothing, shelter, and in some cases, medicinal properties. Plants can be placed in several classifications. Trees, shrubs, and grasses make up a large group of plants with a variety of species in each. There are about 10,000 species of grasses worldwide. Although all grasses and plants contribute to the enhancement of the environment, researchers and scientists in the 1940s highlighted the usefulness of wheatgrass, in particular, for the enhancement of human health.

The Role of Wheatgrass in the Green Health Movement

The Green Revolution refers to the research and development of better farming techniques and increased food production for developing countries in the mid 1900s. It began with the transformation of agriculture in the 1940s and is largely attributed to the life work of Norman Borlaug, an American agronomist — an expert in the sciences of soil management and crop production. In what would become a major catalyst for the movement, the Mexican government created an agricultural research station to develop different types of wheat for feeding the rapidly growing population of the country. It was during the time of the Green Revolution that Ann Wigmore began promoting the health philosophy of the Greek physician, Hippocrates, which purports that the body will heal itself if given the right conditions. Wigmore compared this health movement to the ongoing Green Revolution and termed it the "New Green Revolution." As she wrote in *The Wheatgrass Book*, Wigmore felt that the emphasis of a revolution should be "on the part of people everywhere, on working with nature to prevent illness before it takes hold." She did this herself through her research and practice of using wheatgrass and other raw, green foods to promote good health.

Today, populations continue to expand and the world continues to revolutionize. Scientists and manufacturers have developed various synthetic drugs, multi-vitamins, energy drinks, and food supplements. The versatile wheat plant, however, has remained a constant. "Wheat is the king of all grain foods," states grass expert Dr. Earp-Thomas in Wigmore's book *Why Suffer?* It is a world food staple and continues to be used in a variety of forms. Wigmore encouraged using the full power of wheat in the form of wheatgrass. Wheatgrass has played an important role in human health in the past and is part of the green health movement of today. Many claim wheatgrass to be among the best natural resources of vitamins, minerals, amino acids, and enzymes. Users claim that this simple plant can rejuvenate your system and help you care for your body.

Wheatgrass: Nature's Medicine

At times, our lives become extremely busy. It is difficult to remember to consume five servings of vegetables every day. Sometimes, even if we do remember, it is just as much of a challenge to actually do so.

Although national nutritional guidelines recommend choosing a variety of food sources to meet nutritional standards, according to Wigmore and other cereal grass supporters, one powerful supplement can enhance good body nutrition. They claim that wheatgrass is that single supplement, and the excitement and discussion about wheatgrass in the health world has helped it secure that position. It is used as a nutritional supplement, an energy booster, a blood cleanser, and a natural healing aid. Supporters of wheatgrass believe that using wheatgrass in conjunction with a diet high in quality foods is all that is needed to maintain good body nutrition.

Chlorophyll: the working agent in wheatgrass

Chlorophyll became the highlight of the 1940s as an important and effective drug. In a report prepared by Dr. Benjamin Gruskin of Temple University and published by the *American Journal of Surgery* (1940), an estimated 1,200 patients mentioned in the report were treated with chlorophyll. The ailments ranged from ulcers and skin and gum problems to deep internal infections.

Since that time, a number of researchers have successfully treated ailments with chlorophyll extracts. Despite these events of the 1940s, chlorophyll did not evolve with modern medicine. Though scientists did attempt to create a chlorophyll tablet, it was synthetic and did not work like the original chlorophyll extracts. Its use also resulted in side effects such as nausea and anemia. For all medicinal purposes, this tablet was abandoned and health ailments were treated with more conventional drugs.

Today, chlorophyll, in the form of wheatgrass, can once again take its place in the medical world. Through the work of Wigmore and others, chlorophyll has made a comeback. A large body of information, reports, and success stories attest to the rising power of chlorophyll in wheatgrass as nature's medicine.

Unleashing the power of the grain

The versatile wheat grain was the staff of life and the staple of many diets in the Western world during the Middle Ages. The dried grain was gathered from the wild and provided optimal nourishment as a basic food. It was ground into flour, made into flat cakes and breads, and cooked into porridges. It sustained people in years past as a nourishing grain, and it continues to sustain people today as a healing herb. When the grain is dried, it provides high nutrition as a basic food, containing vitamins, minerals, carbohydrates, and protein. The healing power, however, is released when the dried grain begins to germinate. Germination takes place when a plant emerges from a seed and begins to grow.

Germinated wheat sprouts are an economical and effective tonic to improve general health. The seeds become living food the moment germination takes place. Valuable enzymes are activated at this point. Once eaten, these enzymes become catalysts that perform a variety of functions in the body.

As humans, we need oxygen to survive. Our cells also need oxygen to survive. The oxygen-rich chlorophyll in wheatgrass delivers nutrients to the body's tissue through the blood and helps dispose of bodily wastes. High oxygen levels of chlorophyll in wheatgrass attest to wheatgrass benefits. Many accounts have reported the cleansing detoxifying power of the oxygen-rich wheatgrass. Other components working with chlorophyll help contribute to the healing benefits. Wheatgrass, with its multiple components, offers a number of therapeutic benefits.

Wheatgrass versus conventional medicine

Wheatgrass has been used to treat a number of ailments from cuts and bruises and mouth, eye, and nose infections to hemorrhoids and bronchitis. Some have even claimed that wheatgrass healed their cancer and other deadly diseases, though this is not supported by medical evidence. It is doubtful, however, that wheatgrass will be evaluated and approved as a valuable medicine by the FDA — mainly because it is not a drug. Natural products and herbal supplements are considered dietary supplements and are not regulated under the same set of rules as conventional medicines. There is also the challenge of establishing enough scientific data to prove the value and safety of wheatgrass. Such research is costly and time-consuming and often not supported for natural products.

Many physicians, however, are accepting the positive benefits of alternative medicines — including wheatgrass — and using them in integrative therapy programs along with conventional medicines. While modern medicine depends on chemistry and surgery to correct physical health conditions, wheatgrass therapy aims to rejuvenate the body by nourishing the cells to a state where healing can occur. Physicians are discovering that this physical rejuvenation can have a tremendous effect on the mind and soul as well, promoting overall well-being.

Origin of conventional medicine

Modern medicine did not originate in the laboratory. Early written documents record the use of poultices and herbs as healing aids. Many conventional medicines are actually synthetic replicas of botanical substances. It was Hippocrates, in 400 B.C., who prescribed the leaves and bark of the willow tree for the relief of pain and fever. The antibiotic penicillin is derived from mold. Hippocrates did not believe in the use of drugs for healing, but he did believe that the body could heal itself through natural means. The scientific basis for medicine was formed shortly after by the Greek philosopher Aristotle, who studied medicine from childhood. Aristotle's observations were based on the biology of humans and animals. Later, another Greek physician, Pedanius Dioscorides, began working with medicinal plants and drugs from animal and mineral sources. Aelius Galenus, a Roman physician, also began studying the human body and made several medical observations based on his studies.

Medicine in the Middle Ages, the period of time between the 5th century and 15th century, focused on combining multiple ingredients for use in treating a variety of ailments. The Arabs made major contributions during this time period through their recordings of crude drug preparations. In the 1600s, the Apothecaries of London was formed and prepared and sold medicines; this lead to the importing of medicinal drugs. In the 1800s, the Philadelphia

College of Pharmacy, the first association of pharmacists, was formed. The development of drugs continued with a greater focus on standardization and chemistry, which continued through to the 21st century.

Though pharmaceutical companies dominate the medical scene today, alternative medicine is not a new or emerging theory. Modern medicine originated in nature and only began to be produced in the laboratory during the 19th century with the emergence of the modern drug industry.

Health care expenses are climbing with conventional practices

In a comprehensive study published by *Life Extension Magazine*, conventional medicine is reported by the Nutrition Institute of America as the No. 1 cause of death (783,936 people per year) in the United States, followed by heart disease and then cancer. The institute came to this conclusion based on the findings of a group of researchers headed by health and nutrition expert Dr. Gary Null. According to the researchers' report "Death by Medicine," "Something is wrong when regulatory agencies pretend that vitamins are dangerous, yet ignore published statistics showing that government-sanctioned medicine is the real hazard." The causes of injuries and death through conventional medicine practices include the following:

- Latrogenic injuries, which are injuries resulting from medical treatment or advice and include error in diagnosis
- Drug iatrogenesis, which are adverse effects of prescription drugs, including errors in dosage
- Drug company errors in drug compositions and/or instructions
- Unnecessary surgical procedures, X-rays, and hospitalization, including caesarean sections and screening for breast cancer
- Bedsores
- Malnutrition in nursing homes
- Drug pollution in our water supply

Through his paper, "Error in Medicine" published in the *Journal of the American Medical Association* (1994), Dr. Lucian Leape, professor of health policy at Harvard University, hoped to encourage medical practitioners to face these issues and deal with them in an effective manner, but injuries and deaths continued to happen. Meanwhile, U.S. health care expenditures continue to climb. Advocates of natural medicine propose that instead of spending more money in an attempt to correct such issues with conventional drugs and other medical technology, a more effective plan for controlling disease would include the following:

- Examining stress and how it negatively affects the immune system and other body systems
- Correcting the excessive intake of calories and insufficiency of exercise
- Addressing the problem of the continual consumption of highly processed foods grown in nutritionally depleted soils
- Better addressing the issue of environmental toxins

Applying wheatgrass instead of over-the-counter drugs

Over-the-counter (OTC) drugs have become a major part of the American health care system, with products ranging from acne treatments and cough suppressants to weight control systems. OTC drugs are medicines that can be purchased by the consumer without a prescription. In many recent incidences, some of these drugs, although deemed "safe" by the FDA, have been surfacing with some very "unsafe" features. Children's liquid Tylenol was recalled in early 2010 because bacteria had contaminated the raw materials, according to an April 2010 report from the FDA. There were also reports of metal particles found in the product. Many other cough medicines and suppressants contain drugs such as dextromethorphan (DXM), which has hospitalized babies and enticed drug abuse by teenagers. Other products also contain potentially hazardous chemicals and contaminants. According to Wigmore and other natural health advocates, wheatgrass is a safer solution to addressing common body ailments. Wheatgrass has been known to address the same health ailments that consumers have been looking for relief from in OTC drugs. Wheatgrass has reportedly treated the common cold, headaches, fever, acne, and weight problems without harmful side effects.

Wheatgrass and science

Once again, the advice provided on these pages is for educational purposes only. Scientific research has yet to study wheatgrass and its medicinal properties in depth. You should not use this information to diagnose or treat a health problem or disease without consulting the advice of a medical physician or holistic practitioner. Please consult your physician as well if you have a condition and wish to change your diet to include raw foods and wheatgrass juice as a healing aid.

Health Uses of Wheatgrass

There is nothing new about wheatgrass and healing. These two words have been linked together since the days of the pharaohs in ancient Egypt. Wheatgrass was highly esteemed as a medicinal plant. Since that time, many have explored the healing benefits of wheatgrass.

Cancer prevention

There are more than 100 types of cancers that can develop in the body, and they all begin with the uncontrolled division of abnormal cells. These cells can quickly spread and invade other tissues, causing chaos and destruction in the body's organs. According to the National Center for Health Statistics' 2006 report, cancer ranks second as the leading cause of death in the United States with a mortality rate of about 23 percent. Lung cancer is the most fatal cancer in both men and women, followed by prostate and colon cancer in men and breast and colon cancer in women.

Clinical studies have revealed the importance of a strong immune system for the prevention of the development of cancer. In fact, the stronger the immune system, the less likely the body is to develop cancer. Although regular exercise, stress reduction, and adequate rest are known to strengthening the immune system, they cannot effectively improve the system if a vibrant, nutritionally balanced diet is not in place.

The human body must deal with a multitude of factors in its daily performance. One of its greatest challenges when fighting disease is eradicating free radicals that are formed during the natural process of metabolism. Free radicals are unbalanced molecules that can damage healthy cells by altering them and causing them to malfunction. Damage from free radicals is believed to be the chief cause of cancer development. The greatest weapon the body has against free radicals is antioxidants. These antioxidants confront the dangerous oxidation effects of free radicals and attempt to balance their electric charge. According to the Centers for Disease Control and Prevention (CDC), a diet that is high in antioxidants can decrease the risk of developing various forms of cancer and heart disease. Although a series of 1990s studies by the National Cancer Institute (NCI) have questioned the value of beta-carotene (vitamin A) as a cancer preventative, antioxidants such as vitamins E and C are highly recommended for the diet. Many wheat products, especially wheat germ oil taken from the germ of the wheat kernel, are high in vitamin E. Vitamin C and E can be found in broccoli, oranges, sunflower seeds, and — of course — wheatgrass.

Dr. Chiu-nan Lai of the University of Texas Cancer Center determined through the administration of the Ames Bacterial Mutagenicity Test — a test for determining whether a chemical is mutagenic and potentially cancer-causing — that chlorophyll, an active ingredient in wheat sprout extracts, nullified the metabolic activity of a number of carcinogens, or cancer-causing agents. Along with chlorophyll, the many other antioxidants in wheatgrass can significantly strengthen the immune system, enabling it to effectively ward off the development of cancer. Wheatgrass is noted as a natural prophylactic (preventive measure) in a 1992 antimutagenic study conducted by a team of Warsaw scientists. In this study, wheatgrass extract was shown to significantly reduce cell mutation in cancerous rats. Antimutagenic refers to an agent that hinders mutations or changes to a cell's DNA structure.

Cancer treatment

Just as a strong immune system is of utmost importance in the prevention of cancer, it is also essential for ridding the body of unwanted cancer cells. The results of several experiments are largely inconclusive, leading researchers to continue their investigations into the potential benefits of antioxidants. Recently, however, the relationship between nutrition and cancer has been recognized in a greater way by organizations such as the CDC and the

NCI. An unhealthy diet consisting of processed, high-fat, high-sodium, and low-fiber foods is believed to contribute to the increasing number of cancer cases in the United States. Cells thrive on oxygen. An unhealthy diet can weigh down the entire body, congest organs, and starve cells of needed oxygen. On the other hand, a nutritionally balanced diet, consisting of foods containing high levels of vitamins D and E and plenty of enzymes and antioxidants, can cleanse the system. Such a diet, according to the CDC, opens passageways for the clear transport of oxygen, considerably lowering the risk of a carcinoma, or malignant tumor.

Wheatgrass has been used in the prevention and treatment of a variety of cancers, including prostate cancer. There is no conclusive evidence, but many physicians and cancer patients attest to these treatments based on the positive experiences that they have had. Dr. Mahnaz Badamchian of the George Washington University Medical Center demonstrated how barley grass extract directly hindered the malignant growth of three different human prostate cancer cells. The extract also inhibited human breast and melanoma (skin) cancer cells in vivo (tests conducted within a cell or an organism) as well as in vitro (tests done in a controlled environment outside of the organism, such as a test tube). Human prostate and melanoma cancers were later grafted, or surgically transplanted, onto mice, and these mice later developed cancerous tumors. The tumors were significantly reduced by treatments of barley extract. Barley, a cereal grass, has similar properties to wheatgrass. Because some health practitioners suggest that wheatgrass might be helpful in the treatment of prostate cancer, it might be safe to conclude that cereal grasses have anti-cancer properties. It can be beneficial, therefore, to include wheatgrass in your prostate cancer remedies. The following are other examples of wheatgrass and cancer research:

- American biochemist and researcher Dr. Ernst Krebs, Jr., pointed out the anti-cancer benefits of vitamin B17 (laetrile) found in wheatgrass and other whole foods. In a few studies, laetrile has demonstrated the ability to selectively destroy mutant cells in the body.

- In 1984, Dr. Arthur Robinson of the Oregon Institute of Science and Medicine reported in the *Hippocrates Newsletter* that a living foods diet, including wheatgrass, decreased the effect of cancerous wounds in mice by about 75 percent.

- In 2001, a double-blind test conducted by the U.S. National Institutes of Health studied 180 individuals in Quidong, China. These individuals were treated with a daily one-ounce dose of wheatgrass and experienced an increase in the induction period (time for contracting a disease after exposure to infecting agent) from 20 to 40 years. The province of Quidong experiences the highest rate of liver cancer in the world.

- In a 2002 study of ulcerative colitis patients, those consuming three ounces of wheatgrass juice daily for one month, along with standard medical care, reported a decrease in pain, diarrhea, and rectal bleeding. Ulcerative colitis is an inflammatory bowel disease that can lead to cancer if left untreated.

- In 2005, a rye extract, similar in makeup to wheatgrass, was demonstrated to strongly inhibit cancer growth by 55 percent to 89 percent in five different cancer cell lines using as little as 0.1 percent of the extract.

- Dr. Virginia Livingston-Wheeler determined that abscisic acid (related to vitamin A) was an effective treatment for cancer and used it as a prime supplement in cancer treatments. Abscisic acid is a plant hormone found in wheatgrass.

- In a two-year study of organ cancer patients in Netaji Subhash Chandra Bose Cancer Research Institute in India, wheatgrass juice was concluded to be an effective natural alternative for blood transfusions after iron levels in the blood increased as well as the performance status (time period between transfusions) in patients tested.

- In a 1999 issue of *Harvard Health Letter*, researchers emphasized the first line of defense in the prevention of cancer is a consumption of more deep-green pigmented foods.

- Studies at the CDC in Atlanta, Georgia, reveal that individuals eating a high-fiber, low-fat diet can decrease their chance of developing colon and rectal cancer by 10 percent, and when adding five servings of greens to this diet, risk is decreased by 40 percent. Studies also showed that a diet devoid of these greens increased the risk of developing breast and skin cancer by 25 percent.

In studies conducted as early as Dr. Charles Schnabel's work, the production of the growth hormones in laboratory animals was stimulated by cereal grasses. It is strongly suspected that human growth hormones work in a similar fashion. Hormones are chemical substances produced in the body to regulate the activity of cells or organs. Growth hormones stimulate the production of growth factors (natural substances that promote cell growth), such as the insulin growth factor (IGF). These growth hormones affect the development of each cell in the body. IGF must remain balanced to decrease the risk of developing cancer. These hormones, also responsible for growth in children, can lead to the regeneration of damaged tissues and organs throughout life. Multiple studies have revealed an increased risk of cancer with an increase in IGF. Observations have also revealed that the nutritive properties in cereal grasses can stimulate the production of hormones and inhibit the growth of many cancer cells.

Although many have reported successful treatment of cancer through the consumption of wheatgrass and other cereal grasses, this book does not intend to use these observances as a claim that wheatgrass cures cancer. It simply wishes to emphasize how wheatgrass works within the body, supplying it with all the necessary nutrients it needs to effectively deal with sickness and disease and, eventually, heal itself. Individuals, such as Eydie Mae Hunsberger, former guest of the Hippocrates Health Institute, have attested to such in her book *How I Conquered Cancer Naturally*. According to the American Cancer Society, however, there exist no clinical trials in scientific literature to support such claims.

Chemotherapy

According to Australian physician Dr. Chris Reynolds, patients undergoing chemotherapy have greatly benefited from wheatgrass treatments. In a 2007 study, several patients consuming wheatgrass while receiving chemotherapy did not require extra hospitalization from side effects caused by the chemotherapy. In fact, common side effects of chemotherapy, such as nausea, vomiting, and mouth ulcers, were practically nonexistent.

Myelotoxicity, a potentially life-threatening bone marrow disease caused by chemotherapy, showed significant restriction with wheatgrass treatments. Wheatgrass juice cleansed the blood while regenerating damaged tissues. It is claimed that wheatgrass treatments also decrease the likelihood of contracting hematological toxicity, related to chemotherapy treatments in breast cancer patients. Hematological toxicity is a blood disorder, such as anemia, that can be potentially life threatening. In a 2007 pilot study conducted by Dr. Getta Fried and colleagues at the Rambam Medical Center and Faculty of Medicine, Technion-Israel Institute, wheatgrass was studied as an alternative treatment for the disease based on its effective treatment of other diseases such as rheumatoid arthritis, ulcerative colitis, and thalassemia, which is an inherited blood disorder where the patient has difficulty producing hemoglobin or produces defective hemoglobin. Additionally, the study revealed that wheatgrass juice taken during chemotherapy can reduce the chemotherapy dosage and need for granulocyte colony-stimulating factors (GCSF) support. GCSF is a hormone used to help the blood marrow produce stem cells and white blood cells.

Check out the full picture: Investigate thoroughly

Dr. Virginia Livingston-Wheeler, mentioned earlier amongst the list of cancer research contributors, experimented with cancer and bacteria. She believed that cancer was caused by bacteria in certain individuals and developed a treatment to combat these microbes. She also believed a strengthened immune system was the key to overcoming the cancer. Although her cancer research work in the 1940s was commended and accepted, her 1969 proposal that cancer was caused by the germ Progenitor cryptocides brought great controversy. Livingston-Wheeler developed a complex vaccine made from the cancer patient's urine and blood. This vaccine was meant to strengthen the patient's immune system so that it would overcome the spreading cancer germ. She also developed the Livingston Therapy Program in which the patient was placed on a strict vegetarian diet while given the vaccine and coffee enemas. Caffeine, found in coffee, was believed to be a strong stimulator of the liver and gall bladder. Livingston-Wheeler's work was met with resistance from organizations such as the California Department of Health Services and the American Cancer Society. They stated that the vaccine had not been approved by the FDA, the vegetarian diet was vitamin-deficient, and the coffee enemas were unsafe. Although there are those who continue to support the work of Livingston-Wheeler even after her death in 1990, the Livingston-Wheeler Clinic is no longer in operation due to financial difficulties as well as unsafe practices.

The case of Livingston-Wheeler shows how important it is to examine both sides of an issue when determining whether a nutritional regimen is right for you. It is prudent that not all information discovered be blindly accepted as truth. Researching the topic thoroughly will help you make an informed decision. Readers considering wheatgrass therapy should learn as much about their options as possible before changing their diet. This book can assist you in your research and help you make a decision that is right for you.

Beware of unlicensed medical practice

According to the Liaison Committee on Medical Education (**www.lcme.org**), "In order to practice medicine anywhere in the US, physicians must have received their MD from a medical program accredited by the Liaison Committee on Medical Education." In addition, they must have a graduate-level medical education or completed residency and must be licensed by the state in which they work. The Federation of State Medical Boards defines the "practice of medicine" as, "offering or undertaking to prevent or to diagnose, correct, and/or treat in any manner or by any means, methods, devices, or instrumentalities any disease, illness, pain, wound, fracture, infirmity, deformity, defect, or abnormal physical or mental condition of any person, including the management of pregnancy and parturition." In emergency situations only are non-physicians allowed to fulfill this clause, and certain family members are allowed to administer prescribed remedies to other family members. In spite of these limited allowances, "several practitioners of unconventional cancer treatments have been prosecuted for the criminal charge of practicing medicine without a license," according to the 1990 U.S. government technology assessment, "Unconventional Cancer Treatments." One such example concerning wheatgrass includes the case of Dr. Michael Gerber, a self-proclaimed "orthomolecular practitioner," who inappropriately treated a potentially curable uterine cancer patient "for 27 months with Hoxsey herbs, megavitamins, chelation therapy, Wobe-Mugos enzymes, chaparral tea, pangymic acid, benzaldehyde, wheatgrass juice, coffee or enzyme enemas, apricot pits, red clover, and slippery elm." Because of his actions, the state of California revoked Gerber's medical license in June 1984. According to Chapter 11 of the assessment, the Board of Medical Quality Assurance found him "guilty of gross negligence and incompetence, repeated similar negligent acts, and other similar charges." His guilt was determined by his use of substances not approved by either state or federal authorities for the treatment of cancer and, as written in the assessment, "excessively prescribing and administering diagnostic tests and ineffective drugs and treatments." The authority to license and discipline health care practitioners is based on each state's legal responsibility to protect the health, safety, and welfare of the public. Some states are now developing legislation that would "restrict anyone except registered dietitians or physicians from counseling patients about nutrition, making it illegal for many nutritional advocates and nonphysician practitioners to give nutritional advice."

Blood pressure stabilization

According to the American Heart Association, more than 50 million Americans have high blood pressure. High blood pressure is symptomless in its early stages and many individuals are not aware of the fact that they have a potentially life-threatening disease. High blood pressure can damage the blood vessels and the heart, if left untreated. It can also lead to kidney failure, heart attack, stroke, or other serious health ailments.

Blood pressure rises when the arterioles constrict or tighten. High doses of adrenaline and other hormones cause this tightening to occur. Increased blood volume can also occur when the body retains excessive salt and fluids. These conditions challenge the heart to work harder to pump the blood through the narrowed arteries.

The risk of high blood pressure increases as the body ages due to the reduced elasticity of the arteries. Those with a family history of the disease also have a higher risk. Individuals with family histories including diabetes, obesity, and certain other disorders also have an increased risk of developing high blood pressure. Other possible causes of the condition include excessive alcohol use, smoking, lack of exercise, and stress.

Diet plays a major role in the prevention and treatment of high blood pressure. Often, a high-fat, high-sodium diet is the culprit to the development of the disease. Converting to a low-sodium, high-fiber diet will do much to help stabilize blood pressure. Adding wheatgrass to the diet helps because wheatgrass juice stimulates the capillaries and increases the circulation of the blood. With this improved circulation, valuable nutrients can be distributed throughout the body more efficiently. Chlorophyll combined with oxygen is also able to remove foreign matter from the walls of the blood vessels. According to Dr. Theodore M. Rudolph, chiropractor and author of *Chlorophyll: Nature's Green Magic*, the chlorophyll in wheatgrass is beneficial, along with other accepted methods of treatment, for high blood pressure and hardening of the arteries (arteriosclerosis).

Several types of medications are generally prescribed to treat high blood pressure. Most of these prescriptions come with adverse side effects such as insomnia, leg cramps, and even impotency, in some cases. Because wheatgrass is a completely natural food, it brings about no harmful side effects. Consumers of wheatgrass report that they have experienced a natural spike in energy equivalent to caffeinated coffee but without the crash that comes along with it. Also, wheatgrass does not raise blood pressure, as many popular energy drinks are known to do. Wheatgrass treatment is a great natural alternative for individuals suffering from high blood pressure.

Pain management

Wheatgrass has been used as a therapeutic treatment, either externally or internally, for centuries. There is no secret concerning its positive and powerful effect on the body's immune system. Unlike some immune stimulants, such as ginseng, which can often have an adverse effect — including loss of appetite, anxiety, and insomnia — on the body if consumed over long periods, wheatgrass is safe and can be taken indefinitely.

Wheatgrass has practically no negative side effects. Any adverse effects, such as nausea, decrease as the body becomes acclimated to the product. The combination of cost-effectiveness, remarkable efficacy, and accessibility without a prescription should make wheatgrass an essential product for every practicing physician or therapist. Some medical professionals, such as Dr. Keith Block from the Block Medical Center in Evanston, Illinois, have embraced natural healing principals and do incorporate them into their general practices. Dr. Block offers green foods to cancer patients as part of an integrative therapy program — a combination of conventional medical treatments with alternative homeopathy or naturopathy therapies. Other professionals choose not to incorporate wheatgrass and other natural products into their practice. Wheatgrass can often alleviate problems where no suitable pharmaceutical alternative is applicable. Wheatgrass improves the immune system, and advocates claim that this gives the body the ability to heal itself.

Externally, there are several claims that wheatgrass can solve many skin conditions. Applied to the skin, it is claimed to eliminate itching almost immediately. It acts as an anti-inflammatory. It has also been claimed to soothe skin that has been burned and act as a disinfectant. Wheatgrass can be rubbed into the scalp before a shampoo to alleviate itchy, scalp conditions. People have claimed wheatgrass can treat open sores, boils, insect bites, rashes, poison ivy, and athlete's foot. You can make a poultice (treatment for pain or inflammation) with the grass pulp, and re-apply it to the skin every two hours until pain or itching has subsided. You can also buy ointments containing wheatgrass and/or chlorophyll online and at health food stores for the treatment of a variety of skin ailments.

Wheatgrass has also been used for the treatment of internal pains and has been successfully used for constipation, diarrhea, menstrual discomfort, and even complicated conditions such as peptic ulcers (open sores in the lining of the stomach) and ulcerative colitis (a condition causing inflammation and ulcers in the rectum and large intestine). Of course, outcomes vary from one individual to the next, but many have reported sufficient relief from internal discomforts through wheatgrass treatments.

Chlorophyll, the main ingredient in wheatgrass that promotes healing, also helps soothe pain by keeping the capillaries stimulated and the blood flowing. In the early 1900s, medical and nonmedical people used chlorophyll treatments extensively to treat and alleviate physical discomforts. With the use of antimicrobial products and steroids in recent decades, these treatments have been neglected. Since 1995, however, chlorophyll treatments have come back on the scene. There are a number of successful treatments using a specially formulated wheatgrass extract for both topical and systemic use in numerous medical conditions. Although this treatment is most likely unacceptable to most practicing physicians, it does not nullify the success of the treatments. Clinical observations are supported by both formal clinical trials and anecdotal evidence from a number of sources.

With the increasing body of knowledge concerning wheatgrass and wheatgrass treatments available today, advocates feel that health practitioners or laypersons can help their patients or family and friends suffering from irritations or painful injuries using wheatgrass. Wheatgrass, in liquid or cream form, is a safe, all-purpose healing agent that can significantly facilitate the work of hands-on health professionals. It significantly boosts the immune system, when taken orally, aiding in disease prevention.

A number of clinical observations of the healing of fractures and the rapid re-growth of skin from wounds and burns suggest that wheatgrass activates growth factors. There are four main areas in which wheatgrass works well:

- As a wound healer
- As a hemolytic (an agent that opens red blood cell and releases hemoglobin)/homeostatic agent (agent that controls balance)
- As an anti-inflammatory
- As a skin and connective tissue softener

There exists, therefore, many clinical uses to which wheatgrass can be applied, particularly as a first-aid cream and topical analgesic. Ointments should be used sparingly as it does not take much to perform the task. For acute conditions, it is best to apply the wheatgrass as soon as possible after the injury has occurred or at the onset of symptoms.

Wheatgrass and pregnancy

A question has arisen pertaining to wheatgrass and its use during pregnancy. Is it safe to consume wheatgrass while pregnant? The answer is not a difficult one, but it is one that does bring about some controversy. Wheatgrass is a high-quality food. Any high-quality food can be beneficial unless you suffer from an allergy involving that particular food. With this in mind, many avid wheatgrass users have concluded that it is safe to consume wheatgrass and other greens during pregnancy; they are an excellent source of folic acid and other important nutrients.

According to the CDC, folic acid deficiency is one the most common nutrient deficiencies worldwide. Folic acid deficiency during pregnancy can cause several serious birth defects, including neural tube defects — incomplete development of the brain and spinal cord — such as spina bifida, the incomplete development of the backbone and spinal cord. Several studies, including a 1996 needs assessment test in Southwestern Virginia, revealed that women of childbearing age needed an increase in folic acid for their own health and the health of their babies. In response to this test, an informational campaign was developed and carried out in 1997, alerting women to the importance of correcting this nutrient deficiency. During this time period, it was established that women who took 0.4 mg daily of folic acid before and during pregnancy would lower the risk of having a baby born with a serious neural tube defect by about 50 to 70 percent.

In 1998, it was mandated that "enriched" cereal grain products be fortified with at least 400 mcg of folic acid per 100 grams of cereal grain product. The prior requirement was 140 mcg per 100 grams. The Institute of Medicine advised that women of childbearing age partake of foods from a varied food diet in addition to taking the daily 400 mcg of synthetic folic acid. Recommended foods included enriched grain products, beans, and leafy green vegetables. In 1999, the CDC, along with the National Council on Folic Acid and the March of Dimes Birth Defects Foundation, launched a national educational awareness program to alert women of the important role that folic acid played in their health.

Folic acid is vital for the development of DNA and, thus, cell growth and development and the formation of tissues. One of the best sources of this nutrient is dark, leafy vegetables such as kale, spinach, broccoli, and cereal grasses. One ounce of fresh wheatgrass juice can supply about 8.22 mcg of folic acid to the diet. Dehydrated wheatgrass contains 1,110 mcg of folate per 100 grams compared to the 71 mcg in 100 grams of broccoli and 194.4 mcg in 100 grams of spinach. It goes to work quickly in the system, enhancing immunity as it maintains and cleanses the blood. Also, the naturally occurring digestive enzymes and fiber contained in wheatgrass can be a great help for aiding constipation, which is a common occurrence during pregnancy.

As a side note, women trying to become pregnant can also find wheatgrass beneficial. California biologist Yasuo Hotta is attributed with isolating the P4D1 compound from young cereal grasses. It his studies, Dr. Hotta revealed the ability of P4D1 to "stimulate the production and natural repair of human reproductive sperm cells and DNA," according to *The Wheatgrass Book* by Ann Wigmore. This revelation indicates the potential of wheatgrass and other cereal grasses to increase potency and correct reproductive problems in both men and women.

Safety

Wheatgrass during pregnancy is considered by some to be perfectly safe when used moderately and obtained from a safe source. Many users claim it is not likely to cause any interference with pregnancy in women who have already adopted a high-quality diet. Large therapeutic dosages, however, would not be recommended during pregnancy. Dosages of this volume are normally used for treating illnesses and function as a purgative. Purgatives act on the body as a cleanser, usually evacuating the bowels. This would not be advisable during pregnancy, as it may create an unstable environment for the unborn child, possibly leading to miscarriage. Pregnancy is not the time to begin a detoxification program. If you are pregnant and have never consumed wheatgrass, it is best to begin with only a small amount, perhaps about 10 milliliters. This can be slowly increased until a normal dosage of one to two ounces is reached. More than 2 ounces is not recommended during pregnancy.

As an informed individual, you must determine how you will use wheatgrass during pregnancy. One concern that health professionals might have for pregnant women is possible adverse effects caused by mold. Anyone can grow wheatgrass, but not everyone exercises the effort necessary to grow high-quality, nutritious wheatgrass that is mold-free. Also, some wheatgrass manufacturers have higher sanitary regulations than others. These companies watch closely for mold in their product and have a high level of quality control.

Some wheatgrass sold to consumers is not fit for anyone to drink. Because of quality control (or lack of it), most users suggest only drinking wheatgrass you juice yourself while pregnant. If you buy it fresh intending to juice it yourself, buy organic, buy local, and buy from a reputable dealer. Check for mold around the base of the plant. The color of the grass should be bright and healthy-looking, and the plant and soil should smell fresh, not moldy.

Most wheatgrass juice available at specialty grocery stores, juice bars, and health food stores comes from greenhouse growing stations. In these high-density planting operations, water and soil are often recycled and the normal growing process is accelerated. This wheatgrass is not the nutritional equivalent of outdoor-grown wheatgrass and, many times, contains high levels of mold. Many people are allergic to these molds, and they can cause anything from mild nausea to serious physical reactions. Anything that you ingest that creates an allergic reaction is a cause for concern, especially when you are pregnant. So, if you do consume wheatgrass while pregnant, it is suggested that you stay clear of greenhouse wheatgrass. The best way to determine whether you have a good quality juice is to investigate before you drink.

Wheatgrass and your baby

Wheatgrass provides high nutrition, exhibits curative properties, and acts as an energizer. It is essential to consume a healthy diet during pregnancy, and wheatgrass is an easy way to provide your body with all of the antioxidants, vitamins, minerals, and folic acid it needs. As wheatgrass is so readily absorbed into the bloodstream, your baby is sure to get a good supply of these essential nutrients at the crucial time of development. Some claim wheatgrass to be a great prenatal care product that benefits not only you, but also your unborn child.

Wheatgrass might also benefit your child after he or she is born. Breastfeeding mothers who consume wheatgrass might find that their breastfed babies are less irritable and less susceptible to colds and flus. If you have not been consuming wheatgrass all along, be sure to introduce the product into your diet slowly to be certain it is assimilating well in your baby's system.

Seek medical advice if pregnant

As there is little to no medical research done on the topic of wheatgrass and pregnancy, it is advisable to consult your physician if you are concerned about this topic. Scientific research has yet to confirm or deny the safety of wheatgrass during pregnancy. If you are unsure of exactly how wheatgrass can benefit you and your health, you should definitely do your homework.

The advice provided on these pages is for educational purposes only. You should not use this information to diagnose or treat a health problem or disease, especially during pregnancy, without consulting with a qualified health care provider.

Internal Cleansing

In many instances, the body is like a filter — taking in oxygen and nutrients, releasing toxins and wastes. If a filter becomes clogged, it no longer functions. Likewise, the body will not perform if it becomes impaired. Toxins and wastes become stored inside, hindering the absorption of oxygen and nutrients. This malfunctioning of the body can lead to a host of illnesses and diseases. Just as the external parts of the physical body must be cleaned, cleansing of the internal parts is also important. It is essential to keep the body cleansed in order for it to function at its best. Any internal cleansing program should begin with the colon.

Colon cleansing

Colon cleansing is one of the most beneficial forms of detoxification. It is valuable for the treatment of an existing disease as well as the prevention of future illness. Many people do not adequately care for their digestive systems. If the system becomes defective, it can lead to ailments and diseases such as inflammatory bowel disease, Crohn's disease, and cancer. The colon must function properly to ensure the optimum functioning of all of the body's other systems. A diet that is high in fiber, such as fruits and vegetables, can help eliminate many problems that are related to the colon. In fact, many health advocates claim that overall good health — as well as the degeneration of health — begins in the colon. With this in mind, a high-fiber diet can help with problems, such as heart disease and asthma, that are not directly related to the colon. Unfortunately, many people do not include enough fiber in the diet; consume too many starchy, sugary foods; and do not eliminate waste properly. According to general medical advice, moving the bowel anywhere from once a day to three times a week is normal. According to holistic and other natural health practices, it is essential to eliminate the bowel on a daily basis to prevent disease and maintain good body health. If meal consumption is two to three times per day, bowel elimination should be the same. If elimination is not on a regular daily basis, then the problem needs to be addressed.

The colon is a storage place for waste. As the body absorbs oxygen, nutrients, and water to keep it functioning properly, it also extracts what is not needed from the colon and excretes it from the body. The goal — and challenge — is to prevent a build-up of bacteria and waste in the colon. The created toxins will be absorbed back into the body and will eventually lead to a number of health ailments. The entire body will respond negatively to the effects of a malfunctioning colon. The physical organs that process and transport waste to the colon will especially suffer when the colon is not working well. A healthy colon ensures the optimal performance of the body's systems.

Natural enemas

Irregular, ineffective bowel movements affect the entire body. The constant dumping of inappropriate foods on the digestive system is one of the main problems of constipation. Because this food is not eliminated in a timely manner, it causes a backup in the system, and this leads to problems with the colon, which will lead to a host of other health problems. An enema is one solution for a blocked bowel. An enema is the process of introducing liquids into the colon or rectum by way of the anus for the purpose of elimination. The liquid introduced by the enema causes an expansion in the lower intestinal track, creating a feeling of urgency to evacuate. Usually, the evacuation of the lower intestinal tract is complete.

Enema treatments vary. Each treatment provides a unique solution, according to the complexity of the problem. The use of different enemas can help treat a variety of diseases. The major benefit enemas offer is the gentle removal of harmful substances in the colon that can cause illness. Enemas are also effective in removing heavy metals and toxins from intestinal walls. They have been used to treat headaches and, when used with a tincture, have provided an effective treatment for parasites. Herbal bowel cleaners have proven useful with chronic constipation problems and coffee enemas have been used to increase bile discharge.

Wheatgrass implants

Wheatgrass implants can be used after an enema for the purpose of cleansing the colon. When a wheatgrass implant is placed in the colon, it helps to stimulate the muscles of the colon wall. This process helps to loosen old fecal matter that might have built up in the walls of the colon. The magnesium in the wheatgrass is very helpful in drawing impurities out of the colon wall. Wheatgrass inserted into the rectum for about 20 minutes before being expelled can be very helpful in the case of illness, serious or otherwise, as it stimulates a fast evacuation of the lower bowel. The removal of toxins from the colon is essential to its optimal health. In addition to the removal of toxins, a wheatgrass implant can introduce many important nutrients into the body.

A wheatgrass implant can be used to immediately purge the colon, or it can be used as a retention enema. When used as a retention enema, the juice of the wheatgrass should be held or retained in the bowels for about one hour before it is expelled. In most cases, one implant performed per day is sufficient. In cases where an illness is being treated, the implants can be repeated every hour or two for a period of time. Wheatgrass implants are very effective for cleansing the liver and the colon because the nutrients from the wheatgrass are absorbed into the body. When the wheatgrass is retained, it benefits the small intestine as well as the lower bowel.

Using a wheatgrass implant can be uncomfortable at first. A sterilized syringe is filled with one or two ounces of fresh wheatgrass juice and then inserted into the rectum. It does not take long for the bowels to move after the insertion. This can be done once or twice more. After a second treatment, dried fecal matter should be successfully removed from the colon. Upon a third treatment of the implant, the wheatgrass juice should be retained in the rectum for about 20 minutes, if possible. In this manner, the juice can thoroughly cleanse the bowels. If the colon has been purged before the retention enema, no toxins should be absorbed back into the body. Enemas and wheatgrass implants are safe procedures to perform. Wheatgrass enemas and implants are effective means for cleansing the colon.

Colon hydrotherapy

Autointoxication is an ancient belief that undigested foods accumulate in the colon causing toxic-producing mucus that, when absorbed into the bloodstream, poison the body.

The cleansing of the colon provides the natural detoxification of the entire body, assisting in the healing of any physical disease. Thorough cleansing of the colon opens the door for optimal health and complete physical balance for a strong immune system. Colon hydrotherapy became popular in America in the early 1900s.

Colon hydrotherapy, also known as colon irrigation, eliminates toxins from the colon by flushing the waste matter out of the colon with water. It is not to be confused with colon cleansing, which involves purchasing products to produce the cleansing. These products can be taken orally or through the rectum. Colon hydrotherapy is faster and more efficient than enemas and colon cleansers and leaves the body feeling clean and purified. An effective colonic will cleanse the colon as well as the intestines, as opposed to an enema, which will only cleanse the rectum and lower portion of the colon. Wheatgrass juice mixed with purified water provides an effective irrigation of the colon. The colon must be brought back to its healthy functioning state to eliminate disease and toxins from the body. A wheatgrass colonic will work toward this end.

Colon hydrotherapy is generally performed by a skilled colon therapist in a professional setting and is perfectly safe. One session generally lasts about 45 minutes to one hour. The treatment involves flushing about 20 gallons of water into the rectum through a rubber tube. The abdomen may be massaged while the water is irrigating the system. Fluids are then flushed out of the body through another tube. Colon hydrotherapy not only removes toxins, it also boosts energy by promoting healthy intestinal bacteria and enhancing the immune system.

When seeking a colon therapist, look for one that has been certified by the International Association for Colon Hydrotherapy (I-ACT). These therapists use FDA-registered equipment, disposable speculums (rectal nozzles), and filtered water. I-ACT is the worldwide certifying organization for colon hydrotherapists. It works with local municipalities to regulate colon hydrotherapy by establishing standards and guidelines.

CASE STUDY: THE IMPORTANCE OF A CLEAN COLON

Sister Sarah Moss, colon therapist
Walking in the Spirit
111-36 130th St.
South Ozone Park, NY 11420
Walkingintthespirit2@yahoo.com
Phone: 718-529-5470

Sister Sarah Moss began colon therapy in the late 1970s when she discovered she had stomach cancer. She claims a change in diet and regular colon irrigations helped her to overcome this condition. She has since made it her business to enlighten others about the importance of colon health and is instrumental in helping others to overcome health ailments through good nutrition and colon therapy.

Good health begins in the colon — so does poor health. Moss believes the underlying issue in practically every health dilemma is an unclean, unhealthy colon. The colon is responsible for completing the job of digestion. If it is not working properly, undigested foods will build up and begin to putrefy in the system. This can cause a number of health problems, ranging from constipation and headaches to obesity and cancer. Parasite infestation, which usually accompanies this unhealthy state of the colon, will rob the body of nutrition and energy.

The best way to prevent an unhealthy colon is to maintain a diet of fluids and high fiber foods. Correcting the problem also begins with the diet. Sometimes, however, the condition of the colon is so bad that a diet change is not enough. The individual must undergo a colon cleansing or irrigation to remove old fecal matter, toxins, and mucus that have accumulated along the walls of the colon. Colon irrigation will flush the colon and recondition the bowels.

Moss mostly uses chlorophyll in the colon flushes she administers. Chlorophyll is high in oxygen and has been used as a cleansing agent for ages. Recently, she has begun to explore the use of wheatgrass in colon irrigations as an implant as well as taken orally for a body cleanser and deodorizer. Through her research, she realizes that wheatgrass can help fight toxins by inhibiting the growth of bacteria in the colon. It can also aid in the treatment of a number of health ailments, such as high blood pressure. Wheatgrass is good for replacing good bacteria in the colon. It also improves digestion and is wonderful for blood disorders. Wheatgrass has a healing effect on the skin when used as a cleanser and is good for purifying the liver. Most importantly, wheatgrass is excellent for constipation; it keeps the bowels flowing, which is necessary to prevent the build up of waste matter and hazardous toxins.

Recently, Moss' clients have reported increased energy with the addition of wheatgrass in the cleansing regimen. Others claim they have a better night's rest, better control over body odors, and even improvements in hair condition. It can be easy to fill the body with foods that do not profit, but we must remember to use the things that are provided by nature for our use upon the earth. Wheatgrass is one of those natural things that can benefit us tremendously.

Blood cleansing

Blood is a vital part of the human body. It is a busy transporter, delivering essential nutrients to various parts of the body and, similarly, removing harmful wastes. Without blood, the human body would simply shut down. The quality of our blood has a great effect on our health and energy levels. Low-quality blood — blood not rich in iron and other necessary nutrients — equals poor health and low stamina. Iron-rich blood delivers more oxygen to the cells, preventing senility, the loss of memory usually associated with old age, and promoting youthfulness and vitality.

Blood is a vital part of human life and, because of this, it needs nurturing. It is beneficial to periodically cleanse the body to keep the blood strengthened. This is usually achieved with a special blood-cleansing fast. The consumption of raw vegetables and green drinks — drinks made with green vegetables — one week prior to the actual fast will provide a good launching pad for the detoxification.

To carry the toxins out of the body with a blood-cleansing fast, you should consume at least eight cups of steam-distilled water every day. Steam-distilled water contains no minerals that can interfere with the detoxing process. You can also use herbal extracts to aid the process. Juices made from lemons, carrots, beets, and leafy greens are beneficial at this time. The chlorophyll in leafy greens strengthens the blood by providing essential nutrients.

Wheatgrass juice is an excellent source of chlorophyll. It enriches the blood by increasing the red blood-cell count. It also helps with circulation and lowers blood pressure by dilating the capillaries and other blood pathways. Wheatgrass can restore the blood's alkalinity levels through its store of alkaline minerals, such as calcium and magnesium. Other active enzymes and compounds found in wheatgrass will cleanse the blood and neutralize toxins in the cells. Enzymes are especially important to the process of blood cleansing. In addition to enzymes, the amino acids and bioflavonoids, a type of antioxidant, in wheatgrass help cleanse the blood and its tissues. Amino acids are absorbed directly into the blood and are effective in neutralizing toxic substances.

Liver cleansing

The largest glandular organ of the body is the liver, weighing about three pounds. The liver has many roles in the functioning of the body. It produces amino acids; urea, a substance in the urine; and substances that break down fats. It maintains an appropriate level of glucose, or simple sugar, in the blood; converts glucose to glycogen, a storage place for carbohydrates; and stores vitamins and minerals. Perhaps its greatest task is filtering harmful substances from the blood.

Because of this tremendous job, the liver is considered the major organ of detoxification in the body. Its health determines the health of all other body organs, as well as the blood. The liver functions as a processing plant. Modern foods — especially meat, fried foods, refined oils, and foods with chemical additives — weaken the liver. Alcohol, tobacco, and environmental pollutants make the liver work harder than it was designed to work. Bile, which is stored in the gallbladder, acts as a carrier for older wastes, including excessive cholesterol. Bile is also necessary for proper digestion and assimilation of fats. A mineral-deficient, low-fiber diet tends to produce solid particles from bile components. These components are called gallstones, and they contribute to the weakening of the liver. To regain health and energy, the liver and gallbladder must be cleansed and kept unobstructed in their work. Wheatgrass juice, with its abundance of rich minerals, can do an effective cleansing job on both the liver and gallbladder. Combined with other juices it can act as a cleanser and toner. The following are good juice combinations:

- Other green drinks made from alfalfa sprouts and greens can be combined with wheatgrass to boost the cleansing process.

- Carrot juice stimulates bile flow because it is rich in beta-carotene.

- The citric acids in lemon juice mix well with the properties in wheatgrass juice and can produce an antiseptic, or disinfectant, action.

- Apple juice performs well as a liver stimulant and bile solvent.

- A wheatgrass and beet juice combination provides a powerful liver flush.

For an effective liver cleanse, you should take juices upon rising in the morning before eating. Sip the juice slowly, in small quantities. The high levels of enzymes and amino acids in the wheatgrass work along with the properties of the other juices as a natural detergent to detoxify the liver.

Lung cleansing

The lungs are very important body organs. Not only do they allow us to breathe, but they also act as a cooling agent for the body. Although the body can survive without food and water for a period of time, it cannot survive without the breath of life. If the lungs become congested with excessive carbon wastes and mucus, they will be hindered in the work they have to perform of inhaling and exhaling oxygen. The intake of oxygen into the body is important because oxygen is needed to destroy body wastes.

Every day the air that we breathe is purified by our lungs, so it is important to keep the lungs clean from a build up of toxins. A build up of toxins or mucus in the lungs also puts a strain on the other body organs, such as the colon and the liver. The recommended method for cleansing the lungs consists of consuming anti-mucus foods and practicing simple breathing exercises. Foods such as garlic, fresh ginger, and onions are very good for cleansing the lungs. Wheatgrass juice is also excellent. Because the chlorophyll in wheatgrass juice is similar to the hemoglobin in the red blood cells, it helps in purging harmful toxins and wastes from the lungs. Detoxifying the lungs often result in offensive breath odor, but once the lungs are clean, this odor will pass.

Kidney cleansing

The two bean-shaped organs within the body that are about the size of a fist are called the kidneys. About 200 quarts of blood flow through the kidneys every day. The kidneys cleanse the toxins and wastes from the blood. Excess water, uric acid, urea, and other waste products such as bacterial wastes and pollutants are eliminated through this cleansing process. The kidneys are also important organs for regulating body temperature. The kidneys have the important job of filtering the food and the water that comes into our system. They perform this task through the nephron, the filter in the kidneys. If the workload of the kidneys becomes too extreme, the nephron can become damaged. Sometimes, this is not known until the kidney is severely damaged and unable to function properly. In most cases, a damaged kidney cannot be repaired.

It is important for the cleansing and keeping of the kidney to avoid overly processed foods, excess salt, tobacco, and alcohol. Even coffee, tea, and tap water can negatively affect the kidneys. The recommended procedure for cleansing the kidney is to drink large amounts of green drinks, especially wheatgrass juice, to help the kidneys filter wastes from the body. The chlorophyll in the wheatgrass juice also builds the blood. Other juices that are good for cleansing the kidney include lemon juice, watermelon juice, and beet juice. Sea vegetables, such as kelp and spirulina, are also good for detoxifying and stimulating the kidneys.

Skin cleansing

The skin is the largest body organ. It is also an organ of elimination. Elimination takes place through the pores of the skin. It is important that the pores are not clogged so that the skin can perform its job effectively. When the pores are clogged and the skin is unable to function properly, it affects the other organs of elimination as well.

The body sheds its skin cells periodically. When the skin looks overly dry, it is an indication that it is not performing effectively. The pores need to be opened up, and you can do this by brushing the skin with a natural-bristle body brush in the morning before a shower. Every 27 days or so, the entire surface of the skin is renewed. New skin should look fresh. Heavy detergent soaps and detergents and shampoos can hinder or clog the pores of the skin and create a dry look. The use of natural shampoos, conditioners, and soaps are recommended for keeping the skin clean. You can also rub wheatgrass juice into the scalp and onto the skin to help with the cleansing. Once the wheatgrass juice dries, it can be rinsed off. This treatment should help the pores to open. The wheatgrass juice also will enhance blood circulation and is helpful for treating dandruff.

It is also important to massage the skin periodically. This will help the pores to remain open. By massaging the skin, brushing the skin with a loofah or soft brush, using natural skin products, and eating properly, you will help your skin look radiant and function at its best.

Wheatgrass Therapy

Over the last 20 years, there has been an explosion of information in health and scientific literature supporting the use of natural medicine. Wheatgrass and wheatgrass therapy are often highlighted topics. Wheatgrass therapy embraces the philosophy of the Greek physician, Hippocrates. He taught that it is nature, not the physician, who cures the patient. With the advancement of civilization, it has been easy to look to scientific and technological advances for cures. Wheatgrass therapy is an attempt to get back to nature. According to many, wheatgrass therapy, combined with exercise, proper diet, and less stress, paves the way back to optimal health.

Finding establishments that offer wheatgrass therapy

A number of institutions throughout the country offer wheatgrass therapy as part of their healing plan. The primary object of these centers is to educate individuals on methods and techniques that can lead to enhanced health. Many of these programs are set up so that the visitor is an active participant in the educational process. The hope is that, during the stay, the visitor's health will increase so dramatically that it will make a lasting impact on his or her overall well-being. Wheatgrass juice is the emphasis of many of these retreats.

Many successful wheatgrass therapy programs are based on the historical work of Ann Wigmore. They adopt a balanced approach for the mind and body and incorporate four major healing components:

- **Food.** A raw food diet is established. Wheatgrass is used liberally and is considered the most powerful of the raw food group.

- **Exercise.** Light activities (physical exercise and gardening) designed to stimulate the flow of oxygen into the body are involved in these retreats.

- **Education.** Active involvement in all aspects of food preparation is expected, with the idea that a nutritional food program can be continued at home.

- **Meditation.** This is used to purge the mind and develop coping strategies for dealing with stress.

Services such as colon hydrotherapy, chiropractic care, and massage are usually available at these institutions.

Finding a healing facility that meets your specific needs can take some time. Consult with a naturopathic or holistic doctor to obtain recommendations, visit online forums to determine where others have gone, do an online search to determine whether there are affordable centers in your area, and read reviews to determine whether the offered programs meet your expectations. Modern American society puts an emphasis on beautifying the outer man. A healing facility will focus on strengthening the inner person by building the physical body. This is typically done with rest, exercise, fresh air, and a healthy diet.

Retreats and other treats

Many health retreats have been established across the nation. These retreats have adapted the principles of Ann Wigmore and others, and they use a program that cleanses the body from within. A program that incorporates meditation, exercise, rest, and wholesome life foods helps the body to rejuvenate and recover from illness and disease. Every year, individuals make goals for themselves; for example, many promise they will eat right and exercise in order to get healthy. Many times, just like a New Year's Day resolution, these resolutions are made firmly and sincerely, but before the month is out, the resolution is broken. Many times all the individual needs is a support group to help him or her accomplish the health goals. A trip to a health retreat can be just what you need to accomplish what the mind has set out to do. Being in an environment with like-minded individuals to offer and support and encouragement will help you in a great way to accomplish your goals. The following are a few highly esteemed raw food retreats:

- Optimum Health Institute — Lemon Grove, California/Cedar Creek, Texas; **www.optimumhealth.org**
- Hippocrates Health Institute —West Palm Beach, Florida; **www.hippocratesinst.org**
- Creative Health Institute — Union City, Michigan; **www.creativehealthinstitute.com**
- Ann Wigmore Natural Health Institute — Rincón, Puerto Rico; **www.annwigmore.org**
- Living Foods Institute — Atlanta, Georgia; **www.livingfoodsinstitute.com**
- The Ann Wigmore Foundation — San Fidel, New Mexico; **www.wigmore.org**
- The UK Centre for Living Foods — Ludlow, England; **www.livingfoods.co.uk**

The Hippocrates Institute originated in Boston, but it is now located in Florida. The Ann Wigmore Foundation also came out of Boston, but it has now moved to a desert location in New Mexico. All of the above facilities have been greatly influenced by the historic work of Wigmore and many of them strive to maintain the original program she began in the 1950s. They offer a retreat package of one to three weeks and encourage guests to become immersed in a lifestyle that will outlast the time of their stay.

What to expect at a retreat

Many other health institutes that promote a program in wheatgrass therapy are based on the teachings of Wigmore. She has created a legacy that will continue to live on for people who desire a healthier lifestyle. Usually a healing center is set in a beautiful location where the guest can be in tune with nature. Sometimes, this location is in the mountains or near a lake or a river. The atmosphere is usually serene and welcoming so that visitors relax enough to participate wholeheartedly in the holistic experience. When guests arrive at the compound, their vitals are taken — they might be weighed, given a blood test, and have their blood pressure measured. This allows the instructors to know how the guest will fit into the program. In some facilities, this information helps the center create a customized plan for the guest. Many facilities also set aside a time for an introduction or orientation the first night so that guest can get to know one another.

Some facilities might have oxygen therapy programs, gyms, and other recreational activities such as tennis and golf. Guests are also given opportunities to explore personal hobbies or indulge in new activities, such as crafts or music and drama. The centers teach a variety of classes on many topics, including how to grow wheatgrass, how to sprout, how to relax, or how to cope with stress.

Creating an at-home wheatgrass therapy program

Although most people enjoy a change of environment from time to time, some strongly feel that "there is no place like home." Or, perhaps, you would like to embark upon a program in wheatgrass therapy, but the time and resources necessary for attending a retreat are not possible at the moment. Fortunately, with a little ingenuity, you can establish a wheatgrass therapy program in your own home. There is an ample amount of literature available that can guide you in this endeavor. Consult with a naturopath or holistic doctor experienced in wheatgrass therapy to help you develop a plan. Having a desire to begin is the most important factor.

Programs such as the Ann Wigmore Home Study Program (**http://chidiet .com**) can get you started. This example is a comprehensive course that teaches you how to adopt a living foods diet. It will walk you through the steps needed for a life-transforming experience. It will show you how to prepare raw foods, incorporate exercise into a busy schedule, and deal with stress. The current price for the complete guide, developed by Jim Carey, costs $695. You can also purchase The Ann Wigmore Collection of ten DVDs for about $150. You can also use the information found online and in books to put together your own therapy program. This would be the least expensive way to get started on a health rejuvenation plan.

Home exercises for the colon

Squatting is an important exercise for strengthening the colon. The way people normally sit tends to close the colon, hindering proper elimination. By squatting on an elevated level or platform, the colon can open up and a more complete evacuation can be obtained. Squatting also strengthens the abdominal muscles. This is important to protect the body from hemorrhoids and hernias. Placing your feet up on the toilet bowl and squatting over the toilet bowl is one way to practice squatting while eliminating.

You can also practice the abdominal lift by placing your hands over your knees and bending over slightly. Blow out and hold your breath while you are doing this exercise. Pull in your stomach muscles. Relax while trying to push the stomach back out. Hold your breath and try to increase the area of your stomach (make it bigger). Then stand and relax by taking slow, deep breaths. Begin the abdominal lift again. This should be done ten times to build and strengthen the colon and abdominal muscles. It is best to practice the abdominal lift upon rising in the morning or retiring for the night. This exercise should never be done on a full stomach. The abdominal lift is good for massaging and toning all the internal eliminating and digestive organs.

Deep breathing

Breathing, when done properly, helps to eliminate toxins from the body. It is important to use the lungs in their full capacity when breathing so that the cleansing process can take place. Short, shallow breaths will not do the job. When breathing is done properly, it adds oxygen to the blood. Oxygen-rich blood is important for cleansing and eliminating toxins from the body.

It only takes about ten minutes per day to do deep breathing exercises. You should sit where you are comfortable, using good posture with a relaxed body. Breathe deeply through the nostrils, filling the lungs with as much air as possible. The abdomen should expand. Do not try to hold your breath, but release the air that you have inhaled out of your system slowly and completely. Exhaling should be done through the mouth. Deep breathing might initially cause light-headedness. Begin slowly and build up until you are able to complete the deep breathing exercises ten to 15 times in one sitting.

Wheatgrass as a Natural Energizer

Long-lasting fatigue is abnormal and is largely the result of poor diet. Life can be quite challenging, to say the least. Each day, you deal with situations that zap your energy — energy that cannot be replenished by a nutritionally imbalanced diet. Although a certain amount of fatigue after a long day of work is expected, a good night's rest should leave you feeling refreshed and energized. When you wake feeling as if you had never slept, there is a problem. Your body is not getting what it needs from your diet. Or, perhaps it is getting too many things that it does not need.

Wheatgrass can help your body restore itself to a high energy level in two ways: first, by removing toxins and wastes from your cells, blood, tissues, and organs, and second, by fulfilling nutritional deficiencies. Wheatgrass and wholesome, raw foods added to your diet will supply you with enough energy to tackle the most challenging of days. Wheatgrass will also help to release excess mineral deposits, proteins, and fats that are trapped in your body organs causing sluggishness and slothfulness.

An adult can easily function on six hours of sleep, as long as that sleep is deep and undisturbed. During sleep, the body's goal is to balance and re-energize its cells. This is virtually impossible if the body is overloaded with food, especially heavy, poor-quality food consumed late in the evening before bed. The more out-of-balance your cells are, the more out-of-balance your body is, and the more rest it requires.

Wheatgrass is light and clean and will nourish and cleanse the body. After a few days of drinking wheatgrass while avoiding heavy, clogging foods, your body will be refreshed and you can truly enjoy a good night's rest.

How wheatgrass gives energy

The starch of the wheat grain contains stored energy. When this energy is transformed to simple sugar, it becomes a quick source of energy. One of the greatest benefits of wheatgrass juice is that it is absorbed immediately into the bloodstream, rapidly sending energy throughout the body.

The stress of everyday living can certainly place a great load on the body. Add an acidic diet, and it is no wonder people have difficulty keeping their eyes open during the day. The acid in their diet attacks the red blood cells. The cells cannot withstand this attack for long, so they will eventually die. Death of the red blood cells causes a weakness in the body. It becomes feeble and sluggish. Correcting this problem entails restoring the acid-alkaline (pH) balance of the blood. If the body is healthy, it can overcome an acid-alkaline imbalance for a time by excreting acids through the skin, lungs, and kidneys. The body will also pull alkaline minerals, such as calcium, from the bones to correct this imbalance; although, this can create another set of problems. An unhealthy body will have difficulty correcting the pH imbalance in itself. Correction through the diet is necessary by eliminating acidic foods and consuming more alkaline, mineral-rich foods.

Wheatgrass is one of the most alkaline foods available. It is also easily absorbed into the bloodstream, so its alkaline minerals immediately go to work neutralizing acids. When the acids are neutralized, the red blood cells can get back to their important work of delivering oxygen from the lungs to all the cells in the body. When the cells receive the needed energy from the oxygen, the body becomes energized again. Although many health professionals report that the immune system is the body's first line of defense against illness and disease, in actuality, the pH balance of the blood is the body's first and major line of defense.

The Future of Wheatgrass

Although there are documented studies on the use of wheatgrass as a medical aid, they are few and far between and have not been accepted as scientific evidence or proof that wheatgrass is anything more than a nutritious food. As studies continue concerning wheatgrass and medicine, we look forward to any evidence or results that might determine the future potential of this super food.

CHAPTER 4

Beauty, Age, and Weight Management

"To keep the body in good health is a duty ... otherwise we shall not be able to keep our mind strong and clear."

~ Buddha

Wheatgrass has an unmatched vitality. It is said that 2 ounces of the fresh juice is equivalent in minerals and vitamins to 5 pounds of fresh, organic greens. When taken on an empty stomach, wheatgrass juice is absorbed into the bloodstream in less than ten minutes, and the energy it provides can last the entire day. Many people claim that they can feel the wheatgrass working as it enters their system.

Nature's Plastic Surgeon: Wheatgrass & Beauty

The world's cosmetic roots can be traced back to the ancient Greeks and Egyptians. These ingenious people often used plants and plant parts to beautify themselves. Cosmetics often were made from plants, plant oils, or minerals. Perfumes were made from flowers and leaves. Of the cereal plants, barley and wheat were commonly used as a cosmetic aid. Today, wheatgrass is still used as a beauty aid. Many companies are currently manufacturing products containing wheatgrass and chlorophyll because of their antioxidant and vitamin E content. Wheatgrass has also been used as a skin cleanser and toner. It has been used effectively to clear blemishes and sunspots and enhances blood flow by expanding the blood arteries. The expanded arteries allow vitamins and minerals from wheatgrass to reach the skin cells, stimulating them. The result is a radiant glow. Wheatgrass can also be rubbed into the skin to promote healthy blood circulation.

If you are looking for a lasting glow, it is best to start from within the body. Topical gels and creams cannot give you that deep glow that comes from a body that has been thoroughly cleansed from the inside out. It has been claimed that incorporating a diet of live, raw foods into your lifestyle can help improve your outward appearance.

Wheatgrass juice can be used as a toner for skin. The wheatgrass can be juiced and the pulp can be used as an exfoliant for the skin. Exfoliation is the process of removing the dead skin cells from the surface of the skin. It is a practice that began with the Egyptians and is continued today. Exfoliation of the skin helps to maintain it and keeps it supple. The wheatgrass pulp can also be blended with flowers or fresh herbs to enhance the experience of the exfoliation. The pulp can be scrubbed over rough areas of the bodies, such as the elbow, knees, and heels of the feet.

Wheatgrass pulp can also be used to treat the gums and teeth. Place the pulp over the gums and teeth and leave it on for about 20 minutes. This treatment is helpful if you have recently experienced bleeding in the tooth and gum area.

You can also shape the wheatgrass pulp into small rounds and dry it in the sun. The rounds contain large amounts of vitamin A. Also, the protein in the pulp will increases during the drying process. You can place these vitamin-rich rounds in the bathwater as a skin treatment.

Wheatgrass and the Aging Factor

The young blades of the wheatgrass plant contain many properties that proponents claim can rejuvenate the body's cells. According to Ann Wigmore and other researchers in the 1940s, chlorophyll is a factor in the renewed life of these cells and, thus, a key component in the battle against aging skin.

The enzymes contained in wheatgrass also play a major role in skin renewal as they detoxify bacteria and pollutants from the cells. In particular, the enzyme superoxide dismutases (SOD) is especially effective in the anti-aging process. SOD is found in almost all of the body's cells. It plays a major role in nullifying excessive amounts of superoxides, which are natural by-products of metabolism. Too many superoxides in the body can cause cell damage, stimulating aging. SOD keeps the superoxide balance in check, giving cells a chance to regenerate.

Wheatgrass juice, when consumed regularly, can suffice as a beauty treatment that slows down the aging process. Because wheatgrass is an effective blood cleanser, it will immediately go to work rejuvenating aging cells. Some users claim wheatgrass can tighten droopy, sagging skin. Wheatgrass juice can even be used on the face as a cleanser to further promote a more beautiful, youthful appearance. Using wheatgrass on a daily basis can work wonders on your body. Your hair, skin, and nails will benefit from such treatment because the minerals and enzymes in wheatgrass saturate lifeless cells and perk them up. Users claim nails will grow stronger and hair color can be restored. Ann Wigmore claimed that her gray hair was completely restored to its natural brown color after turning to wheatgrass and other life-giving foods. Wheatgrass treatment on the scalp also benefits the hair by giving it a healthy luster.

As the body gets older, it will experience a natural degeneration in the function of its body parts. Pollutants in the environment, stress, and a number of other factors will add to the degeneration process. Adopting a chlorophyll-rich diet can fortify the body and enable it to better cope with the changes that are a part of life. Well-nourished cells help body parts to function at their best. Wheatgrass is a good source of chlorophyll and, when added to the diet with other life-giving foods, can help the body better deal with the aging process.

More Secrets to a Healthier You

Body odor is highly embarrassing, and no one wants to be found in a position where he or she is avoided due to unseemly odors. It is important to cleanse the body systems on a regular basis. Many times those chocolate-covered donuts or that pineapple upside down cake can be the culprit causing embarrassing odors. The white flour used in certain foods builds up in the intestines and is hard to eliminate. This can create toxins that will be eliminated in the form of intestinal gas. It is often said, "You are what you eat." If you continue to consume poor-quality foods, foods that are unhealthy and unprofitable to the body, you will suffer from the effects of these foods. No amount of bathing or scrubbing the skin can correct a problem that stems from within. Though little research exists on the exact correlation between certain foods and body odor, it is thought that body odor is often the result of poor eating habits. Many high-fat, sugary-laden foods are difficult to digest and remain in the body decaying. This produces toxins that are harmful as well as odorous. Odorous toxins can escape the body through the skin, hair, breath, and bowels. You can overcome these odor problems by correcting bad food habits. The chlorophyll in wheatgrass juice has been proven to be an effective deodorizer for the body. Adopting a diet of wheatgrass juice and other raw foods helps solve the problem of body odor, according to some claims.

Wheatgrass and alopecia

Alopecia areata is a skin condition resulting in patchy and sometimes complete hair loss. It usually occurs on the scalp, but it can also affect other parts of the body. The condition is considered to be due to autoimmunity, a condition where the body's immune system attacks and damages normal body tissue. This can occur at any age. In many situations, the hair follicles beneath the skin simply stop functioning.

There is no permanent cure known for alopecia areata, but wheatgrass juice is claimed to be an effective treatment in a number of cases. Wheatgrass reportedly heals the hair follicles the same way muscle tissue and skin is healed following injury. The hormones and minerals in the wheatgrass stimulate growth factor — a substance that stimulates cell growth and division — activity. These factors are vital for promoting proper cell function, including cell renewal and division. Supporters claim wheatgrass juice can help re-activate hair follicles, promoting regrowth of the hair, when applied to the affected areas.

There are many other ways that wheatgrass juice can be used if it is applied to the skin. It can help with itching, scratches, and other skin lesions. You can rub the pulp of the wheatgrass into the skin, or you can juice the wheatgrass and apply it to the skin.

Wheatgrass help for other problems

Some have claimed that wheatgrass has the ability to purify water from pollutants. Just one ounce of wheatgrass in a gallon of fluoridated water — water that contains fluoride, a form of the chemical element fluorine — can transform it into good, usable water. Although many public water supplies are fluoridated, there is some controversy about the safety of fluoride in drinking water. According to the U. S. Environmental Protection Agency Headquarters' Union and other health-conscious groups, adding fluoride to water is an unreasonable risk. Though moderate amounts of fluoride promote tooth health, too much fluoride can cause dental fluorosis, which often stains teeth and can cause cracking in severe cases. The addition of wheatgrass to the water makes it suitable for consumption. Wheatgrass can also be included in bathwater. The juice can help relieve stress, as tired skin will eagerly soak up the rejuvenating properties. It also adds softness to the face and hands.

Wheatgrass and Weight Management

Obesity is a major concern in the United States today. Although most people do not want to be overweight, they generally do not regard obesity as a serious problem. Obesity is a serious problem, however. It is a disease that can lead to many other health problems such as depression, heart disease, high blood pressure, and cancer. There are more than 50 million obese people in America alone. Obesity is also a leading cause of mortality in the United States, according to the American Obesity Association.

The difference between being overweight and obese is generally determined by the body mass index (BMI) of an individual. This is a calculated number using the weight and height of a man or a woman. Obesity in children is determined by individual examination. One is considered overweight if his or her BMI measurement is between 25 and 29.9. If the BMI measurement is over 30, the person is considered obese. Obesity may be the result of many factors, including genetics, medical conditions, an inactive lifestyle, and lack of energy balance. Lack of energy occurs when caloric intake is greater than energy output. Many people have a slow metabolism. The best way to combat this problem is to become more physically active and consume foods that allow for better circulation. Another common recommendation is to avoid processed foods, including sugar, red meat, and dairy products.

Although drinking wheatgrass juice will not make you slim by itself, it can help to combat the problem of excess weight. Wheatgrass is effective at helping you to control your appetite. It also eliminates excess fat in the body. The many different enzymes in wheatgrass aid the body in getting rid of unnecessary poundage. Wheatgrass juice can also provide an excellent source of iodine, which is necessary for the formation of thyroid hormones. Thyroid hormones regulate the metabolism, which affects a person's weight. This addition to the diet will have a tonic effect on the body and will help tremendously in losing weight safely. You can start a weight loss routine gradually by consuming wheatgrass juice on a regular basis while also consuming foods that are fresh and light. Crash diets are not healthy. A diet rich in organic, raw food and plenty of wheatgrass juice can set you up for the best weight loss diet you have ever had.

Wheatgrass help for the underweight

Not everyone suffers from the problem of obesity. Some individuals are extremely thin due to an overactive metabolism. Individuals with a BMI below 18.5 are classified as underweight. Wheatgrass can help correct this problem by enabling the body to better assimilate the nutrition in food. Wigmore suggested digestive stimulation, which involves adding more enzymes when meals are consumed. Adding enzymes to the diet for weight gain might seem like a contrary concept; however, some individuals are unable to properly synthesize protein due to an abundance of cortisol in the body. Cortisol is a hormone manufactured by the adrenal gland in response to stress. One of its main functions is to assist protein metabolism. Too much cortisol in the body results in too little protein. Too little protein hinders the building of tissues and muscles. Digestive enzymes go to work lowering cortisol levels.

Additional enzymes at mealtime also stimulate the existing enzymes in the lower intestines, encouraging them to more fully absorb nutrients and calories from the food. Digestion stimulation paired with relaxation is beneficial for slowing down metabolism. The large quantity of enzymes — especially the digestive enzymes protease, amylase, and lipase — as well as other nutrients in wheatgrass make it the perfect food for those needing to put on weight. Wheatgrass helps with weight gain in the following ways:

- Clears accumulated mucus from the intestinal tract
- Allows greater absorption of the nutrition in food
- Relaxes the nervous system
- Stimulates the digestive tract
- Improves blood quality

Some individuals gain weight because of stress. Others do not eat well and, thus, do not benefit from the food they intake. A relaxed nervous system can reduce the effects of stress, helping these individuals to eat better and put on weight. Increased blood quality can also help with weight gain. As the blood cells become oxygenated, the body is energized and able to perform physical tasks that, perhaps, were impossible to tackle before, such as exercise. This physical exertion of the body opens the appetite, naturally leading to weight increase. The chlorophyll in wheatgrass is also good for stabilizing blood sugar levels. Increased blood sugar can cause weight gain. Of course, those who are underweight due to illness such as hypoglycemia, a condition in which blood sugar levels are too low, should approach the weight-gain issue from the angle of addressing the illness. As stressed elsewhere in this book, individuals looking to correct an illness should consult with their medical physician before embarking on a wheatgrass regimen.

Incorporating Wheatgrass into Your Current Diet

Wheatgrass can be very easily adapted into any diet. Whether you feast on chips and soda in the mornings or meticulously choose fresh fruits and homemade yogurt, you can include wheatgrass in your regular routine. Of course, the fresh fruits and yogurt would allow the wheatgrass to better perform its restorative and healing function. If you are adding wheatgrass to a poor diet in hopes of offsetting some impending disease, you are probably deceiving yourself. Wheatgrass alone cannot prevent or treat disease. It works along with other nutritious foods and life-changing practices, such as exercise, to bring about results. If you are eating moderately well and wish to include wheatgrass juice to boost the nutritional value of the foods, you can benefit from the wheatgrass. If you are experiencing a few symptoms that are unnatural to the body, such as low-energy, headaches, and irregular bowels, adding wheatgrass to your diet can be beneficial. It will help your body become more alkaline and move toward health improvements. The body functions optimally when it is pH balanced. The pH scale ranges from 0 to 14, with the more acidic substances with a pH of less than 7 and the more basic, or alkaline substances, with a pH higher than 7. Seven is a neutral pH. The body normally has a blood pH of 7.35 to 7.45 and operates best with a 7.4 pH. Many factors contribute to this pH level, but the body can face serious problems if the pH becomes too acidic or basic.

Problems with high-protein diets

There are many different diet regimens and weight-loss plans offering false hope for those wishing to lose weight. Dieters, in frustration, often flit from one diet plan to the next with little or no success. High-protein and low-carbohydrate diets, in particular, should be a cause for concern. These diets encourage a high consumption of chicken and lean beef and almost no carbohydrates, which cannot be a healthy action. A high intake of fats and proteins and a low intake of carbohydrates produce ketone toxins. These can lead to ketosis, a toxic condition in the body that can cause organs to fail. Doctors recommend consuming at least 100 grams of carbohydrates a day to prevent ketosis.

A high-protein diet creates temporary loss of weight, mostly from losing water weight. The body is attempting to dilute and flush out the manufactured toxins of the extra protein. After a few days, the weight loss ceases. The dieter then abandons the diet and picks up the lost weight and perhaps a few more pounds. This type of diet is also dangerous as it can cause kidney damage brought on by the ketosis. Gout can also become a problem as well as liver disease, cancer, and heart issues. High-protein diets can also cause constipation and dilute the vitamins and minerals that are in the body, causing tooth decay and bone loss. Wheatgrass should not be paired with a high-protein diet, as it will not be able to work effectively.

Pairing wheatgrass with other foods

Although wheatgrass is best consumed alone and on an empty stomach, you can use it in meal preparation to boost the nutritional value of the meal, as well as to tone down the intense flavor of the wheatgrass. Technically, wheatgrass should not be cooked as cooking destroys the enzymes in food. Wheatgrass juice and powders have been used in the following ways:

- Wheatgrass juice or powder can be added to sauces, gravies, and dressings. It is better to add the wheatgrass to the food after the dish has been cooked to preserve the wheatgrass's nutrients, preferably just before serving.

- Wheatgrass can also be added to baked goods, such as bread recipes, muffins, and pizza dough. If using a bread machine, add the wheatgrass powder to the flour before adding the yeast.

- Powdered wheatgrass can be sprinkled on hot and cold cereals, popcorn, and salads. Wheatgrass sprouts can also be used in salads.

- Chapter 1 noted how wheatgrass can be used in juices and smoothies. The powder can also be used in soymilk to create a wheatgrass shake.

Food chemists are currently conducting taste and nutritional tests to compare wheatgrass flours to conventional wheat flours. The USDA Western Regional Research Center (WRRC) in Albany, California, is conducting food evaluation on intermediate wheatgrass grain, which has nutritional qualities similar to wheat and rye. By comparison, the wheatgrass grain has a higher protein level than regular wheat. The sweet, nutty taste of the wheatgrain flour was also preferred to regular wheat flour in taste tests conducted by chemist Robert Becker in Albany, California.

Establishing a New Lifestyle with Wheatgrass

Although life is full of changes, it does not mean that it is easy to embrace the change. Adopting a new lifestyle can be difficult. If you are interested in experiencing the maximum benefits of wheatgrass to improve health or to prevent or treat a disease, a new lifestyle might be in order.

A new lifestyle includes a new diet. The Living Foods Lifestyle® was developed by Ann Wigmore; it is a program devoted to teaching users how to restore health through detoxification, quality nutrition, and exercise. The principle of the Living Foods Lifestyle lies in the theory that the body can and will heal itself if given the proper tools. If you find yourself in a situation where you have a potentially life-threatening disease, simply including wheatgrass into your current diet might not be sufficient. After consulting with your physician, of course, you might decide to adopt an entirely new lifestyle. A thorough internal cleansing would be the first order of business. You would need to adopt and maintain a high-quality diet of high-fiber, low-fat *living* foods. Living foods are natural, unprocessed foods that are full of nutrients and retain their original enzyme content. Wheatgrass should be a major part of this diet. Plenty of exercise and rest are also essential.

The living foods diet

The Living Foods Diet, the Wheatgrass Diet, the Hippocrates Diet, and the Ann Wigmore Diet are essentially the same. They should not be confused with the wheatgrass fast that is discussed later. The wheatgrass diet is not a whimsical weight-loss program that calls for drinking gallons of wheatgrass juice throughout the day. The diet is a structured regimen that includes the addition of wheatgrass and other raw and living foods such as seeds, grains, sprouted nuts, fruits, and vegetables to improve or correct health. Diet developers say that wheatgrass juice has a vital life energy that is generally destroyed when the grain is cooked or processed. Some food researchers, such as enzyme specialist Dr. Edward Howell of Chicago, stress the importance of active enzymes in the diet. Howell said that enzymes are destroyed once food is heated above 212 degrees Fahrenheit. Some raw foodists — those that eat 75 percent or more raw and living foods — claim that destruction begins at as little as 106 degrees. Dr. Howell points out that acid secretion in the stomach is minimal for at least 30 minutes when food is first consumed, giving the enzymes in the food the chance to perform the work of digestion. After 30 minutes, when the acid juices begin to freely flow, enzymes in the food can still perform digestive work because they can tolerate certain acid conditions. This self-digestion saves the pancreas the work of over-producing the enzymes necessary for food digestion. By eating a diet rich in living foods, you can help strengthen your immune system, which will aid the body in self-recovery.

What are raw and living foods?

Raw and living foods are foods that contain a wide range of nutrients and enzyme activity. Enzyme activity is the catalytic effect created by an enzyme. These foods help the body to alleviate health problems, working with the body to bring about its natural healing. Raw and living foods also help with weight maintenance and enhance activities of the brain. These foods provide nutrients that can enable the brain to function better. Raw nuts and seeds, especially walnuts and sunflower seeds, increase memory and boost brainpower. Oxygen-rich blood — provided by raw and living foods — increases mental health. Most people use the terms "raw" and "living" to refer to the same foods. There is, however, some differences between the two terms. Living food is food that is still growing. Living foods have a higher enzyme content that is readily available upon consumption of the food. Raw foods tend to lose their nutritional value as they age. Also, raw foods, such as nuts, must be "activated" to gain the highest benefits of their enzyme content. This can be done by soaking the nuts in water for about 24 hours. Once the nuts begin to sprout, they are considered living foods. For the greatest nutritional benefit, living foods must be organic, or grown without pesticides.

Food history began during a time when humans did not cook their food. They survived on foods provided by nature such as seeds, nuts, and fruits. They also were able to consume certain roots and leaves. Cooked foods were introduced into the diet sometime after the discovery of fire. Since that time, cooking has become more and more advanced to the point of using microwave ovens, steamers, and deep-fryers. These cooking devices not only cook the food but, because of their high temperatures, often also cook the vitamins and minerals in the food. If the nutrients are destroyed, the food cannot benefit the body. The living foods diet is concerned with offering nourishment to the body at the highest level. Living foods are those foods that still have the nutrients — vitamins, minerals, and enzymes — intact. The diet mainly consists of fruits, vegetables, greens, sprouted grains, nuts, seeds, chlorophyll juices, fermented foods, and raw honey. Fermented foods are foods produced or preserved by microorganisms. Microorganisms are organisms that cannot be seen with the naked eye. Organisms such as yeast have been used for years in food and beverage preparation. The Living Foods Diet is void of any foods that are unsafe for human consumption. Raw, living foods are prepared in ways that are healthy as well as palatable.

Benefits of eating fresh fruits and vegetables

The fruit is the part of a plant that contains the seeds. Water makes up 80 percent or more of most fruits, but they still offer much in the way of enzymes. Fruits work to cleanse the body, regulate metabolism, and provide energy. Mild acids contained in the fruit help the body to eliminate toxins and waste. Though fruits can be eaten at any time of the day, it is best not to eat fruit immediately after a non-fruit meal so that the fruit will not interfere with the body's digestion. Supporters of the food combination approach, which pairs certain foods together based on their nutrient and chemical make-up, say that the sugar in the fruit needs little, if any, digestion and might ferment if allowed to linger in the stomach with others food that require longer digestion. According to this approach, sugars mixed with starches can also cause gastric problems. Conventional nutrition information does not include guidelines about which foods should be combined.

Fruits are great for snacks and desserts. Dried fruits are especially good for snacking and can be substituted for fresh fruit when it is not available. Soaking dried fruit in water before consuming it will help the body to digest it better. Unsulfured and unpasteurized dried fruits are the best to consume. These can be found at health food stores. Sulfured and pasteurized fruits can be difficult to digest. These fruits contain sulfur dioxide as a preservative. Scientists have examined the possible negative effect of the chemical compound sulfur dioxide. Excess consumption of the compound can lead to bloating, gas, and other digestive problems. It can also cause asthma in sensitive individuals. Most governments either regulate the amount allowed in food or have suggested guidelines in place. The process of pasteurization uses high temperatures to destroy bacteria in foods. These temperatures can also destroy the nutritional content of some foods, causing them to be no more than nutritionless calories. This can lead to weight gain. It is also suggested that dried fruits be washed to eliminate dust and possible insect eggs.

Modern vegetables are derived from herbs that grew in the wild. Vegetables and greens are valuable to the body. They contain good amounts of vitamins and minerals that help the body to grow and develop. Vegetables also help the body eliminate wastes and toxins. They provide natural fiber that helps the colon to function properly. Raw salads provide the body with roughage, also called fiber, which helps with the elimination process. You should eat greens and vegetables in abundance daily. They supply the body with calcium, iron, and other nutrients. Sprouts, raw greens like spinach, avocados, and nuts and seeds are all a part of the living foods group that benefits the body.

What do the critics say?

Not everyone supports the idea of eating raw, living foods for health and well-being. Many nutritionists feel the Living Foods Diet is extreme, stating that most enzymes — whether cooked or uncooked — are naturally destroyed by the gastric juices in the stomach and, therefore, are not benefited by the body as they are not absorbed by the small intestine. Wheatgrass critic Frederic Patenaude points out in his article "What's Wrong with Wheatgrass" that the enzymes destroyed in food are not the same enzymes required for the digestion of food. Food enzymes, Patenaude claims, are for the benefit of the growth of the plant and are not needed in the human digestive process. Nutritionists also advocate that many raw foods, such as sprouts and unpasteurized dried fruits, are unpalatable and can even be unsafe to consume. Many nutritionists also say claims about wheatgrass benefits are too far-fetched.

Benefits of chlorophyll juices

Fresh fruit juices are an important part of a living foods diet. They are filled with nutrients, are low in calories, and can be assimilated easily by the body. Chlorophyll juices, unlike fruit juices, are juiced from green vegetables filled with chlorophyll. *See Chapter 2 for a look at the importance of chlorophyll and how it works in the body.* Chlorophyll juices are also rich in vitamins, especially iron, which is important for the prevention of anemia. The iron comes from the leafy greens that you use to make chlorophyll juice, so the iron content will change depending on the source of the juice. Chlorophyll juices are non-toxic and can be consumed in abundance on a daily basis. (You should not suddenly start consuming large quantities of wheatgrass because of its detoxifying effects. If you use wheatgrass to make the juice, start consuming it in small amounts initially and work your way up to larger doses.) Chlorophyll juices should be juiced fresh and consumed immediately after the juicing. You should juice them with a slow-turning juicer. Slow-turning juicers are built to handle the strong, fibrous texture of grasses and greens. The low-speed operation also preserves the enzymes and other plant nutrients, because the juicer does not create heat from friction. The nutrients in chlorophyll juices are good protectors from pollutants and toxins in the body. Good vegetables for making chlorophyll juices include collards, dandelions greens, kale, and wheatgrass. Other vegetables can be added such as carrots and squash to enhance the flavor of the juice.

Benefits of sprouted seeds, nuts, and grains

Nature provides an abundance of seeds, nuts, and grains. They are best used by the body when they are eaten raw or when they are sprouted; otherwise, these foods can interfere with the body's digestive system. Sprouts, such as alfalfa, clover, and sunflower seeds, are inexpensive and provide good nutrition for the body. Sprouting grains such as wheat, rice, and oats brings them to life, boosting their nutrient value. Sprouted seeds, nuts, and grains are easily digested, and their high enzyme content actually helps with digestion. Sprouts are often referred to as vegetables, although, according to Ann Wigmore, they are really in a class of their own. Sprouts are more nutritionally dense than most vegetables. The sprouting process also makes the seed or grain easier to digest. You can use sprouts in a variety of ways, and they are especially good on raw salads. You can also blend them with other fruits and vegetables. Sprouted grains can be used to make bread or crackers. Nuts and seeds can be eaten raw or soaked before eating. Soaking the nuts and seeds before eating provides the greatest nutritional value. Seeds and nuts can be used in a variety of dishes. Nut milk, especially, is good to drink and is beneficial for the body. You can make nut milk yourself from nuts and seeds.

What are fermented foods?

Fermenting is the chemical decomposition, or breaking down, of organic substances. This process breaks fats, starches, and proteins into smaller substances for better consumption. If food is fermented outside the body, it is often referred to as "predigested" food. For example, both pickles and sauerkraut are treated before you eat them. Fruits and honey are also considered predigested because nature ripens, or predigests, them. Raw honey provides the body with energy, food enzymes, and other nutrients. These types of foods require less work for the body to digest than cooked foods. Fermented foods are useful, when used without meat, in correcting the acid level in the colon, which is needed for the colon to function at its best.

The use of sea vegetables

The living foods diet also incorporates sea vegetables in its rejuvenating plan. Sea vegetables are various types of sea plants, like seaweed, that grow in the ocean. They contain a great supply of minerals and nutrients. Humans can easily digest the organic mineral salts in the sea vegetables. These minerals and elements come from the sea or coast where the vegetables have been harvested, making them a valuable addition to the human diet. In fact, sea vegetables contain the greatest amount of trace elements and minerals of all the food groups. Fresh or dried, sea vegetables are beneficial to the diet because they are raw and unprocessed. Sea vegetables also can add flavor to your dishes. Because they contain a percentage of mineral-rich sea salt, sea vegetables eliminate the need for the large quantity of salt that many recipes require.

Kelp and dulse are the most common sea vegetables used in the living foods diet. You can purchase them at most health food stores and some supermarkets. Kelp can be crumpled and added to soups and salads. Kelp can also be ground into a powder, and when mixed with dried wheatgrass powder, it can boost the nutritional value of the foods. You can also use kelp powder as a salt substitute. *Read more about kelp in Chapter 9.* Dulse seaweed is high in vitamin B and other vitamins and rich in protein and fiber. You can add dulse to soups or salads or eat it as a snack. Soak sea vegetables in warm water to soften them. This allows the vegetables to be sliced and used for roll-ups or wraps in sushi rolls. You should never consume the soaked water from the sea vegetables due to its high salt content. Sea vegetables can also be included in a variety of dishes to enhance the taste as well as the nutritional value of the dish. See the following websites for recipes and ideas using sea vegetables in dishes:

- Inner Self (**www.innerself.com/recipes/sea_veggies.htm**) is a motivational site encouraging individuals to better themselves in order to excel in life. The food and nutrition section offers a number of healthy recipes incorporating sea vegetables to boost nutrition.

- Mitoku: Macrobiotics and Organic Foods (**www.mitoku.com/ recipes/index/seavegetables.html**) is a leading exporter of traditional Japanese foods. The site has an expansive recipe section that elaborates on the benefits of various sea vegetables and how to use them in meal preparations.

- Julie's Raw Ambition (**www.juliesrawambition.com/category/ recipes/sea-vegetables**) demonstrates creative dining through raw and living foods. Recipes including sea vegetables are included in the mix of healthy, gourmet meals.

The use of condiments

Many people are used to cooking with different spices or seasonings. These seasonings and spices can really bring a recipe to life. The living food diet also uses herbs and spices. Lemon juice, sea salt, raw honey, and certain other herbs and spices can all be used to flavor different foods. Although not all herbs and spices have medicinal and nutritional value, if used sparingly, they can enhance a meal without harming the body. With the living food diet, you do not use traditional table salt that you purchase from the supermarket. The diet uses salt in the form of miso or tamari, flavorful Japanese condiments made from aged soybeans. Sometimes, a little sea salt can be fine. Fresh lemon juice on salads can provide a delightful flavor. You should avoid strong spices like powdered or fresh onion and garlic powder, especially if you have digestive problems. If you do use different spices or herbs as condiments, use them sparingly. Remember they are meant to enhance the flavor of the foods, not mask it.

Food combining

The body must digest food to use it properly. It takes about 24 to 72 hours to complete the process of digestion beginning with the ingestion of the food and ending in the elimination of waste products. It is important to chew the food properly when consuming it, because the salivary glands play an important part in the digestive process. Food must be masticated, or chewed, thoroughly. The saliva secretes enzymes that aid in food digestion. This is called pre-digestion. If the food is not masticated properly, it makes the digestion process difficult and all body parts involved must work harder. Some foods, like melons, other fruits, wheatgrass, and other chlorophyll juices, are absorbed directly into the body's system. A great percentage of food, however, is not digested before moving into the small intestine. This can result in indigestion problems such as gas, bloating, and constipation.

At times, people do not think about the foods they eat and how their choices will affect their digestive system — they just eat. Many times, however, the foods clash when combined in the digestive system. This creates distress that can lead to gas or stomach ailments. The theory of food combining, developed by Dr. William Howard Hay in 1911, addresses these issues. This theory states that each food type requires different conditions to digest properly. According to the food combining approach, certain foods should not be mixed because some foods take longer to digest than others. Other foods should not be mixed because they require different enzymes for digestion or different pH balances of the digestive juices. Proponents of the approach say proper food combining is very important for enhancing health. Benefits include better digestion, weight loss, increased energy, and a sense of well-being. If you are embarking on a new health regimen, you must not overlook the importance of food combining. It does not matter that the foods all end up in one place — when foods clash in the stomach, this puts a strain on the entire gastrointestinal tract. This can affect the whole process of food digestion. To ensure that the digestion of food, the assimilation of food, and elimination of food are efficient, you should not overload the digestive system.

The small intestine helps absorb nutrients from the food. The small intestine uses finger-like projections called villi located within its walls to soak up nutrients. Once absorbed, the nutrients travel to the liver. The liver filters nutrients into the blood where they are converted into elements that can be assimilated by the body. These nutrients leave the liver by way of the blood system and are sent to the lungs and other parts of the body. The entire food digestion process can be hindered and result in heartburn or other digestive ailments if the food is not digested properly. Starchy foods need to be paired with plenty of alkaline digestive juices to be digested and assimilated properly. Protein foods, however, require the acid juices of the stomach for proper digestion. If the two substances cross, they will neutralize each other. This will slow down the digestion of the meal and lead to indigestion.

If you want to begin a living food and raw food diet using the food combining approach, you will need to develop a plan for your diet. Nomi Shannon, in her book *The Raw Gourmet*, and Ann Wigmore, in her book *The Hippocrates Diet and Health Program*, suggested the following tips for adhering to a food combining diet:

- Do not mix vegetables with fruit in the same meal. The acids and sugars in the fruits will slow down the digestion of the starches and vegetables, which can cause gas and bloating.

- Do not mix acidic fruits, such as oranges, with sweet fruits, such as bananas and pears. Consume one or the other. Do not eat breads or grain products with acidic fruits on a regular basis.

- All sprouts and vegetables can be mixed together, including greens and avocados. Nuts and seeds also mix well with vegetables, sprouts, and greens. Do not try to crowd too many of these foods into one meal because they might distress the digestive system.

- It is important not to eat sprouted grains and nuts with acidic fruits.

- Sprouted seeds and nuts can be eaten together.

- All melons should be eaten alone. They do not combine well with other foods, or even other fruits, because their digestion time is very brief — only 20 to 30 minutes.

- Never drink while you are eating as this hinders the gastric juices from working. Juices or water should be consumed half an hour before or half an hour after you consume the meal.

- Always chew your food thoroughly to mix foods and juices of the saliva.

- Do not eat foods that are excessively cold because they will have a negative affect on the diaphragm, which can cause pain in the chest. Foods should be eaten at room temperature.

- Eat the raw food in the meal before eating the cooked foods. If this is not done, the cooked food will keep the raw foods from being digested immediately, which can cause intestinal gases.

- Do not eat while stressed. The body needs to be relaxed so that all digestive organs can function at their best.

Is food combining really necessary?

Not all nutritionists and health food advocates agree with the concept of food combining. Many state there is no scientific evidence to support such a concept and that all foods are in themselves combinations. Beans contain protein and fiber as well as sugars and starches. Critics insist that the digestive system is well-equipped to handle all digestive situations in a timely fashion and that enough enzymes are present to do an effective job. Nutrition expert Dr. Gabriel Cousens, the founder of Tree of Life Rejuvenation Center and author of *Conscious Eating* and *Spiritual Nutrition*, believes if mostly enzyme-rich raw foods are consumed, there is no reason to be concerned about food-combining rules. Many agree that these rules can be confusing, and trying to follow them can be stressful. Furthermore, in a study published in an abstract by the Division of Therapeutic Patient Education for Chronic Diseases, a diet of food combining was compared with a regular diet of balanced foods and both achieved similar weight-loss results.

Another concern that many health professionals have with the food-combining concept is the idea that water hinders the gastric juices from digesting food. Mayo Clinic gastro-enterologist Dr. Michael Picco and others believe that water can actually aid digestion when consumed with a meal. Water and other liquids, especially warm liquids, help food to disintegrate, making the job of the digestive system easier.

The purpose of fasting

Fasting is the temporary abstinence or rest from all or some food and/or beverages. A fast could last only one day or extend over a number of days. The body takes advantage of this period of relief and uses it to cleanse and rebuild itself. It is important that fasting is not misused for the sole purpose of weight loss. Used in this fashion, it is potentially harmful. If deprived of foods for extended periods of time, the body will begin to process its own fats and protein for energy. This process, called "autolyzing," can result in a weakening of the entire body system. According to many health advocates, medical doctors, and spiritual leaders, fasting can be beneficial to the body. As the Greek physician, Phillipus Paracelsus, one of the fathers of western medicine concluded, "Fasting is the greatest remedy — the physician within." According to Stephen Harrod Buhner, in his article "The Health Benefits of Water Fasting," and Kevin Secours, in his document "The Benefits of Fasting," fasting can:

- Improve mental awareness
- Help the body to lose weight
- Balance the nervous system
- Restore energy levels and increases sensory perception
- Revitalize body organs
- Improve skin tone
- Help breathing
- Increase cell oxygenation and balance metabolism
- Rejuvenate the digestive system and improve bowel function
- Eliminate toxins from the body
- Stimulate the taste buds
- Help the body overcome illness, disease, and addictions

According to Ann Wigmore, withholding nutrition from the body for extended periods of time too regularly can be harsh on the body. Although fasting has many benefits for the body, fasting too frequently or for extended periods of time can also pose health problems.

Types of fasts

Fasting is an ancient practice and was often related to some type of religious ceremony or event. Many times, fasting was complete abstinence from food or drink, challenging individuals to penitence and purification. In other cases, fasts were encouraged to induce fertility or to avert catastrophes. Today, fasting is still practiced by many cultures. The norm, however, is more selective fasting rather than complete abstinence. As a word of precaution, it is highly recommended that you consult with a health care professional before embarking on a major fast. Those with severe health ailments, such as diabetes, and pregnant women especially should seek professional medical advice, as fasting is not recommended in these situations.

The water fast

Fasting with water can last for one day only or up to 40 days. The ten-day water fast, encouraged by health advocate Paul Bragg, is a popular fast for cleansing the body and encouraging weight loss. It involves the complete elimination of solid food from the diet and the ingestion of only water. Distilled water is recommended due to its magnetic properties and ability to absorb toxins. Distilled water has been purified of toxins through the process of distillation — boiling to produce steam, which is condensed for consumption. Because distilled water has no impurities, it is helpful in flushing toxins from the body. Distilled water also has the ability to absorb carbon dioxide when exposed to air. The magnetic properties are also helpful in suspending flushing toxins from the body. Water fasting claims to remove toxins rapidly from the body. Because water has no calories or nutritional value, this might be a difficult fast for some. It requires mental preparation as well as physical preparation and should be performed when only minimal pressure and responsibility are present in your daily routine. Some advise drinking fruit juices or eating raw fruits the week before the fast to ease into the detoxification process. It is also recommended that a water fast begin and end with a two to three day juice fast. You can read more about the ten-day water fast in Paul Bragg's book, *The Miracle of Fasting*. His website EvolutionHealth.com (**www.evolutionhealth.com/bragg_miracle_fasting .html**) includes information on fasting as well.

The juice fast

A 30-day juice fast, recommended by European health facilities, claims to remove toxins from the body while supplying energy to the body. It is a corrective procedure, because juices are easily absorbed into the system, allowing more energy for the body to heal and rejuvenate. Because your only calories come from the juice, the less juice you consume, the more intense the detoxification process will be. Use fresh fruits and vegetables for the juice fast, and do not mix them together. Some say the 30-day juice fast and the ten-day water fast deliver the same results. Individuals hoping to lose weight might find diluting the juices with water helpful.

The lemonade fast

The lemonade fast, sometimes called the Lemon Cleanse or Master Cleanse Diet, was originally developed in the 1940s by alternative health practitioner Stanley Burroughs as a cure for ulcers. It entails consuming lemon water sweetened with maple syrup and flavored with cayenne pepper for a period of ten to 40 days. The diet is still popular today as a means of detox and weight loss. Learn more about the lemonade fast on the All About Fasting website (**www.allaboutfasting.com/master-cleanse.html**).

The wheatgrass fast

Fasting with wheatgrass allows the body to experience the benefits of fasting without compromising safety. The three-day wheatgrass fast, as described in *The Wheatgrass Book* by Ann Wigmore, not only incorporates the powerful wheatgrass juice, it also involves consuming other high-quality green drinks from nutritious vegetables such as greens and sprouts. These juices assimilate quickly into the bloodstream, delivering oxygen to the cells and encouraging elimination. Rejuvelac, a fermented wheatberry drink developed by Ann Wigmore, is often used in the fast and daily enemas or implants are helpful. The wheatgrass fast offers enough nutrients to the body to enable fasters to perform their regular activities. Care should be taken, however, not to overextend oneself. The fast should not be performed on days filled with appointments and errands, as rest is highly recommended. Additionally, the wheatgrass fast is gentle on the body, allowing the individual to ease into and out of the diet without the "healing crisis" that is so often associated with many fasts. The healing crisis can produce vomiting, diarrhea, and other undesirable symptoms as the body is plunged into a harsh fast without adequate preparation. The more toxic the body, the greater the healing crisis. Wigmore claims that the wheatgrass fast, although lacking in calories, will cause no negative effect on the body if kept to a period of three days or less. In fact, she said many would benefit from the loss of excess weight and waste a three-day fast would bring about. Caution should be taken when breaking the wheatgrass fast — as with all fasts — to allow the body to readjust to solid foods slowly. A moderate amount of fresh fruit (one or two apples and a few grapes, for instance) is recommended once you have completed the fast.

Dangers of Fasting

Many critics, such as Dr. William T. Jarvis of National Council Against Health Fraud (NCAHF), are quick to point out side effects and potential dangers of fasting. Although this has been a method of cleansing and healing for centuries, fasting is now met with skepticism and criticism, especially in the Western world. Dr. Jarvis points out that fasting does not relieve the liver, but "overworks the liver by saturating it with toxins produced by fasting itself." Headaches, muscle aches, and nausea can be directly related to fasting. Prolonged fasting can lead to kidney problems, liver problems, and anemia. In extreme cases, death has been associated with fasting. Water fasting, primarily used for detoxification purposes, is said to lead to vitamin deficiencies, loss of muscle, and blood-sugar problems. The juice fast, although actually full of nutrients and protein, leads to metabolism disturbances. The slowing of the metabolism causes weight gain. Because wheatgrass is low in caloric value, many experts deem it unsafe for fasting purposes. Some critics claim that what many are calling detoxification is actually starvation. According to a 1998 report from the Clinical Guidelines on the Identification, Evaluation and Treatment of Overweight and Obesity in Adults, safe weight loss should be about one to two pounds per week over a period of weeks or months. The sudden loss of excess weight associated with the wheatgrass diet also makes it an unsafe plan of action. All fasters should beware of the "healing crisis" associated with fasting, which is a reaction of the body to the detoxification process and results in symptoms such as cramps, headaches, diarrhea, and skin lesions. Although many believe the healing crisis to be a natural part of fasting, fasters must know when to draw the line, as potential danger exists with such "crises."

Wheatgrass and exercise

Everyone knows the importance of exercise. Exercise helps lower blood pressure and cholesterol levels. It also helps prevent the development of many diseases, such as diabetes, cardiovascular disease, and cancer. Daily moderate exercise can also lower the risk for developing osteoporosis and break the depression-obesity cycle. Dutch researcher Dr. Floriana S. Luppino of Leiden University Medical Center and other physicians have noted a strong link between depression and obesity. According to Dr. Luppino, this link has led to a negative cycle where depressed individuals seek comfort in binge eating, leading to excess weight gain. They then become depressed because of the weight gain and resort to more eating. Although many people know about the dangers of obesity, statistics from the U.S. government and health sites, such as the U.S. Department of Health and Human Services and the Office of Disease Prevention and Health Promotion, concur that people of all ages do not exercise as much as they should.

Why is exercise such a neglected practice in so many lives? Everyone is different, but the following are some of the commonly cited reasons people do not exercise on a regular basis, according to a 2009 U.S. News & World Report article:

- No time
- No interest
- No energy
- No money for gym membership or equipment
- Lack of discipline
- Frustration
- Embarrassment
- Lack of knowledge
- Exercise is hard
- Exercise is inconvenient
- Too old
- Too fat
- Too thin
- Too out-of-shape
- Arthritis

Exercise is work, and in many cases, the body is not prepared to perform this type of work. With the convenience of modern transportation, people are not used to walking as a primary mode of transportation. Today's sedentary lifestyle does not naturally encourage exercise. People must put aside time for exercise and cultivate a desire to exercise to keep themselves motivated. However, exercise is necessary for healthy living. Exercise and nutrition work together to create harmony within the body. Food and stored fat need the oxygen derived from exercise to be converted into energy. Without energy, the body feels tired and sluggish.

The thought of adding exercise to your daily routine might seem overwhelming. However, by easing wheatgrass into the diet and eliminating some energy-sapping foods, including white flour, white sugar, and hydrogenated fats, the body can better begin the process of establishing a regular exercise routine. As mentioned in Chapter 3, wheatgrass provides energy for the body. Wheatgrass can open the door to an entirely new way of life, making exercise an activity that is welcomed and enjoyed.

Benefits of exercise

Although maintaining a healthy diet is important, it will not benefit the body unless you also embrace physical activity. Exercise is very important for the body. It is just as important as diet and body cleansing. Exercise can improve blood circulation and help with waste elimination. It can also open the appetite for healthy, wholesome foods. Exercise also strengthens the immune system and helps with mental clarity. If you are not used to exerting energy beyond getting up in the morning, then it is time to expand yourself in this area.

Effective exercise can be as simple as walking for 30 minutes a day. Light exercise and deep breathing are also helpful. As with a change in diet and body cleansing, beginning a program of exercise should not be a haphazard endeavor. It should take some thought and some planning. If you are not used to heavy exercise, you should not immediately begin a strenuous exercise program such as weightlifting. Begin with moderate exercise that can be increased gradually. Light exercise, when done consistently, will greatly benefit the body. It will help with food digestion and weight control. Light exercise also is excellent for dealing with stress — and it can be fun. It might be hard to start at first, and it might be difficult to remain consistent, but if you persevere, you will see and feel the benefits of exercise in your life.

The importance of good rest

Just as a healthy diet and proper exercise are important, it is also important that the body gets good rest. Although the organs of the body are able to rest during a time of fasting, it is also important that the body physically rest, in sleep, for it to function optimally. The best rest is deep, undisturbed sleep. Many times, the body does not get a chance to reach this stage of sleep because it just cannot relax. Some people have to get up in the night to eat, drink, go to the bathroom, or perhaps tend to a baby or small child. Sometimes, anxiety can keep you awake, preventing your mind and body from relaxing. If the body has consumed a heavy meal too late, the body might not be able to rest because the digestive system is busy working throughout the night. When sleep is constantly disturbed, the body does not prosper. Although it has laid down to rest, the body will arise exhausted. During sleep, the body can balance itself and the cells can energize. According to the National Sleep Foundation, adults need seven to nine hours of sleep and school-aged children (5 to 10 years old) need ten to 11 hours of sleep for the body to benefit. Ten- to 17-year-olds need a recommended 8½ to 9¼ hours. Sometimes, an afternoon nap of one hour is beneficial, if you are able to do so. Researchers funded by the National Institute of Mental Health agree that a power nap can work wonders for a tired body. According to Wigmore in *The Wheatgrass Book*, adults who adopt a wheatgrass and live foods lifestyle will naturally benefit from less sleep, and only need to sleep six hours or less. Wheatgrass juice and light foods added to the diet, especially consumed as the evening meal can help the body relax and rest properly. If you are constantly on the go, it might be difficult to slow down. Rest, however, is important. Your entire body needs to rest to profit from a good night's sleep.

Is Wheatgrass Enough?

Wheatgrass is not a magic potion. Although it is full of vitamins, minerals, and many other needed nutrients for the body, it is not designed to be a one-step cure-all. Anyone looking to reap the total benefits of a wheatgrass regimen must be willing to adopt an entire health-promoting lifestyle. Once again, this includes incorporating living foods, whole body cleansing, and exercise into one's daily life. There are a number of other diets, apart from the Living Foods Diet, that emphasize nutrition as a means of physical body repair. The Gerson Diet, a low-sodium, low-fat, low-protein diet developed by Dr. Max Gerson in the 1920s, addresses chronic and degenerative diseases through immunonutrition. Immunonutrition is a specific nutrient feeding solution believed to rejuvenate the immune system, causing it to rise up against disease. This diet does not incorporate food balancing and uses an abundance of cooked foods as well as raw. The Gerson therapy of immunonutrition is still in use by the Gerson Institute located in San Diego, California. Other diets, such as the natural hygiene diet, the pH healing diet, the hallelujah diet, and the alleluia diet also purport health restoration through nutritious foods, fasting therapies, and detoxification. Wheatgrass can be successfully incorporated into any of these diets.

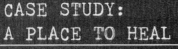

```
CASE STUDY:
A PLACE TO HEAL
Brian Clement, Ph.D., LNC, director
Hippocrates Health Institute
1443 Palmdale Court
West Palm Beach, Florida 33411
www.hippocratesinst.org
info@hippocratesinst.org
Phone: 561-471-8876
Fax: 561-471-9464
```

Dr. Brian Clement is a leading expert in the field of natural health. He has conducted numerous lectures, seminars, and educational programs, traveling extensively throughout the United States and to more than 25 countries around the globe to promote the Hippocrates philosophy, which is "the belief that a pure enzyme-rich diet, complemented by positive thinking and noninvasive therapies, are essential elements on the path to optimum health."

The Hippocrates Health Institute has been in operation since 1956 and is the oldest natural health center on the earth. It has its beginnings in

HIPP◯CRATES
HEALTH INSTITUTE

Boston where founder Ann Wigmore brought wheatgrass into preeminence. Ann had healed herself of colon cancer in the 1950s when told by Harvard University that she had only had six months to live. The healing tool was wheatgrass. Wheatgrass is a main herbal treatment and has been a popular health food for over 25 years. Wheatgrass is also a vital healing aid in the "Life Change Program" at Hippocrates Institute, now located in West Palm Beach, Florida.

The Life Change Program is the "definitive blueprint for changing over to a healthier lifestyle." It offers hope. Hope for individuals faced with an uncertain future based on a fatal medical diagnosis. If offers knowledge. Knowledge for individuals seeking to develop a healthier lifestyle for themselves and their families. It offers life. Life for all who enter the program with an open mind and a desire to turn away from deadly health choices to a vibrant, living solution of a better way.

Dr. Brian Clement, Director, Hippocrates Health Institute.

The Hippocrates Health Center and its Life Change Program help guests realize that excellent health is obtainable. It all begins with the desire to change. Coming to an institute, such as Hippocrates, to implement the change is essential for several reasons:

- It allows the individual to get away from the stressful routine of daily living.

- It allows the individual to relax as he or she becomes harmonized with nature.

- If offers a professional assessment of each individual case.

- It offers individually tailored treatment in the form of nutrition and exercise for optimum recovery.

- It offers a support group to challenge and provided necessary encouragement for implementing the change.

- It fosters the development of new friendships and strengthens prior relationships.

- It provides an education that will last a lifetime.

Hippocrates *is* an education center. It teaches people how to live in harmony with their bodies and how to strive for better health in life. Unique life skills are taught that were not a part of childhood training and were not acquired in secondary institutions of learning. These important principles are essential for successful living in today's world of environmental imbalance and deteriorating health. Hundreds of thousands of individuals have found help upon entering the doors of Hippocrates. They have learned how to heal themselves of disorder, preventing illness and prolonging their lives. Many have stayed on to attend the Health Educator Program, equipping them with the necessary tools to educate others about this healthy, natural way of life. All of these individuals have attributed life changes to their stay at the facility. They also recognize Hippocrates for what it is: a "community that offers a natural path for you to heal your body, reconnect with your spirit, and rejuvenate your health." Striving for optimum health alone can be difficult; striving for it in a professional, thriving environment with like-minded individuals can yield unlimited rewards.

CHAPTER 5

What to Know Before You Grow

"Stay close to nature and its eternal laws will protect you."
~ Dr. Max Gerson

*T*he previous chapters have outlined the principle behind using wheatgrass as food and medicine. If you are convinced that wheatgrass is good for you, and you wish to grow your own, there are a few things that you should consider before beginning the growing process. As with many activities, growing wheatgrass will only be perfected through experience. A basic knowledge of what to expect and how to go about the process, however, will help you avoid some common pitfalls.

Beginning the Process

Before you begin growing wheatgrass, you need to locate a storage area for the seeds, soil, and other tools necessary for the growing process. Seeds should be stored in a secure, airtight container to keep out moisture and weevils. Weevils are small beetles that sometimes attack wheat and other grain products. You also need to determine where you will sprout and grow the seeds. Ideally, the wheatgrass should grow in indirect sunlight and have a warm place to begin the sprouting process during the winter months. A temperature of 65 to 75 degrees Fahrenheit is recommended. The easiest place to set up a growing system might be in the kitchen, where you have access to running water. You can also use the basement, garage, or porch. Basements, however, tend to hold moisture so this might not be the best place for storing the wheatberries (wheat seeds). A greenhouse would be a perfect set up for a growing system. Apartment dwellers can grow wheatgrass in a window box or on a balcony, fire escape (if your landlord agrees), or rooftop. The rooftop might be a bit of a challenge as far as watering is concerned, but it certainly can be done. No matter your location, you can grow wheatgrass if you try. Ann Wigmore, herself, grew wheatgrass in her Boston apartment.

You will also need to decide whether you will be using soil, which is recommended, or an automatic sprouter. An automatic sprouter will allow you to grow the wheatgrass plants hydroponically, or without soil. An automatic sprouter is a growing tray (or trays) designed for sprouting grains easily. Wheatgrass seeds are planted in the same manner as with soil, but they might require a different method for watering. Instead of getting nutrients from the soil, the wheatgrass receives nutrients from a solution made from water and liquid kelp or some other natural product. A timed mist generator is often included to provide water and air to the sprouts. Although wheatgrass can be grown hydroponically, soil is the recommended growing method because young plants tend to look for nutrients from the soil after about three to four days. Some wheatgrass growers, however, report that there is little difference in the two growing methods, as you can always add a mineral product such as liquid kelp to the growing solution. *The different planting methods are discussed later in this chapter.*

Materials and Costs Associated with Growing Wheatgrass

Many people turn to growing their own wheatgrass because they are natural gardeners and enjoy the growing process. Others begin growing wheatgrass because it can be costly to continuously purchase trays of wheatgrass averaging about $20 per tray or shots of wheatgrass juice at $2.50 per one-ounce shot. Although there can be some initial expense involved in purchasing the various tools and equipment needed to begin growing wheatgrass, many of the materials are reusable. Once you get started, you will be able to produce wheatgrass trays very inexpensively. According to master grower Michael Bergonzi of the Hippocrates Health Institute, growing wheatgrass at home will only cost you about $1 per week.

Grains, seeds, kernels, or wheatberries?

The first step is finding the main ingredient — wheatgrass seeds. You will need to purchase organic hard winter wheatberries for sprouting. You should buy these from a sprouting seed house or professional wheatgrass grower. Check online for a grower in your area. You can also purchase seeds online if there is not a grower in your area. This is recommended because seeds purchased from a supermarket or health food store might not be fresh or of the best quality. It is important to purchase a good quality seed because bad seeds will not produce good wheatgrass and can also be the cause of mold.

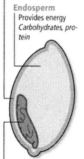

Whole grain kernel

Bran
"Outer shell" protects seed
Fiber, B vitamins, trace minerals

Endosperm
Provides energy
Carbohydrates, protein

Germ
Nourishment for the seed
Antioxidants, vitamin E, B-vitamins

Used courtesy of U.S. Department of Agriculture, MyPyramid.gov.

Wheat kernels average about $1 per pound, slightly more for organic kernels. A 1½-pound bag of wheat kernels will produce about 64 standard trays of wheatgrass. A standard tray is about 11x21 inches, but sometimes larger trays are used.

There are two main categories of wheat grain — winter wheat and spring wheat — and a variety of different types. Hard winter wheat kernels are generally used for sprouting wheatgrass. A good quality grain will be high in protein content and low in moisture. You should inquire about the protein and moisture content before purchasing the seed. Although hard red and hard white winter grains are both sold, you should purchase the hard *red* winter wheat. The color of the grain should be deeply golden. If you are purchasing from a professional wheatgrass grower, simply specifying "grains for wheatgrass growing" should be sufficient.

At this point, you might be wondering what the difference is between grains, wheatberries, wheat seeds, and wheat kernels. The difference is in theory. Grains are the seeds of cereal grasses. The wheatberry is the entire kernel of the wheat plant minus the hull. It is made up of the bran, the outer coating of shell; the germ or embryo, the part that grows into a new plant if germinated; and the endosperm, the main part of the seed from which white flour is processed. Kernel refers to large cereal seeds and, as you probably know, plants develop from seeds. A seed consists of an embryonic plant, its food store, and a covering called the seed coat. The terms grains, seeds, kernels, and wheatberries are generally used interchangeable and refer to the same thing.

Importance of an Organic Crop

Many suppliers will tell you that there is no difference between organic wheatberries and wheatberries that are not organic. Organic wheatberries are those grown from plants that have not been treated with chemicals or synthetic fertilizers. Non-organic seeds have been treated. To obtain the highest quality product possible, you must use organic wheatberries. Organically grown seeds from a natural foods store are recommended because they have not been exposed to potentially toxic sprays and fertilizers. Synthetic fertilizers are often derived from hazardous waste products and petroleum. If the soil has an imbalance of nutrients, it will cause the same imbalance in plants grown in it. Organic wheatberries are also derived from plants that have been grown in organic soil — soil that is nutritionally balanced. This allows for a nutritionally balanced product.

Organic wheatberries are also void of poisonous pesticides. Organic products are not treated with such pesticides. Organic growers use natural minerals, soil enzymes, and earthworms to promote soil fertility. They also rely on a number of biological means to control weeds and insects, such as composting crop residues and crop rotation. Crop residues, such as the stalk, leaves, and stems of the plant, are the materials left in the field after a crop has been harvested or the material remaining, such as the roots, seeds, and husks, after a product has been processed for use. This material is composted, or turned into a soil-like substance by decomposition, and used to kill weed seeds and plant pathogens. Pathogens are organisms that cause disease. Crop rotation entails growing different types of crops in the same area but at different seasons to avoid a decrease in soil fertility or the development of pests and pathogens in the soil. According to USDA standards, food labeled "organic" cannot be treated with synthetic, or man-made, pesticides. Foods grown organically are balanced, meaning they are grown in soils that have a balanced nutrient content. This is important for establishing a balanced diet. If you are trying to begin a new, healthy lifestyle, you certainly want to avoid ingesting harmful pesticides, which would defeat the purpose of the new lifestyle.

Wheatgrass Shelf Life

Hard winter wheat has a shelf life of about two years if stored properly. A cool, dry, dark space with low humidity is generally required. You can use glass, hard plastic, or aluminum containers, but they must have tight-fitting lids. Seeds can also be refrigerated or frozen for extended shelf life. However, if any condensation forms, it will shorten the shelf life of the seed. Once germination takes place, the seed begins its growing cycle and the shelf life is decreased. Generally, you will harvest the wheatgrass after six to 12 days of growth, when the grass has reached a height of about 7 inches. Harvested wheatgrass should be consumed immediately or refrigerated. Refrigerated grass is best stored in glass or plastic containers with lids or in eco-storage plastic bags. Standard plastic bags are shapeless and do not allow enough air to pass through to the grass and can suffocate the harvest. Plastic and glass containers have some airflow space at the top. Regular plastic bags also do not drain properly and can cause mildew and bacteria to develop. Refrigerated grass, if properly stored, can last about two weeks according to Steve Meyerowitz, commonly known as the Sproutman. All grass should be juiced before it begins to turn yellow. Once the grass is juiced, it should be consumed immediately or frozen. If storing wheatgrass juice in the freezer, it should be placed in plastic or glass containers. If you use a glass container, make sure the container can withstand freezing temperatures and be sure not to overfill it. This could cause it to break. Frozen wheatgrass has a shelf life of about one year.

Growing Medium

Wheatgrass is generally grown in a soil medium. Though it might be easy to find a gardening supply store or florist shop where you can purchase topsoil, peat moss, and/or compost, it might be challenging to determine the quality of the soil. Soil quality is extremely important when growing wheatgrass. Ann Wigmore recommends using a combination of topsoil and peat moss or topsoil and compost. Pre-mixed soils available at gardening shops are generally acceptable. Light and airy organic soils that include perlite and vermiculite work well. Some growers advise against using bagged organic soil, as it tends to be acidic and wheatgrass prefers more alkaline conditions. If you do use an organic soil, be sure that the organic substances in the soil are completely decomposed, meaning there is no visible organic matter, such as foods, twigs, or leaves, to avoid problems with mold. Good quality compost should be moist, dark in color, and have a loose, granular texture. Wood or bark pieces should barely be present. Also, beware of companies selling processed sewage sludge as organic compost. Sludge is taken from sewage systems and industrial waste plants. Although it has been treated and used in agriculture for more than 80 years, some health-conscious gardeners and farmers are petitioning that it be removed from land application, as it might contain contaminants and toxins. According to a 2009 report by the EPA, sewage sludge, labeled "biosolids," can be harmful to your health.

Approximate costs of soils from online sellers in 2010 are as follows:

- **Topsoil:** $2 to $5 per 25-pound bag
- **Organic topsoil:** $5 to $9 per 25-pound bag
- **Compost:** $7 for a 25-pound bag
- **Organic compost:** $6.50 to $13.50 per 3-cubic-foot bag
- **Peat moss:** $7 to $13 per compressed 4.4-cubic-foot bale
- **Lime:** $3.50 to $5 per 5-pound bag
- **Organic lime:** $5 to $6.50 per 5-pound bag

A standard 11x21-inch tray uses about two quarts of soil. Soil should be leveled to about 1 to 2 inches in the tray.

Of course, you can also use the topsoil from your garden if it is rich and fertile. Remember that gardening soil contains bugs that you might not want to bring inside your house. Gardening soil can also be contaminated with animal manure, which is fine for your garden flowers, but you might want to avoid using it in your wheatgrass due to bacteria and possible pathogens. If you do take the soil from outdoors, mix limestone in the soil to offset its acid level. Outdoor garden compost should be sifted completely before mixing with topsoil to remove sticks and large stones. As with garden topsoil, compost that has been treated with animal manure is not recommended for growing wheatgrass. If you are not using compost, you can mix peat moss with the topsoil. Peat moss helps keep the soil light and airy. It also helps absorb water and nutrients added to the soil and releases them over time into the soil. A good soil formula includes 40 percent compost, 50 percent topsoil, and 10 percent peat moss. You can also mix the compost with the soil for a 25 percent to 75 percent soil to compost ratio.

Before you start growing, it is important to determine how many trays of wheatgrass you are going to produce per day. If you plan correctly, you will have enough soil, compost, and peat moss ready when you begin the growing process. To produce one tray of wheatgrass per day, you will need two barrels of topsoil (about eight to 12 25-pound bags) and about half a bale of peat moss. You also need two empty barrels or a compost bin if you are interested in recycling the used plant mats. Plant mats are the intertwined root mats from the wheatgrass blades after they have been harvested. You can read more about composting on the EPA's website at **www.epa.gov/epawaste/conserve/rrr/composting/index.htm**.

Automatic sprouters

Wheatgrass can also be grown in an automatic sprouter. Automatic sprouters allow the wheatgrass to be watered automatically and can even control airflow. With an automatic spouter, wheatgrass can be grown without a soil requirement. Instead, a nutrient solution is used. A nutrient solution consists of water and a variety of minerals. This type of growing is referred to as hydroponic growing. Hydroponic techniques have a long history. Many believe the Hanging Gardens of Babylon used hydroponics, and the Aztecs also used this technique to create floating water gardens in the 10th and 11th centuries. It is used extensively today for crop production. First-time wheatgrass growers might have an easier time with growing plants in this manner. Growing wheatgrass hydroponically can save time and be more convenient. This method works well if you have or are working in a small space. Wheatgrass growing comparisons conducted by Steve Meyerowitz and most other growers have concluded that there are no real disadvantages to growing wheatgrass without soil; the nutritional value of the two crops are identical. Dr. Chiu-Nan Lai of the University of Texas did report stronger carcinogenic activity with soil-free wheatgrass. Many expert growers such as Michael Bergonzi of the Hippocrates Health Institute in Florida, however, still prefer growing wheatgrass with soil and believe it to be the better method.

Wheatgrass grown hydroponically alleviates problems with insects and soil-born diseases. Many users claim that hydroponically grown wheatgrass has a taste similar to the taste of green tea, compared to the super sweet taste of soil-grown grass. Wheatgrass growers are still debating whether growing in soil or without soil is the better method. However, it cannot be disputed that growing without soil is certainly more convenient. There is no composting to worry about. There is no soil to mix, and there are very few, if any, fruit flies to combat. *Fruit flies and other pests will be discussed later in this chapter and in Chapter 6.* There are also fewer problems with mold. *Mold, a common problem for wheatgrass growers, is discussed in greater detail later in this chapter.* The hydroponic-grown grass also has a milder taste. Deciding which method is best for you and your circumstances can take some thought. As far as nutrition goes, the wheatgrass is still beneficial. Cost can be a consideration, as a two-tier automatic sprouter averages about $100.

Lighting

Any plant needs light to thrive, and wheatgrass is no exception. Light is important for creating chlorophyll, and the greater the exposure to light, the richer the chlorophyll in the plant. During the first four days of germination, little or no light is needed for the wheatberries. Sprouts germinate in the dark or a shady area. Covering the seedlings with a second tray or with newspaper after four days of germination is recommended. The trays are then placed in indirect sunlight or a bright area. Direct sunlight should be avoided initially — too much sun can damage the grass, causing it to rot and develop bacteria and mold. It is important that growing conditions are ideal, especially for the first five days, as most growing problems develop during this time. If the grass is exposed to continuous light, it should be watered frequently to prevent it from drying out. The grass should also be placed near an open window, if possible, so that air can circulate through the blades. Air circulation is important to prevent mold from growing. It is recommended that all the plants get about three hours of sunlight per day. If you do not have sunlight or direct light available, you can buy spectrum grow lights. Growing wheatgrass during dark winter months requires a grow light. The price of grow lights can range from about $15 to $80, depending on the bulb wattage and whether the bulb is attached to a fixture or automatic timer.

Jars, bags, trays, and racks

Wheatgrass sprouting takes place in jars and growing takes place in trays or other suitable containers. Standard sprouting jars can be purchased for about $5 per jar. These jars have ready-to-use lids for rinsing the wheatberries. You can also assemble your own sprouting jars. If using Mason jars or other wide-mouthed jars, you can purchase some type of screening (nylon mesh or cheesecloth) from a hardware store. Affix this screening to the jars with heavy duty rubber bands. Sprouting lids can be purchased separately for about $3 per lid. A dish draining rack will work well for draining the wheatberries. Wheatberries (about one cup per jar) should be rinsed and placed in jars with about two cups of water. Jars should be covered with screens and left to soak overnight or for eight to 12 hours. Wheatberries are then drained, rinsed, and left to sprout for another eight to 12 hours. Jars should be inverted at a 45-degree angle for the best drainage during the sprouting time. Wheatberries should also be rinsed twice daily — once in the morning and once in the evening — during the sprouting time period. Some growers prefer hemp and flax sprouting bags to jars, as the wheatberries can breathe and drain more effectively in these containers. You can buy a sprouting bag for about $12.

Once sprouted, you will need to place the wheatgrass in growing trays. These hard plastic trays can be purchased from sprouting nurseries or restaurant supply stores for about $2 or $3 per tray. You will need a tray with drainage holes for planting the sprouts and a bottom tray to catch the drained water. Some growers use a third tray to cover the sprouts during the first three to four days of growth, but brown wrapping paper can work just as well. A growing stand or rack can be helpful if you are growing more than one tray per week. Growing stands, also called "sprouters," are simply free-standing shelving units that allow you to grow multiple trays of wheatgrass at once. Sprouters can be automatic, where the watering is done for you, or manual. Growing stands can cost anywhere from $80 to more than $300, depending on whether the tray is muti-tiered, has wheels, lights, and a watering and drainage system. If you are handy, you might be able to build your own stand. Instructions for doing so and for purchasing some hard-to-find parts are available on the Grow Wheatgrass website (**www.growwheatgrass.com**).

The Effect of Climate

Although wheatgrass is not difficult to grow, it is important to achieve ideal conditions to successfully grow your plants. A temperature range of 65 to 75 degrees Fahrenheit is recommended for producing a good crop. Lower temperatures hinder plant growth and higher temperatures can scorch grass and even encourage mold growth. Wheatgrass grows for about seven to ten days before it is ready for harvest. The actual growing time for the wheatgrass will vary from climate to climate and season to season. Temperatures tend to fluctuate according to climate, and indoor temperatures vary depending on which household appliances are in operation. When choosing a location, consider how any appliances, like refrigerators or ovens, will affect the plant. A regular garden thermometer can be helpful in monitoring growing temperatures. These are available at garden centers ranging from $10 to $20.

Growing indoors

Growing wheatgrass indoors allows for an around-the-year crop. It also allows for better control of the growing environment. The trays of grass are generally grown in greenhouses or under fluorescent lighting. When grown in this fashion, the growing time is accelerated. Many people report

Tray of indoor-grown wheatgrass shoots.

that tray-grown grass has a concentrated sweet taste, which is probably due to the accelerated plant growth. Because the plant reaches the nutritional peak so quickly, the simple sugars do not have a chance to convert to complex carbohydrates. Thus, the indoor-grown grass is sweeter. This concentrated growth and sweet taste might also contribute to the quick energy burst experienced by some users. The tray-growing method causes the plant to place most of its effort on growing leaves rather than developing the root system. The tray-grown grass is not as nutrient dense as field-grown grass. Some people grow wheatgrass indoors for consistency in production and maximum safety, meaning protection from the elements, pests, and disease.

The mold issue

One of the biggest problems of growing wheatgrass indoors is dealing with mold. There are several varieties of mold, and it is almost impossible to avoid all mold types at all times. The type of mold that generally grows on wheatgrass is nonpathogenic, meaning it is does not cause harm to the human body. It is still under debate, however, whether it is the mold that causes feelings of dizziness and nausea in some wheatgrass users or whether it is the detoxing effect of the juice itself. For all types of mold, the mold is on the wheatgrass or its roots and not in the wheatgrass, thus, it can be rinsed off. The wheatgrass can also be cut off above the mold and used. Mold that is harmful to humans is also harmful to the plant and the wheatgrass will not survive under the attack of these molds.

Most growers try to avoid mold on their plants by keeping a clean, controlled environment. Tips for avoiding mold, according to Master Grower Michael Bergonzi and other expert growers, include the following:

- Soak the wheatberries for no more than eight hours.
- Spread the wheatberries in a thin layer without overlapping to avoid crowding.
- Add grapeseed extract, colloidal silver, or baking soda to the rinse water to keep mold at bay.
- Circulate air through the wheatgrass blades as they grow.
- Keep growing temperatures between 65 and 75 degrees Fahrenheit.
- Clean trays with bleach or hydrogen peroxide after each use.
- Use only quality wheatberries.

If you have a known allergic reaction to mold, it is recommended that you do not consume wheatgrass or wheatgrass products.

A word about fruit flies

Another issue indoor growers might have to contend with is chasing off fruit flies. These annoying pests are generally attracted to ripening or fermenting fruits and vegetables. They are also attracted to wheatgrass mold. Eliminating fruit flies is a daunting task that will require diligence and plenty of patience. You can try using an exhaust fan to discourage the flies or fly paper to trap them, but getting rid of the flies is difficult. The best way to handle this problem is to strive to grow mold-free wheatgrass.

Growing outdoors

You might have noticed that quality wheatgrass grown outdoors is grown in its natural habitat. Kansas is one of the best places for growing cereal grasses in the United States because of its ideal climate.

Wheatgrass field.

Growers claim that this boosts the nutritional content of the plant. Soil quality is also important, and soil scientists agree that the central plains of Midwestern states are the most fertile for crop production. Wheatgrass can be grown outdoors in the spring and fall. Winter wheat grown outdoors takes about 200 days of slow growth to reach the nutritional peak of 7 inches. The result is a thicker, more nutritionally dense blade compared to tray-grown grass. Ann Wigmore noticed in her grass experiments that wheatgrass grown outdoors in the shade brought forth sturdier stalks. The color was also richer, the roots were more extensive, and the juice had a more pleasant taste and aroma. The full plant and wheat will only grow about one inch during the first month, and an extensive root system is developed that will sustain the plants during the cool, winter months. During the course of the 200 days, the simple sugars are converted to complex carbohydrates, vitamins, and other nutrients. Carbohydrates are important for providing the body with the energy needed to function properly. Complex carbohydrates starches, allow stored energy to be released over a period of time; the body does not experience the sharp rise and fall of blood sugar levels and energy of the simple sugars. The conversion of the simple sugars into complex carbohydrates contributes to the milder taste of the field-grown grass.

Many companies try to capture the essence of the field-grown grass by dehydrating it and selling it as powders, capsules, or tablets. If you have the space and would like to try growing wheatgrass outdoors, it can be a profitable venture. Keep in mind, however, that you will have to contend with insects, birds, and pets that are attracted to the wheatgrass.

Is it really fresh?

Wheatgrass companies claim that their outside-grown wheatgrass is very high in nutrition because it receives 200 days of sunlight. Technically speaking, wheatgrass or any plant growing through the winter cannot see 200 days of actual sunlight. Depending on the growing climate, there will be snowfall and heavy rain. This could pose a problem with the outdoor method, as these elements can possibly damage the wheatgrass.

Additionally, the plants can only be harvested for a few days out of the year. How fresh can wheatgrass powder be that was harvested one year in advance? This is a question that indoor growers are asking. Outdoor-grown wheatgrass is also subject to the environment, which means the wheatgrass could have problems with bugs, birds, and rodents. Outdoor growers, however, contend that growing in the field is the best method for wheatgrass production.

Field-grown vs. tray-grown — which is best?

Everyone is entitled to his or her own opinion and such is certainly the case when it comes to field-grown versus tray-grown wheatgrass. Generally, each grower claims that his or her growing method is best. The following comparisons outline the differences between the outdoor and indoor methods. Look at both and decide which is best for you.

Field-growers vs. Tray-growers	
• Slow outdoor growth of about 200 days	• Accelerated indoor growth of seven to ten days
• Gains nutrition from the soil and sun energy	• Not subject to pests, diseases, and critters found outdoors
• Mold-free due to the frigid winter temperatures and the sunshine and fresh air of spring	• Not subject to damage from sun or winter frost; enzymes remain intact
• Freeze-dried for preservation	• Harvested fresh for immediate consumption
• No need for juicer for consumption	• Need juicer for consumption
• Nutrients include complex carbohydrates for easy assimilation	• Nutrients include simple sugars, which can cause spike in blood level
• Consumed for nutritional benefits	• Consumed for therapeutic benefits
• Cost under $1 per serving	• Cost over $1 per serving
• Mild flavor	• Intense flavor

Incidentally, another group of growers claim that in order to get maximum nutrition from the wheatgrass plant, the roots must also be consumed. Auxin, P4D1, and other important nutrients found in wheatgrass roots encourage damaged cells to repair themselves. Auxin is a substance that aids the growth cycle of plants and also stimulates cell reconstruction. P4D1 also works with defective cells, encouraging DNA repair. Wheatgrass that is consumed totally (roots and leaves) is grown using the aeroponic growing system. This system grows plants using air as opposed to soil, as is used in tradition growing methods, or water, as is used in hydroponic growing. Roots grown in soil cannot be cleaned well enough to be safely used. For more information of aeroponic growing, visit Thin Air Growing Systems website (**www.thinairgrowingsystems.com/what_is_aeroponics.htm**).

CASE STUDY: WORKING WITH NATURE

Tom Stem, owner
DynamicGreens Wheatgrass
161298 9th Line, Stouffvile, Ontario
L4A 7X4 Canada
www.dynamicgreens.com
Phone: 877-910-0467

DynamicGreens Wheatgrass is a family business that has been growing and juicing wheatgrass since 1972. The family members actively participating in the business are Tom, Janice, and Derek Stem. DynamicGreens is sharing their personal experiences. It is important to note that these statements have not been evaluated by the Federal and Drug Administration and their product is not intended to diagnose, treat, cure, or prevent any disease.

DynamicGreens
the wheatgrass juice experts

Tom Stem at the farm.
Photo use courtesy of DynamicGreens.

Having both the breast cancer gene and a long history of blood sugar problems, the Stem family faced the same health issues that many others are facing today. The use of wheatgrass juice was initiated by Tom and Janice to find ideas, experience, and education regarding a health crisis. The end result was the adoption of a raw food centric approach that is thoroughly detailed in the book *How I Conquered Cancer Naturally* by Edie Mae Hunsberger.

Janice followed this program precisely and experienced the same results as the author and, after nine months of wheatgrass juice use at 8 ounces per day, she was given a clean bill of health.

In the 1970s, relatively little was known about growing wheatgrass. To hone their skills, Tom and Janice participated in sprouting groups across Canada and the United States. The methodology at the time was to grow in shallow trays indoors, and the Stem family faithfully grew and juiced their wheatgrass in this fashion.

It was at this time that the Stems made a significant discovery. After two years of use, Janice, who had been diligently consuming the juice, began to find it increasingly difficult to tolerate. It began with the smell, which created a strong aversion to drinking it, and later developed into an allergic reaction. As luck would have it, renovations were taking place on the house during this time. This resulted in the greenhouse being inaccessible, so the wheatgrass was planted in the garden instead. The difference in the taste and tolerability of the juice grown outdoors in the garden was simply amazing. It tasted delicious, it smelled fresh and clean, and it was easily consumed. In seeking to understand the difference, the Stems thoroughly experimented with the wheatgrass. It became clear that the mold so often battled with indoor, tray-grown wheatgrass was the culprit. Despite being diligent growers, cutting high on the plant and washing it as thoroughly as possible before juicing, mold could not be avoided. The decision to move to growing outdoors for a natural, mold-free crop was an easy one. The importance of growing the wheatgrass outdoors also led to another development: the freezing, and later flash freezing, of the juice in order to capture the best possible plant and maintain the potency of the juice.

Grateful for the benefits of the juice and delighted with the quality of the field-grown plant, the Stems shared their experiences. Before long, family, friends, and neighbors began actively seeking the juice. The Stems shared the wheatgrass juice freely; however, as interest in the juice grew, the local demand became impossible to keep up with.

Eventually, it became necessary to sell the juice to make the capital investments to meet demand. In 2000, Derek Stem, Tom and Janice's son, experienced his own wheatgrass intervention, which caused new ripples of excitement. The result was that the family joined forces to actively grow the business and spread the news about wheatgrass. The DynamicGreens Wheatgrass company was formed, and Tom, Janice, and Derek have been shipping wheatgrass juice into the North American market ever since.

The Stems learned even more as they expanded growing operations and started using rigorous testing methodologies. One of those findings was related to the nutritional content of the juice. Not only is the field-grown wheatgrass free of mold, it has far higher phytonutrient content. Plants have many environmental responses, like a flower turning toward the sun. When subject to the variable conditions of the Ontario climate, the plant releases different phytonutrients to cope with heat, cold, wind, rain, drought, overcast skies, or intense sun light. These phytonutrients are the nutritional backbone of the plant and are critical to fulfilling its full potential as a super food.

Growing outdoors and strictly avoiding chemical use does introduce some unique challenges such as weed control. Weed control is resolved through hard work in the summer and the assistance of freezing cold in the winter. During the summer months, weeds are kept at bay through fallowing, or leaving the ground unattended for a period of time, and continuous cultivation of the land until the fall crop is planted. The spring crop is planted in early August, which allows the wheatgrass to establish a good root system and crowd out any weeds that might be present. The winter months do the rest. Wheatgrass embraces the winter and literally springs back to life in the spring; however, any weeds present do not survive the winter season.

DynamicGreens'
frozen wheatgrass packaging.

DynamicGreens does not use any pest control because there is no issue with pests on young wheat. They point out that plants become interesting to pests when they begin to die and decompose. Wheatgrass is harvested at the opposite end of its lifecycle, when it is in the prime of its life. They also note that additional steps are taken to ensure the clean nature of the grass and the juice. These include custom designed cutting equipment. This keeps the cutting process low but still completely off the ground so no microorganisms that might be a part of the soil are present. In addition, a thorough washing of the harvested grass ensures the production of an extremely clean juice.

DynamicGreens firmly believes in the superior quality of the field-grown wheatgrass. Having worked with both indoor and outdoor methods of growing, it is a conclusion based on personal experience. They continue to strive to produce great-tasting, nutrient-rich wheatgrass for the availability of all.

CHAPTER 6

The Cultivation Process

*"There would be no advantage to be gained by sowing a field of wheat
if the harvest did not return more than was sown."*

~ Napoleon Hill

O nce you understand the basics of the process, you are ready to embark upon the adventures of growing. If you have been studying wheatgrass for a while, you will realize that there are several ways to cultivate the nutritious blades. Everyone involved in wheatgrass growing has an opinion on the best way to grow the grass. There are several choices available to you. After you have gone through the basic process a few times, you can experiment with different growing styles and determine which method is best for you. At this point, you should have already decided whether you will be working with an indoor kit, gathering supplies for indoor growing, or facing the challenge of an outdoor garden.

Soaking and Sprouting

Whatever your chosen growing method, the seeds will need to be soaked to prepare them for sprouting. This will soften the wheatberries and promote the sprouting process. Generally, the seeds should be washed before sprouting to rid them of any dirt or grime they might have accumulated. Once the seeds have been washed, they can be presoaked and sprouted. The amount of wheatberries to soak depends upon the size of the tray that you are using. You can loosely measure these seeds by placing them in the tray before washing to get a feel for the amount to use. In most cases, two cups of grain is enough for a 10x11-inch tray. The seeds should then be placed in a jar with pure water for about nine to 12 hours. During summer months or in hot climates, place the soaking jar in the refrigerator. Once the seeds are soaked, they should be completely rinsed and the jars should be placed in a location where they can drain. This is the germination period, which will last about two to three days. The seeds should be rinsed twice daily with fresh water and drained between rinses. Place jars on a 45-degree angle after rinsing to provide the best drainage. Draining should take place in the dark, because the seeds are sprouting. Not all seeds require darkness for germination, but darkness simulates an underground environment for many seeds. It also helps keep the seeds moist, which is a requirement for germination.

Setting up an indoor garden

Your indoor grow room should have access to light, water, and a good area for working. Shelves can be built or you can use existing shelves in a room. A window shelf, a wall that has shelves, or a bookcase can be used for storing the planted wheatgrass trays. A shelf by a window allows the plant to benefit from the indirect sunlight passing through the window. If you wish to build a growing system with several shelves, this is also possible. Shelves are convenient and can save space if you need to store multiple trays. Inexpensive racks can also be purchased at a hardware store. A table, however, can also be used if shelves or racks are not available. If you are interested in producing a continuous supply of wheatgrass, you will need to prepare a place that can hold at least three trays of grass at a time.

There is no need to invest in an extensive lighting system, but a simple grow light can enhance the growing process. No light is required in the first four days of growing after germination. Direct sunlight must be avoided after uncovering the trays; intense sunlight can scorch the grass, and it will not be able to recover. If you place the plants in an area that receives several hours of sunlight, make sure that the wheatgrass has sufficient water. If the blades look limp or the soil is dry, a watering session is in order. An open window can provide a nice breeze for the wheatgrass trays. Remember, airflow is important for preventing mold. An oscillating fan can also be used, but care must be taken that large gusts of air do not blow directly on the blades, as they can be damaged. The soil also must be monitored when using a fan so that it does not dry out.

If possible, indoor gardening should consist of more than just wheatgrass. Vegetables, especially leafy greens, are vital for human health and are easy to grow at home. When the greens are combined with fresh sprouts, they offer excellent nutrition to the diet. Growing greens at home is especially useful during the winter months when fresh store-bought produce is scarce or expensive.

Planting the Sprouts for Indoor Growing

Plant the seeds after they have germinated. While the seeds are germinating, you can prepare the soil for planting. Although there are many soil options, a mixture of 40 percent topsoil, 50 percent compost, and 10 percent peat moss is recommended by expert sprouter and grower Steve Meyerowitz.

After a two-day period of germination, the seeds are ready for planting. You will notice that the sprouted seeds have a small root emerging from the grain and several spidery roots extending from this main root.

There are a variety of ways to plant the sprouted wheatgrass seeds. Every grower has his or her preference, and you might need to experiment to see what works best for you. A general tip is to place 1 to 2 inches of soil in the bottom of the tray and spread the germinated seed evenly across the top of the soil. The seeds can touch each other, but should not be placed on top of one another. If you have used 2 cups of wheatberries this should be enough to build a 10x11-inch seedling tray. Some growers suggest covering the sprouts with a thin layer of soil to keep them moist, but this is not necessary.

Some growers also suggest placing a layer of strong, unbleached paper towel in the tray before spreading the soil in the bottom. This keeps the soil from falling through the drainage holes in the tray and the roots from growing through the drainage holes. This step is not necessary. The roots will not be damaged if they should grow through the drainage holes, and if the soil is compacted, it will not fall through. A second tray placed underneath the growing tray can also help with soil control. Remember, the planting tray should have drainage holes to prevent the tray from becoming too saturated with water, which could ruin the seeds. After you have spread the seeds, water the entire tray with a spray bottle of purified or filtered water. Take care to water only enough to moisten the soil. This is especially important if you are using a tray that has no drainage holes or a paper towel under the soil. Too much water can create mold. After watering the tray, cover it with a second tray and set it aside for two to three days in order to keep the wheatberries warm and moist while protecting them from light. Some growing instructions will recommend using a plastic bag or newspaper for covering the newly planted seeds as opposed to using a covering tray. Covering the seed with the newspaper is not advisable, as chemicals and toxins can leak onto the plant from the wet newsprint. Wet, soggy newspaper can also encourage mold. Even using a plastic bag as a cover can encourage mold. If you do not have a covering tray, try using brown wrapping paper to cover the seeds. If you do this, be sure to tuck the paper around the edges of the tray. The wheatgrass should be checked daily and watered during this time only if the soil is dry. Remember to mist the seeds lightly when evenly moistening the soil.

Maintaining the Sprouts for Indoor Growing

After two to three days of growing, the sprouted wheat should be about 2 inches in height. The trays should then be uncovered, watered, and placed in indirect sunlight. The seedlings will be pale yellow or white, because they have not yet been exposed to light. Monitor the amount of sunlight that the wheatgrass receives. Direct sunlight at this point will stunt the growth of the plant and dry out the soil quickly. Fourteen hours of indirect sunlight will produce a thriving grass crop, as long as other conditions, such as temperature and moisture, are favorable. Watering should now take place every day or every other day, depending on the temperature of your location. If you are growing in a hot climate, you might need to water more frequently. You can also add powdered kelp to the first or second watering to boost the mineral content of the water. The wheatgrass is ready for harvest after about six to 12 days, depending on the climate. Wheatgrass should be about 7 to 10 inches tall, and the blades should begin to develop second stems. This will look as if the blade is splitting into two pieces. It is important to harvest the wheatgrass at this time, because it is now entering the jointing stage. To get the most nutrients out of the wheatgrass, it must be cut and juiced before the jointing stage — when the grain begins to develop. The plant begins to mature at this point, and the energy of the plant will now be directed toward developing the grain.

About watering

It is important to use the highest quality water available to water your wheatgrass. A home purifier is recommended because it is the most convenient. You can also purchase distilled water or bottled water, but this is inconvenient and can be expensive. Adding liquid kelp or certain other minerals, such as plant teas, can boost the mineral content of the water, which is especially important if you are growing hydroponically, or without soil. Water temperature should also be monitored when working with the wheatgrass. Water that is too warm will encourage mold. Room temperature is best. For more information about plant teas, visit The Herb Companion website (**www.herbcompanion.com/ Gardening/Plants-Need-Tea-Too.aspx**).

Most wheatgrass growers suggest keeping the soil moist by misting the soil twice a day — once in the morning and once in the evening. If you forget a misting session, the plants will continue to thrive as long as the soil does not dry out. To determine whether there is a greater water need, lift the wheatgrass from the tray. If the roots are damp, the plant is sufficiently watered. A sufficiently watered crop will also produce shimmering beads of water on the tips of the blades in the mornings. If the blades of wheatgrass look wilted or pale in color, they are not getting enough water. The blades of grass at this point should be deep green in color. Any sign of mold can be an indication of too much water. It can also be an indication of an unhealthy plant that probably will not make it to harvest. Your plant might have mold if you spot a white, cottony substance, blue-gray fuzz, or brown roots.

Quick Reference for Indoor Growing

For a quick reference to the sprouting and planting processes, refer to the following points:

- Prepare the soil mixture — a good ratio of 50 percent compost, 40 percent topsoil, and 10 percent vermiculite will work.
- Wash the wheatberries, and then soak for 12 hours and sprout for 12 hours.
- Prepare the trays with soil and spread sprouted wheatberries over the soil.
- Water the sprouted berries and cover the tray for two to three days.
- Uncover the tray after the third day and place in indirect sunlight. Mist the tray as needed.
- Harvest the wheatgrass when it is mature in about seven to ten days. It should be 7 to 10 inches tall.

Working with Nature

If you are interested in taking your wheatgrass crop outdoors, you can easily do this in a few different ways. The easiest method is simply to transfer the planted trays to a greenhouse after uncovering them on the third or fourth day. The sprouts should be about 2 inches tall. You can also place your wheatgrass on your porch or other shaded garden area.

Growing in a greenhouse is a valuable space saver, especially if you are working with more than one tray. Set up the planting trays as mentioned earlier and monitor the plants until the time of harvest. Humidity, air circulation, and light are important things to remember when growing wheatgrass in a greenhouse. A greenhouse is a great way to grow plants in a controlled environment. The plants will thrive in the warm, humid sanctuary even when the outside atmosphere is experiencing less than favorable growing conditions. The greenhouse will offer protection from the elements, such as extreme temperatures and excessive rain, which can damage the wheatgrass. The greenhouse can also help keep the wheatgrass clean by keeping out insects, cats, and other predators. When growing wheatgrass in a greenhouse, your biggest concern is keeping the wheatgrass cool during hot summer months.

If you do not have a greenhouse, you can place the planted trays on a porch or patio or in a shady garden after the third or fourth day of growth. It is important that the chosen area have plenty of shade as the trays can absorb heat from a hot ground surface, causing damage to the wheatgrass roots. Wheatgrass can also be grown in an outdoor garden, but remember that you will not be as in control of the environment. The germinated seeds can be sown directly into the ground under a one-inch layer of soil. In this manner, it can be grown for juicing or ornamental purposes. Grass grown outside and exposed to the natural elements does not tend to grow mold. It must, however, be protected from the elements as well as birds, cats, and other predators.

Wheatgrass for decorative purposes

Wheatgrass generally conjures up images of a dark-green fluid in a shot glass — not very picturesque. Wheatgrass, however, is also grown and used for decorative purposes. Growers strive to create authentic works of art for a variety of uses including photo props and centerpieces on tables for weddings and other events. These "living" decorations are not only lovely, they also improve the air quality in the room. For more information and how-tos on using wheatgrass for decorative purposes, visit DIY Wedding (**http://diy.wed-central. com/?p=6**). To order custom-designed floral arrangements, visit The Wheatgrass Grower (**www.wheatgrassgrower. com**). Wheatgrass can also be grown in the garden as an ornamental grass.

"Daisy Square."

Photo courtesy of The Wheatgrass Grower website.

"Daisy Round" floral arrangement designed by Val Calpin for The Wheatgrass Grower.

Photo courtesy of The Wheatgrass Grower website.

Time frame for planting

If you are interested in cultivating an outdoor wheatgrass garden, you should plant in the fall when the temperature is cool. You should also plant early enough so that the germinating seed will not be damaged by frost. If evenings are a little cool, the seedlings can be covered with plastic or burlap sacks. Because of the long outdoor growth period, you will harvest the grass in the spring when it is also cool. Once the wheat is planted in the fall, the blades will grow about 1 inch during the first month. The roots, however, will develop extensively in order to absorb an abundance of nutrients from the soil. These nutrients will sustain the practically dormant plant during the cold, winter months when growth is very slow. For about 200 days, the wheatgrass will grow, utilizing the energy from the sun on the warmer days of winter. When spring arrives, the grass blades are able to take full advantage of warmer weather and growth accelerates, as the blades are able to convert more sunlight into energy, developing a root system that absorbs minerals from the soil to nourish the blades. The longer the grass remains in the soil, the more nutrients the roots will absorb. The wheatgrass will also benefit from prolonged exposure to the sun. Be sure to harvest the wheat at the jointing stage, when the second blade appears. The grass should be about 7 to 10 inches in height.

Using existing soil

Nutrient-rich garden soil is one of the greatest benefits to planting wheatgrass in an outdoor garden. You can tell that the topsoil is fertile if earthworms appear when you till the soil. Earthworms are beneficial to garden soil. Their waste products add valuable nutrients, such as nitrogen, to the soil. Nitrogen is a major plant nutrient benefiting plant growth. Earthworms also keep the soil aerated, allowing air to circulate through the soil, and hydrated with their burrowing action. An increased amount of water and air contribute to the richness of the soil. To grow the best wheatgrass crop outdoors, the soil should be organically rich and free from pesticides and synthetic fertilizers. The soil should be a rich, dark color without too much clay or sand. You can enhance the soil by adding organic compost. This will ensure that it is organically rich. You can also use liquid kelp as an organic fertilizer for outdoor growing.

Watering

Watering your outdoor wheatgrass garden can be as simple as watering your lawn every day. Use a low-pressure nozzle when watering or an oscillating sprinkler. More water is required for an outdoor garden, especially on dry days, as the roots run about 12 inches under the ground. Watering should take place in the early morning so that the blades can absorb the water before it evaporates. If the grass is pale in color, water is needed. Of course, if you live in an area that gets plenty of rain, you will not need to water the wheatgrass every day. If the soil is moist, the wheatgrass can survive without daily watering. Watering during winter months is also unnecessary. Rainfall and snow are sufficient for watering the wheatgrass during periods when the heat from the sun is not so severe. Wheatgrass can thrive under heavy snowfall, but ice can pose a problem as it might damage the growing blades.

Weed control

As with all gardening that takes place outdoors, weeds can be an issue. They come in all sizes and forms and grow haphazardly. Controlling weeds in a wheatgrass garden can be especially challenging because of the initial difficulty of distinguishing between grass-like weeds and the wheatgrass. Once you do become familiar with the smooth, even-growing blades of the wheatgrass, this will not be a problem. It is important to eliminate the weeds, because they will compete with the wheatgrass for the nutrients in the soil. They can also carry pests and diseases that will ruin your crop. The following websites offer more information about pests and diseases of the garden:

- BBC — Gardening — Advice: Pest and Disease Identifier (**www. bbc.co.uk/gardening/advice/pests_and_diseases**): BBC is a world news site aimed to enrich people's lives with programs that inform, educate, and entertain. The site offers a gardening pest and disease identifier that helps diagnose and treat problems in the garden. Their gardening forum is also available for advice and opinions.

- Planet Natural (**www.planetnatural.com/site/garden-pests. html**): This site helps you identify garden pests and shows you how to control them naturally.

- Denver County Extension Master Gardener: Insects and Pests (**www.colostate.edu/Depts/CoopExt/4DMG/Pests/pests.htm**): This site covers insects and other pests in and around the home, plant diseases, and pesticides and controls.

Although some weeds are actually edible and beneficial, such as dandelions and Japanese knotweed, harvesting weeds with your wheatgrass at the end of the growing season is not an ideal plan of action.

The best way to prevent weeds is to make sure that your selected spot is weed-free before planting. If weeds do appear, you must remove them manually. Herbicides, or chemical weedkillers, should not be used on the wheatgrass to eliminate weeds. Natural weedkillers, such as those made with vinegar or lemon juice, are safe to use. The following websites offer helpful information concerning natural pest and weed control:

- Eartheasy (**http://eartheasy.com/grow_nat_pest_cntrl.htm**) offers advice for natural gardening and pest control.

- Organic Garden Pests (**www.organicgardenpests.com**) provides tips for organic pest control.

- No Dig Vegetable Garden (**www.no-dig-vegetablegarden.com/ organic-garden-pest-control.html**) offers information on natural gardening.

- The Organic Gardener (**www.the-organic-gardener.com/organic-weed-control.html**) provides information on organic weed control.

Harvesting Wheatgrass

It is important to harvest the wheatgrass when it has reached the jointing stage. At the jointing stage, the plant is most nutritious. This takes place between six to 12 days in warm weather for indoor-grown grass. The wheatgrass will be about 7 to 10 inches in height at the time of harvest. Wheatgrass might require a few additional days to mature if grown in cooler weather. If you are unsure about judging the time period for harvesting, go with the number of days the plant has been growing, which will be between six to 12 days in warm weather and up to 15 days in cooler weather. Also, look for signs, such as divided blades, that the wheatgrass is entering the jointing stage. The blades should be a rich, green color and stand upright. If the wheatgrass crop begins to lean over or blades turn yellow in color, you have missed the time to harvest. Yellowing can also be the result of inadequate watering, inadequate light, or overwatering. Once the grass has reached a height of about 7 inches, yellowing is most likely due to a depletion of the nutrients in the soil. Old or matured wheatgrass will not be beneficial to the body.

Technically, all the grass in a single tray should be ready to harvest at the same time. To harvest the wheatgrass, hold the blades with one hand while cutting as close to the soil as possible to capture the nutrients concentrated at the base of the plant. A clean pair of kitchen shears can be used to cut the grass, but a long, sharp knife works best. Grass harvested from outdoors should be rinsed and dried before juicing. The wheatgrass should be juiced and consumed right away. Unjuiced blades can be refrigerated for about two weeks.

What to do with the mats

Some individuals advocate growing a second batch of wheatgrass from the cut wheatgrass mats. The mats are the intertwined roots left once the wheatgrass has been harvested. The wheatgrass will grow again, but the nutritional level will not be the same as the original grass. Remember, all of the energy of the seed went into producing the original crop. The soil has also been depleted of nutrients. The grass that will grow from the harvested mats will be less nutritious than what has already been cut. It would be better to start the process again with new seeds and fresh soil. Outside growers need to replenish the soil with organic nutrients or consider crop rotation. Learn more about crop rotation at the Green Your blog (**www.greenyour.com/home/lawn-garden/gardening/tips/practice-crop-rotation**). The used mats can be added to a compost bin with other biodegradable scraps. They can also be used for chicken feed or as mulch around trees and garden plants.

How to compost the wheatgrass mats

Composting is a great way to recycle the used mats from the wheatgrass harvest. Composting is the biological breakdown of organic wastes by microorganisms and earthworms. The process creates a rich humus that can be used for other gardening purposes such as mulching. Composting is a way of restoring the balance of nature. Compost also helps improve and maintain the quality of the soil. The nutrients that the wheatgrass absorbed from the soil can be returned to the soil through the composting process. The composting matter, if properly done, will create a new soil that can support new plant life. This "new" soil, or the compost, can then be added to nutrient-lacking soil to make it usable.

You can buy a composting bin for about $50 to $300, depending on the complexity of the bin. Some come with multiple trays or devices for churning the compost. There are several types of containers for composting, but you can easily make a bin out of an empty barrel that has holes drilled all around it. Several websites and publications explain how to make a composting system at home, including the University of Missouri Extension (**http://extension.missouri.edu/publications/displaypub.aspx?p=g6957**). Some people simply build a compost pile in a corner of the yard, but it is hard to control the composting smell, as well as insects, with this method. Break up the used wheatgrass mats and place them at the bottom of the barrel. Other organic material, like kitchen scraps and pulp from the juicer and dry leaves, can also be added to the mix. Add a few earthworms and the compost mix is ready. The barrel should be covered and left to sit for two or three months. This can be done year round, but the composting process is faster in warmer weather. Stirring the mix once a week will hasten the composting process. After a two- or three-month period, peat moss can be added to the compost. Peat moss helps to aerate the compost and speeds up the composting time. Composted soil can be used in the garden to enhance the topsoil or used for potted houseplants. Some growers use the compost with the wheatgrass growing process, but others advise against it unless you can be certain that the compost is disease-free. This advice applies to any consumable plants that you might be growing. If the compost carries disease, the plants will be affected. You can determine whether your compost is safe to use in the following ways, as suggested by the University of Minnesota's Sustainable Urban Landscape Information Series:

- Place a handful of the compost in a plastic bag and seal for 24 hours. If there is an offensive smell when the bag is opened, the compost should not be used.

- Determine whether the compost was kept at a minimum of 131 degrees Fahrenheit for 48 to 96 hours during the composting period.

- Obtain a soil test kit or have the soil tested by a laboratory. The following websites offer soil testing or information about soil testing:

  » Organic Gardening (**www.organicgardening.com/soiltest/ 1,7775,s1-0-4,00.html**)

  » Texas Plant and Soil Lab (**www.texasplantandsoillab.com**)

You can learn more about composting from Eartheasy at its website, **http:// eartheasy.com/grow_compost.html**.

Buying Wheatgrass from Manufacturers

There are a number of wheatgrass products on the market today, including some previously mentioned powders, capsules, and tablets. If you are purchasing these products from a manufacturer, you should make certain that the products come from high-quality manufacturing to be most beneficial for the body. It is not enough just to grow organic wheatgrass on organic soil — the entire process of harvesting and preparing the product for human consumption is important. High-quality producers will monitor the produce at every phase of production and ensure it does not lose important enzymes. This is mainly a concern for field growers who manufacture wheatgrass powders, capsules, and tablets. The harvested grass must be dried in a low-temperature dehydrator to ensure the preservation of the enzymes. It is also important that the wheatgrass that is used is only harvested once. Some growers advocate regrowing the wheatgrass back to its full height after it has been harvested, but nutrients are depleted from the soil after the first growing. The grass should be quickly transported from the harvest field to the juicing, dehydration, or freeze-drying facility to prevent contamination. If the harvested wheatgrass is left in the field, it will become contaminated or bleached by the sun. There are usually no real contamination problems with indoor-grown grass if it is grown in a clean, safe environment.

When you are purchasing wheatgrass products, it is important to research and find the best products possible. Investigate the company to find out about their harvesting methods. Because you ultimately decide what to consume, researching food-producing companies can be beneficial for your health. It is important to know whether the grass was rinsed or washed from the fields and whether the grass was dried without heat and chemicals. Field-grown grass can collect dust and can possibly be exposed to animal wastes, so it is important to wash it before processing. Chemicals and heat can destroy the enzymes in wheatgrass. It is also important to know the methods of pest control. If you are purchasing a tray of wheatgrass, you should inspect it for mold, if possible. Ask growers how they deal with mold and other contaminates. Be aware of every step of the wheatgrass-growing process. Wheatgrass can also bruise very easily during transport. What is the handling procedure from the greenhouse to the juicer or from the field to the processing plant? Do not purchase trays of wheatgrass that carry bruised or damaged grass, as the nutritional value of the plant may also be affected. You should be able to visibly determine whether the blades are damaged. It might seem like a daunting and exhaustive task to try to answer all these questions. It is important, however, to obtain the very best product for your health.

CASE STUDY:
MAKING IT WORK FOR YOU

Pam Free, president
Grow Wheatgrass
5750 Via Real, 303
Carpinteria, CA 93013
http://growwheatgrass.com
freepam@gmail.com
Phone: 805-684 4071
Fax: 805-684 4071

Pam Free has been growing wheatgrass for a number of years. One of her greatest initial concerns was developing a system where growing multiple tray of grass could be managed effectively. She developed and began marketing a portable six-tray sprouting system that can provide enough wheatgrass for three to four ounces of juice a day. A step-by-step DVD shows you exactly how to build the sprouter as well as how grow your own wheatgrass.

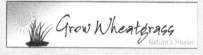

I started growing wheatgrass in 2001 when I wanted to become healthier. I realized that it is not as easy to grow as many people claimed so I developed my own system with a sprouter that I built myself. When it was successful, I was determined to sell it on the Internet. I am now selling the sprouters to people all over the United States and helping people grow wheatgrass in many different environments.

Wheatgrass is a great product and works fantastically well for some people. For me, it detoxified my body after I found that I had mercury toxicity, which was affecting my health. Many of my customers told me of amazing results with cancer and in combating the sickness caused by conventional cancer therapy. It also gives me energy and a sense of taking care of myself. It is harder to eat junk when you are taking the trouble to grow wheatgrass for the sake of your health. Increased energy, increased stamina, increased mental power, and more aliveness are the benefits that I would attribute to using wheatgrass.

Ann Wigmore, who created the concept of juicing wheatgrass, recommended using 2 ounces of wheatgrass per day for healthy people and as much as possible for sick people. She also recommended wheatgrass juice during pregnancy. My daughter-in-law used it for greater health and well-being during pregnancy.

I grow my own wheatgrass. It is fresher and cheaper, and growing wheatgrass yourself provides a more regular supply. The tools needed for growing include trays, a shelf unit to hold the trays, growing medium, and seeds. I grow the grass indoors in a sprouter. Growing outdoors is not practical for most people.

The best time to harvest the grass is ten days after, before it begins to turn yellow — the sign of lost life force. You can count on 6 ounces of juice per tray. If this is your first time drinking wheatgrass, give the body some time to get used to it. Do not overdo it. This goes for growing as well. Give yourself time to get used to the process. Do not get frustrated from your beginning efforts. As far as the taste of wheatgrass is concerned, it is sweet but there is an aftertaste that I do not enjoy. You either like it or you hate it. Sucking on a lemon slice after downing the juice is helpful.

Sometime people encounter problems with mold when growing wheatgrass. I sell a product called Citricide, made of grapefruit seeds, that helps to contain the mold and keep it under control. However, it is a force of nature and cannot be eradicated.

People should definitely use wheatgrass. Leafy green food is necessary to be vibrantly healthy and rid the body of toxins. I told a customer in Hawaii that it would be difficult to grow there because of the humidity, but he persisted and was successful in averting a prostate operation with it.

CHAPTER 7

Consuming Wheatgrass

"The only way to keep your health is to eat what you don't want,
drink what you don't like, and do what you'd rather not."

~ Mark Twain

*T*here are many ways to consume wheatgrass. The best way to consume the grass is to juice it, but you can also consumer it with food. If you are going to grow your own wheatgrass, it is important to know about juicers and other appliances used to consume wheatgrass. Purchasing a juicer can be a major investment, but if you are serious about growing and juicing wheatgrass, you will need good equipment.

Juicers

There are several different types of juicers on the market today. Some will juice fruits and vegetables. Some will make nut butters. Some will make flour and pasta, and some will make frozen desserts. Not all of them, however, are capable of juicing wheatgrass. Choosing an appropriate wheatgrass juicer is important because the job of grinding and extracting the juice from the fibrous plant is not an easy chore. Common juicers or blenders will not work for the purpose of juicing wheatgrass. You need a juicer with a powerful motor and that is durable, convenient to use, easy to assemble, easy to clean, and most importantly, able to efficiently extract juice from the wheatgrass. The best device would be a slow masticating or slow-turning unit that has a screen for separating the juice from the grass pulp. Electric and manual juicers are available. Although an electric model is more expensive, it will churn out the juice faster and will be less work for you. When choosing a juicer, remember to consider both your budget and your lifestyle. You will need to use it on a regular basis, so it must be manageable for you to be beneficial. Manual juicers can cause tiredness in the arm from turning the handle of the juicer. It also takes a longer time to extract the wheatgrass juice with a manual machine.

Using the juicer should not be difficult. With a typical upright model, simply place a handful of wheatgrass into the hole on the top of the juicer. Some of the juice may come out of the front of the juicer followed by the pulp. The bulk of the juice will come out of the spout at the bottom of the machine. Machines work differently, so be sure to consult the machine's directions. You can take the pulp and place it back into the juicer two or three additional times to get as much juice as possible. After the juicing session, take apart the juicer and thoroughly wash and dry all the parts.

Other appliances

If you want to start a living foods regime, you will need other appliances to prepare your meals. In addition to your slow-turning wheatgrass juicer, you also need a fast-turning juicer for juicing fruits and vegetables. A good quality blender is also important. These will be useful in making yogurts, soups, cheeses, and dressings. Blenders cannot be substituted for juicers, because they perform two different jobs. The juicer works to juice food products by separating the juice from the pulp in fruits and vegetables. The blender pulverizes the fruits and vegetables so that they can be used as a drink or as food products for other dishes.

You will also need kitchen supplies for making your wheatgrass dishes including bowls, graters, and cutting boards. Though your individual needs will vary based on your diet, some common items will help you get started. A large slow cooker or large bowl will be necessary for preparing many dishes, such as sauerkraut and fermented vegetable dishes. This bowl can also be used for powdering herbs for spices and other seasoning. It also will be helpful to have a small hand grinder for smaller spices. A coffee mill, or grinder, will work well and can also be used as a nut and seed grinder. You will need to invest in a set of sharp vegetable knives of varying sizes. You will also need a cutting board and vegetable grater for preparing salads and other chopped vegetables. It might be an expensive investment, but a dehydrator would be best for drying food to create dried fruits, fruit crisps, and vegetable chips.

In a living-food kitchen, you will need several types of food, particularly grains, seeds, nuts, fruit, beans, and vegetables. You should keep wheatberries for planting as well as for sprouting and grinding into flours. Many seeds are good for sprouting including sunflower seeds, buckwheat, sesame seeds, and alfalfa. Raw almonds are particularly useful to have because they can be used to make almond milk. Dried and fresh fruits should be available as well. Ripe fruits can be stored in the refrigerator, or they can be peeled and frozen for use at a later date. Fruits that need to ripen can be placed in paper bags until ripe. You should purchase a variety of vegetables, especially green, leafy vegetables, frequently. If these vegetables are not eaten immediately, they can be placed in the refrigerator in plastic storage containers or glass containers. Growing vegetables at home is an option that many enjoy. Greens, squash, peppers, and tomatoes are some favorite vegetable that are not too difficult to grow in a indoor or outdoor home garden. Many herbs, such as thyme, rosemary, basil, and oregano can also be grown at home.

Buying Wheatgrass Food Products

Grains can be nutritious but some grains can be unhealthy. Grain that is turned into highly processed flour is no longer healthy. Refined grains, which are grains that have been significantly modified and include white rice and white flour, have been associated with myriad physical, mental, and emotional problems. All grains that have been processed and turned into flour — even whole wheat — can lead to problems with blood sugar. This is because grains have a lot of starch, and starch becomes sugar when it is digested. This can lead to cravings for other refined grains and sugars. Individuals who are diabetic or sugar-sensitive should avoid foods made with these starchy grains. A diet that is high in processed grains will also cause the growth of candida yeast. Candida yeast is a fungus that causes an infection in the body often referred to a yeast infection.

However, grains also can be very beneficial to the body. Diets that include whole grains help lower the risk for diseases such as diabetes and heart disease. Grains are seeds, which, when grown properly, can provide an abundance of food. Sprouting and making wheatgrass juice are healthy, positive ways to use the wheat grain. Wheatgrass is a complete food in itself but can be paired with other foods for a variety of meals. Many manufacturers are capitalizing on the sprouting and wheatgrass phenomenon by providing a variety of food products that include sprouts and wheatgrass for consumer purchase. Sprouted breads and seeded crackers are popular foods that include wheatgrass. Wheatgrass smoothies and shakes are also popular. There are even wheatgrass pet treats. You can also buy wheatgrass juice powders online and in health food stores.

When purchasing wheatgrass flour products, it is important to check the freshness date. Do not be afraid to inquire about the freshness of the food if it is not labeled. Food products that have been sitting on the shelves for months will not do you any good, even if they do contain wheatgrass.

Wheatgrass Recipes

Thus far, this book has outlined the health benefits and the various vitamins, minerals, and enzymes that make up the potent plant. Now it is time to get creative and see how many fun recipes you can design using the nutritious wheatgrass. Wheatgrass clippings from your wheatgrass supply can be added to salads and soups. You can sprinkle wheatgrass powders over cereals and soaked grains. Whole grains such as oats can be soaked for about 45 minutes in juice or milk before consuming. Grains prepared this way are beneficial because soaking starts the sprouting process. Powders can also be added to whole grain bread before baking. You can mix wheatgrass juice into other juices, soups, and fermented foods. Soaked wheatberries can be tossed onto salads for a crunchy, nutty flavor. The possibilities are endless. Consuming wheatgrass does not have to be a bore or a chore. Get creative and see what you can dish up. The following are a few recipes to get you started. Enjoy!

Juices, smoothies, and shakes

You do not have to drink wheatgrass juice straight each time you consume it. Of course, if you are treating a disease, this is the best way to consume the juice because it should be taken on an empty stomach for therapeutic purposes. To vary your wheatgrass consumption, mix the wheatgrass with different vegetables to create palatable drinks that you, your family, and your friends can enjoy. Juicing the wheatgrass and adding it to other vegetable drinks can be a good way to introduce wheatgrass to children or friends. The other flavors of the drink will absorb the strong taste of the wheatgrass. If you use wheatgrass in the right measure, you can still benefit from some of its nutritional properties. A 1-ounce dosage of wheatgrass per 8-ounce glass is generally recommended. You can experiment with wheatgrass and different fruits and vegetable combinations to create your own recipes. This is simple to do, just remember the recommendation for food combining in Chapter 4. You will receive many health benefits from wheatgrass juice, so it is beneficial to learn how to incorporate the juice into your daily diet in a variety of ways. This does not have to be a complicated process — many recipes using wheatgrass are quick and easy to make.

When juicing fruits and vegetables, cut them into small pieces before putting them in the juicer. As long as the fruit is organic or has been properly washed, you can leave the peels on the produce. After the food products have been juiced, you can pour them into a stainless steel strainer to separate any pulp left by the juicer. It is best to peel any fruits that will be blended for shakes or smoothies. Peel the fruits thinly, because most of the nutrients are just under the skin of the fruits. Remember to remove cores and large seeds or pits before blending or juicing. Many of these recipes require a slow-churn wheatgrass juicer, a high-speed juicer, and a blender or Vitamix. Be sure to use filtered or spring water in recipes that call for water or ice. Fresh juices should be consumed immediately but can be stored for one day in the refrigerator if not completely consumed. Just like other juices, wheatgrass juice begins to lose potency immediately after juicing, so it should be discarded if it is not consumed within 12 hours.

In the following recipes, please note that wheatgrass crop is measured in inch rounds by the circumference of a handful. Also, when working with wheatgrass, always add the wheatgrass at the end of the blending to ensure the freshest drink possible.

Wheatgrass-spinach booster

Wheatgrass and spinach make a powerful combination. Add a few other natural ingredients and you have a nutritious drink that can help boost your energy level for the day. This juice can be diluted with water as necessary for taste and texture.

Ingredients:
- 5 stalks celery
- 3 small cucumbers
- 5 fresh spinach leaves
- ½ c. fresh parsley
- 3-inch round wheatgrass
- Water, as needed

Instructions:
1. Cut the celery and cucumbers into small chunks that can fit into the juicer.
2. Juice all ingredients, except wheatgrass.
3. Juice wheatgrass separately in a slow-churn wheatgrass juicer.
4. Add freshly juiced wheatgrass to mix.

Wheatgrass cleanser

This is a good drink to use during a juice fast or before starting a water fast. The enzymes will nourish the body while it is being detoxed.

Ingredients:
- 2 apples
- 2 carrots

- 1 celery stalk
- Thin slice of beet
- ¼ medium cucumber
- 1 small piece of ginger
- 1 oz. wheatgrass juice

Instructions:
1. Blend all ingredients except wheatgrass, in juicer or Vitamix.
2. Juice wheatgrass in a wheatgrass juicer.
3. Add to mix and reblend.

Veggie combo drink

This is another enzyme-rich drink that can add energy to your day. The addition of carrots and beets add extra vitamin A and folic acid to this drink. This combination of ingredients is good for cleansing the kidneys and gallbladder and helps with constipation.

Ingredients:
- 3 stalks celery
- 2 large carrots
- ½ red beet
- 5 fresh spinach leaves
- ½ c. alfalfa sprouts
- ½ c. parsley
- 3-inch round wheatgrass
- Water, as needed

Instructions:
1. Chop up all vegetables (including alfalfa sprouts) and place in blender with water.
2. Juice and dilute with water as necessary for texture and/or taste.
3. Serve with more alfalfa sprouts in the glass.

Apple-grass juice

Apple juice does wonders for the taste of wheatgrass. This beverage is light and refreshing as well as nutritious.

Ingredients:
- 3 large apples
- 3-inch round wheatgrass
- Water, as needed

Instructions:
1. Chop apples small enough to fit through juicer and juice.
2. Juice wheatgrass separately in wheatgrass juicer and add to apple juice.
3. Dilute with water as needed.

Wheatgrass carrot juice

This is a high-nutrition drink because the wheatgrass juice, carrots, and apple provide vitamins A, B, and E, as well as calcium and many other minerals. This is a good drink to consume when pregnant or breastfeeding.

Ingredients:
- 1 pound large carrots, washed and peeled
- ½ peeled lemon
- 1 apple
- 1 or 2 large lettuce leaves or carrot greens
- ½ oz. wheatgrass juice

Instructions:
1. Run all ingredients, except wheatgrass, through your juicer.
2. Juice wheatgrass and add to mix.
3. Add more apple pieces for extra sweetness.

Orange-carrot-grass juice

This recipe offers a different twist on carrot juice. It is good for boosting the immune system and helps correct problems with vision.

Ingredients:
- 2 oranges
- 2 medium carrots
- 3-inch round wheatgrass

Instructions:
1. Chop carrots to a size that can fit into blender.
2. Add the oranges and wheatgrass.
3. Juice and serve.

Wheatgrass swirl

Blueberries and wheatgrass are high in antioxidants. Add vitamin C (oranges) and potassium (bananas) and you have a super tasty, super energy drink.

Ingredients:
- 4 oranges
- 2 bananas
- 1 c. fresh blueberries (other berries can be substituted)
- 4-inch round wheatgrass
- 3 to 4 c. ice cubes

Instructions:
1. Juice oranges and wheatgrass.
2. Add other ingredients to the mix.
3. Blend until mixture is a smooth texture.
4. If mixture is too thick, add a little orange juice.

Tropical grass delight

For a delightful taste of the tropics, try this fun combination. Feel free to get creative and add other tropical fruits, such as mango and coconut, for variety.

Ingredients:
- 1 c. diced pineapple
- 2 kiwi fruits
- 1 diced guava or papaya
- 1 orange
- 5 strawberries
- 1 oz. fresh wheatgrass juice *or* 1 sachet organic wheatgrass powder

Instructions:

1. Juice the orange.
2. Blend all fruits together with orange juice.
3. Juice fresh wheatgrass and add to mix or add wheatgrass powder.
4. Garnish with strawberries and serve over ice.

Wheatgrass-banana smoothie

Smoothies are great for getting extra greens into your diet. The combination of spinach and wheatgrass in this smoothie will boost your energy level while it oxygenates your cells. This drink is also helpful for anemia and high blood pressure.

Ingredients:
- 2 large bananas
- 2 handfuls of spinach
- 1 c. fresh wheatgrass juice
- ½ c. red grapes
- ½ bunch of parsley
- ½ c. soaked chia
- 1 tsp. spirulina

Instructions:
1. Blend all ingredients in Vitamix, adding water as necessary.
2. Drink immediately.

Green fruit smoothie

Frozen bananas turn this healthy smoothie into a refreshing treat. Wheatgrass can be added in juice or powder form. One or two cubes of frozen wheatgrass juice can also be used instead of the fresh juice or powder.

Ingredients:
- 2 frozen bananas
- 4 medium apples (Gala or Fuji are good types)
- 2 medium peaches
- 1 oz. fresh wheatgrass juice or 2 sachets of organic wheatgrass powder

Instructions:

1. Cut apples, peaches, and frozen banana into small pieces.
2. Blend together, adding water or ice for desired consistency.
3. Add wheatgrass and reblend.

Green vegetable smoothie

This vegetable smoothie is just as delicious as a fruit smoothie. The nutritional content is boosted by the powerful flax seed, which offers rich omega oils and beneficial fiber.

Ingredients:
- 2 c. chopped spinach or kale
- 1 banana
- 2 c. frozen low-fat yogurt
- 2 tsp. flax seed powder
- ½ oz. fresh wheatgrass juice or
- 2 sachets of organic wheatgrass powder

Instructions:
1. Blend all ingredients, adding wheatgrass last.
2. Add water or ice, if desired.

Wheatgrass booster

Give your diet a boost and keep colds and flues at bay with this citrusy beverage. Add a slice or two of fresh pineapple for an extra kick.

Ingredients:
- 2 oranges
- 1 ripe banana
- 1 lime
- 2- to 3-inch round wheatgrass
- 12 crushed ice cubes

Instructions:
1. Juice oranges, lime, and wheatgrass.
2. Blend juices and other ingredients in blender until smooth (about 30 seconds).

Tropical green shake

A variation of the tropical grass delight drink, the apples and banana make this version less tart but just as nutritious.

Ingredients:
- 1 c. crushed pineapple with juice
- 1 c. diced apples
- 1 c. lime juice
- 1 guava
- 1 medium ripe banana
- ½ oz. fresh wheatgrass juice or
- 1 sachet organic wheatgrass powder

Instructions:
1. Blend all ingredients, adding wheatgrass last.
2. Serve over ice.

Wheatgrass energy shake

This creamy beverage is simple enough to make every day. Whip it up quickly on days when time is scarce. At these times, using wheatgrass powder would be more convenient than fresh juice.

Ingredients:
- 1 c. vanilla soymilk
- ½ c. frozen berries
- ½ ripe banana
- 2 tsp. raw honey
- ½ oz. fresh wheatgrass juice or
- 1 sachet organic wheatgrass powder

Instructions:
1. Blend all ingredients, adding wheatgrass last.
2. Sprinkle with nutmeg or cinnamon.

Wheatgrass soups

Soups are light, refreshing, and easy to prepare. They also digest very well. Soups can be served with salads, crackers, or an entire meal. Soups can also make a nice breakfast dish. Preparing soup the living foods way keeps all the fruit's and vegetable's nutrients and enzymes intact. These soups are not cooked but are blended. A vegetable or a fruit is used as a base and other vegetables and fruits are added to the blend. Because they are not cooked, these soups do not stay fresh for long. They should be consumed immediately and leftovers should be discarded. When preparing soups, remember the food combining recommendations as pointed out in Chapter 4. Vegetables and fruits should not be combined — make it all fruit or all vegetables.

Cucumber soup

Cucumbers have a long list of nutritional benefits. They are helpful for individuals suffering from stomach, chest, and lung problems and are useful for controlling blood pressure, eczema, arthritis, and gout. Cucumbers also offer relief from those suffering with diseases of the kidney, liver, bladder, and pancreas and are helpful for the skin and eyes. The addition of wheatgrass to this soup makes cucumbers even more beneficial.

Ingredients:
- 2 large cucumbers, peeled and chopped
- 1 c. grated cheese
- ¼ c. chopped parsley
- 1 scallion
- ½ tsp. cumin powder
- 1 oz. fresh wheatgrass juice
- Spring or filtered water

Instructions:
1. Place all ingredients, except water and wheatgrass, in blender and blend at medium speed, adding enough water to obtain a soup consistency.
2. Add freshly juiced wheatgrass and re-blend quickly.
3. Serve with bread or crackers.

Spinach soup

Spinach is a versatile food that can be found all over the world. Added to this soup recipe, it creates an antioxidant-rich dish that is good for your eyes, heart, and brain. This dish is served cold or slightly warmed.

Ingredients:
- 1 c. fresh, raw spinach
- 1 medium avocado
- 1 c. water or vegetable stock
- 2 unwaxed cucumbers
- 2 green onions
- ½ red bell pepper
- 1 clove garlic
- ½ red bell pepper
- ½ tsp. curry seasoning
- ½ oz. wheatgrass juice
- Sea salt to taste
- Fresh lime juice to taste

Instructions:
1. Blend avocado and ½ cup of water or vegetable stock to make a puree.
2. Add other ingredients, one at a time, blending to desired thickness.
3. Thin with remaining water, if necessary.
4. Top with sun-dried tomatoes (optional).

Chowder with corn and a hint of wheatgrass

Chowders date back to the 16th century, but they are still quite popular in many parts of the world. There are many types and various ways to prepare them. This chowder uses corn and adds a touch of wheatgrass to boost the nutritional value. It is also quick and easy to prepare, as no cooking is involved.

Ingredients:
- 2 ½ c. almond milk
- 5 ears corn on the cob, shaved

- 1 small avocado
- ½ oz. wheatgrass juice
- Sea salt to taste

Instructions:
1. Set aside one cup of corn.
2. Blend milk, avocado, and rest of the corn in a blender at medium speed.
3. Pour into a bowl and add the cup of corn that was set aside.
4. Add wheatgrass juice and stir well.
5. Add sea salt to taste.

Simple oil and vinegar dressing

The use of oil and vinegar on greens and vegetables goes back as far as ancient Babylonia. The dressing was used to enhance to flavor of the vegetables, which were often bitter. This recipe takes little effort and is a lot healthier — and cheaper — than vinaigrettes purchased in the supermarket.

Ingredients:
- ½ c. safflower oil
- ¼ c. olive oil
- ¼ c. cider vinegar
- ¾ tsp. or less salt
- ¼ tsp. pepper
- ¼ tsp. organic wheatgrass powder

Instructions:
1. Combine ingredients in covered jar.
2. Shake and serve immediately.

Lemon French dressing

Here is another simple dressing but with a little more "zing" created by the lemon. The lemon was widely used in traditional medicine, especially by the Romans, for its healing properties. It is good for treating all types of digestive disorders.

Ingredients:
- 6 tbsp. fresh lemon juice
- 6 tbsp. flaxseed oil or walnut oil
- ½ tsp. sea salt
- 1 tsp. Bragg's liquid aminos
- 1 tsp. maple syrup (optional)
- 1 tsp. fresh wheatgrass juice
- Pinch of pepper

Instructions:
1. In a small bowl, whisk together lemon juice, oil, and salt.
2. Add liquid aminos, maple syrup, pepper, and wheatgrass juice.
3. Serve immediately.

Wheatgrass salads

Salads are a good way to consume the sprouts and raw vegetables needed by the human body. According to Ann Wigmore and other natural food advocates, you should eat a large salad of a variety of greens and fresh vegetable sprouts every day. When purchasing vegetables and salads, it is important to get the freshest ingredients possible. The absolute best vegetables are grown organically at home. If this is not possible, look for greens that are crisp and broccoli and carrots that are firm. Vegetables should not look limp or wilted. Peppers, celery, and cucumbers should be purchased without a wax coating. Vegetables are usually presented for consumer purchase with this, as it makes them look more appealing. However, to most people the waxed vegetables look artificial, and the wax is extremely difficult to remove. Avoid hothouse, or greenhouse, tomatoes, as they have been associated with a number of plant diseases. Vine-ripened tomatoes — tomatoes ripened on the vine — are recommended by raw foodists, as commercial tomatoes are sometimes picked green and ripened with ethylene gas, which is an odorless hormone that causes fruit to ripen and decay. Wash all vegetables before they are used and scrub hard vegetables with a vegetable brush. Leafy greens can be soaked or dipped in lemon water or salt water for a thorough cleansing to remove debris and small insects caught within the leaves. Rinse the vegetables thoroughly afterward to get rid of the excess lemon and salt. All vegetables for salads should be cut in small pieces for easy consumption. Lettuce and salad greens, however, should be gently torn by hand unless using a stainless steel or plastic blade. Other metals can cause accelerated browning and affect the taste of the salad. Lettuce and greens should also be dried well before adding to the salad.

When preparing fruit salad, it is important to use ripe food that is very fresh. Fruits should be naturally ripened. Fruits salads should be consumed immediately as oxidation will occur if they are left out. When air interacts with the food, in the process of oxidation, the food turns dark, such as when apples turn brown after they are sliced. Leftover fruit salads can be refrigerated for a short period of time; although, their color will be distorted. Sprinkling lemon juice over the salad will keep it looking fresh longer. Fruit salads that are not consumed within 24 hours should be discarded.

The following are fun, easy-to-prepare salad recipes.

Quick and easy cucumber salad

This salad brings the benefits of cucumber, lemon, and wheatgrass to the table. Use it as a dinner side dish or add a few slices of tomato and have it as a quick and light lunch.

Ingredients:
- 1 cucumber sliced
- ¼ c. fresh lemon juice
- 2 large romaine lettuce leaves
- ½ tsp. dill
- Sprinkling of wheatgrass clippings
- 8 oz. sour cream
- 3 tsp. raw sugar
- Pinch of salt

Instructions:
1. Dissolve the raw sugar into the lemon juice.
2. Add salt, dill, and sour cream to the mixture.
3. Mix in the cucumbers and sprinkle with wheatgrass clippings.
4. Serve over the lettuce leaves.

Watercress and lentil sprouts

Watercress is good for adding vitamin B6, vitamin C, and manganese to your diet. Lentils are high in fiber but low in fat. They also provide good protein. The regular consumption of this salad can help stabilize blood sugar levels and benefit the heart.

Ingredients:
- 1 c. watercress
- 1 c. buckwheat greens
- ½ c. lentil sprouts
- 1 medium celery stalk, chopped (approx. ½ c.)
- 1 avocado, cubed (approx. 1 c.)
- 1 lemon, juiced
- 1 tsp. fresh wheatgrass juice

Instructions:
1. Measure the greens by pressing them into a measuring cup.
2. Tear them into bit-sized pieces.
3. Toss with lentil sprouts, chopped celery, and avocado cubes.
4. Mix freshly juiced wheatgrass with lemon juice and sprinkle over the top of greens.
5. Serve immediately.

Garden salad

A typical garden salad consists of lettuce and tomato. Adding carrots, a few sprouts, and wheatgrass can boost the nutritional value of the salad and add variety to your meal.

Ingredients:
- 2 c. spinach, torn into small pieces
- 1 c. romaine lettuce, torn into small pieces
- 1 c. alfalfa sprouts
- ½ c. cabbage sprouts
- ½ c. cabbage, thinly sliced
- ½ c. carrots, shredded

- 1 large tomato, sliced
- Handful wheatgrass clippings

Instructions:
1. Toss all ingredients, except carrots and tomato, in large bowl.
2. Place tomato slices on top.
3. Sprinkle carrots over entire salad.
4. Serve with lemon French dressing.

Carrot and beet energy salad

Red beets are known for their high level of anti-carcinogens and carotenoid. Anti-carcinogens are substances that fight against cancer. Carotenoids act as antioxidants, which also fight against cancer. Beets also provide quality iron. Cabbage is an excellent source of fiber. Use this salad as a blood-builder, to fortify the cells, and to relieve constipation.

Ingredients:
- ¼ head cabbage, shredded
- 3 large beets, scrubbed and grated
- 3 large carrots, scrubbed and grated
- ½ c. soaked unsulphured raisins
- ¼ c. soaked pumpkin seeds
- ¼ c. soaked sunflower seeds
- Sprinkling wheatgrass clippings

Instructions:
1. Combine all ingredients thoroughly.
2. Serve as is or with vinegar oil dressing.

Fruit salad with wheatgrass granola cereal

Fruit salads are not only healthy and tasty, they are also light and refreshing. This salad, full of vitamins and minerals, can be served for breakfast or as a dessert dish after dinner.

Ingredients:
- 1 apple, chopped
- 1 orange, peeled, sectioned, and chopped

- 4 large strawberries, sliced
- ½ c. high-quality vanilla soy yogurt
- ⅔ c. tropical flavored juice
- Sprinkling of unsweetened shredded coconut

Instructions:
1. Mix all ingredients together.
2. Sprinkle with wheatgrass granola cereal.

Wheatgrass sauces

Sauces and dressings can be used in any number of ways, such as over salads and entrées or as a base for soups. In the early days of cooking, sauces were used to disguise the taste of foods that were losing their freshness. Today, sauces are used to add flavor and moisture to foods as well as to enhance their visibility. When preparing and using sauces, remember to employ the concept of food combining to avoid a conglomerate of foods in the digestive system at once.

Honey-wheatgrass sauce

This sauce is easy to make and can be served with fish or other entrée dishes. You will need a food processor. Prepare the sauce after the main dish is ready to ensure freshness and benefit from the wheatgrass.

Ingredients:
- 1 c. fresh wheatgrass
- ½ c. heavy cream
- 3 tbsp. honey
- Salt and pepper to taste
- 3 tbsp. olive oil

Instructions:
1. Combine wheatgrass, honey, and cream in food processor.
2. Slowly add olive oil, briskly whisking to emulsify into the other ingredients.
3. Press the sauce through a fine mesh strainer.
4. Add salt and freshly ground black pepper to taste.

Quick-and-easy wheatgrass dressing

Most people enjoy dressings on their salad. Unfortunately, most dressings purchased in supermarkets are high in sugar and cholesterol. This tasty, healthy dressing can be quickly whipped up and served over salad greens or other vegetables.

Ingredients:
- ½ tsp. organic wheatgrass powder
- 3 tbsp. flax seed oil
- 1 tbsp. lemon juice
- 1 minced garlic clove
- Salt and pepper to taste, optional

Instructions:
1. Mix all ingredients in a bowl or jar.
2. Add to salad or serve over vegetables.

Dairyless alfredo sauce

Alfredo sauce originated in Italy, but it has become quite popular in the United States. Traditionally, this creamy white sauce is made with butter, parmesan cheese, and, sometimes, heavy cream. This version is healthier and has fewer calories. You can freely use it with your favorite pasta dishes.

Ingredients:
- 1 c. tofu
- ½ c. soymilk
- 1 tbsp. tahini
- 1 tbsp. pesto
- ¼ tbsp. cayenne pepper
- ¼ tbsp. sea salt
- ¼ tbsp. black pepper
- 1 minced garlic clove
- 1 tsp. organic wheatgrass powder

Instructions:
1. Blend together all ingredients, except wheatgrass.
2. Heat through, but do not let boil.

3. Prior to serving, mix in wheatgrass powder.

Peanut-wheatgrass sauce

This unique sauce is rich in protein and can be served with crackers or eaten with bread. It can also be spread into celery or used as a vegetable dip.

Ingredients:
- ⅓ c. crunchy peanut butter
- 1 tbsp. honey
- 1 tbsp. rice vinegar
- 1 tsp. ground coriander seed
- 1 tsp. organic wheatgrass powder
- Cayenne pepper, to taste

Instructions:
1. Stir all ingredients together thoroughly.
2. Serve with crackers, bread, or raw vegetables.

Pesto sauce with wheatgrass

Pesto sauce can be used with pasta, on pizza, in bean dishes, salads, and seafood. The all-important basil leaf that makes up this popular sauce was referred to as the "royal herb" by the Greeks. The addition of wheatgrass to this sauce makes it especially high class.

Ingredients:
- 2 ¼ c. basil leaves
- ¼ c. pine nuts
- ¼ c. hemp seeds
- 1 tbsp. minced garlic
- 1 tbsp. organic wheatgrass powder
- ⅔ c. hemp oil or extra virgin olive oil
- ¼ c. chopped parsley

Instructions:
1. Mix all ingredients, except parsley and wheatgrass, in food processor.
2. Stir in parsley and wheatgrass.

Wheatgrass cereals

The following recipes detail how wheatgrass can be used in cereals.

Blended oats cereal

This dish can be served in a dish topped bananas and/or wheatgrass granola.

Ingredients:
- ¼ rolled oats
- 1 c. soymilk
- ¼ c. non fat yogurt
- ¼ fresh or frozen berries
- Half of a banana
- 1 tbsp. organic wheatgrass powder

Instructions:
1. Blend all ingredients.

Wheatgrass granola cereal

This recipe can be kept frozen for up to one month.

Ingredients:
- 1 ½ c. jumbo porridge oats
- ⅔ c. dried cranberries or 1/2 c. raisins
- ½ c. unsalted sunflower seeds
- ⅓ c. sesame seeds
- ⅓ c. chopped almonds
- ¼ c. ground flaxseeds or linseeds
- 1 tbsp. ground cinnamon
- 2 tsp. grated orange zest
- ½ tsp. sea salt
- 1 large egg white
- 1 tbsp. vegetable oil
- 1 tbsp. clear honey
- 2 tsp. frozen orange juice concentrate
- 1 tsp. organic wheatgrass powder
- 1 tsp. vanilla essence

Instructions:

1. Preheat the oven to 375° Fahrenheit.
2. Mix the oats, apple, sunflower seeds, sesame seeds, almonds, flaxseeds or linseeds, cinnamon, wheatgrass powder, orange zest, and salt together in a large bowl.
3. In a small bowl, whisk together the egg white, oil, honey, orange juice concentrate, and vanilla essence. Pour this into the oat mixture and toss until thoroughly coated.
4. Turn mixture onto a shallow baking tray lined with nonstick parchment and spread evenly.
5. Bake for 25 to 30 minutes, turning the mixture once with a spatula halfway through baking time, or until mixture is golden brown.

Wheatgrass pizzas

Almost everyone enjoys a good pizza. It is fun to eat and equally fun to make. Pizzas, however, can be full of calories, fat, and sodium and practically void of nutrition if not created with "health" in mind. It is possible to enjoy a healthier pizza, but most likely, you will have to make it yourself. The following are some basic recipes to get you started.

Pizza dough

This healthy pizza dough recipe can be used as a base for a variety of toppings. Adding tomato sauce adds lycopene, an antioxidant helpful for preventing disease. Use cheese sparingly. Forgo sausage and pepperoni, which are high in fats and add roasted chicken, turkey, or a mixture of your favorite fresh vegetables.

Ingredients:

- 2 ¾ c. bread flour or whole wheat flour
- 1 package active dry yeast
- ¼ c. organic wheatgrass powder
- ½ tsp. salt

Instructions:

1. Pour the water into a medium-sized mixing bowl and sprinkle in the yeast.

2. Stir gently with a fork until the yeast has dissolved.
3. Add 1 cup of flour and the salt.
4. Mix thoroughly with a wooden spoon.
5. Add the second cup of flour to the ¼ cup of wheatgrass powder and mix well.
6. After the second cup of flour-wheatgrass mixture has been mixed in, the dough will should begin to form a soft, sticky mass. It is now ready to be kneaded.
7. Measure out the last ¾ cup of flour.
8. Sprinkle some flour over the work surface and generously flour hands.
9. Remove all of the dough from the bowl and begin to work the mass by kneading the additional flour in a bit at a time.
10. Knead until dough no longer feels sticky and is smooth and elastic.
11. Lightly oil a 2-quart bowl with vegetable oil.
12. Roll the ball of dough around in the bowl to coat with oil.
13. Tightly seal the bowl with plastic wrap and place in warm draft-free area.
14. When the dough has doubled in bulk (45 to 60 minutes), punch it down and knead again (two to three minutes).
15. Return dough to bowl and refrigerate for 15 minutes before shaping.
16. Shape by stretching the dough into desired format. Do not use a rolling pin.

Wheat and honey pizza crust

This whole wheat pizza crust offers the nutritional value of three forms of wheat and honey. Wheat, as we have learned, is rich in an entire range of vitamins and minerals. Wheat germ, itself (the embryo of the wheat grain), is a concentrated source of many of these vitamins as well as protein.

Ingredients:
- 1 package active dry yeast, ¼ oz.
- 1 c. warm water
- 2 c. whole wheat flour
- ¼ c. wheat germ

- 1 tbsp. honey
- 2 tsp. organic wheatgrass powder
- 1 tsp. salt

Instructions:
1. Preheat oven to 350° Fahrenheit.
2. In a small bowl, dissolve yeast in warm water. Leave until creamy, or for about ten minutes.
3. In a large bowl, combine flour, wheat germ, and salt. Make a dent in the center and add yeast mixture and honey; stir well to combine. Cover and set in a warm place to rise for about 15 minutes.
4. Roll dough on a floured pizza pan.
5. Use fork to make several holes in dough.
6. Garnish with your favorite toppings or use the following recipe.
7. Bake in preheated oven for five to ten minutes or until desired crispness is achieved.

Thai pizza with peanut-wheatgrass sauce

This unique recipe is as healthy as it is tasty. It is beneficial in a number of ways including building the bones, enhancing the blood, and strengthening the eyes.

Ingredients:
- 1 pizza crust
- 2 c. chopped spinach
- 1 c. shredded carrots
- ¼ c. shredded Colby jack cheese
- 1 batch peanut-wheatgrass sauce
- 1-inch round chopped wheatgrass

Instructions:
1. Spread peanut sauce over pizza crust.
2. Sprinkle cheese, vegetables, and wheatgrass over pizza.
3. Bake for about 20 minutes in oven under low heat until cheese has melted.

Wheatgrass bread

Bread has an interesting history. It has been one of the principal forms of food since ancient Egypt. You can actually see 5,000-year-old loaves of bread and wheat grains preserved in the Egyptian galleries of the British Museum. According to legend, the first loaf of bread was made by accident. An Egyptian slave who was making water cakes fell asleep, letting the fire go out before the cakes were done. The resulting product was light and fluffy compared to the hard, flat cakes that were expected. From then on, the cakes were experimented with in many ways. Many other legends surround the history of bread, and it is still a favorite food today.

Wheatgrass loaf bread

This delicious recipe can be used as a basis for other recipes. Add cinnamon and raisins for raisin bread or garlic and onions for onion bread. Once you get used to making this loaf bread, it will be easy to come up with a variety of variations.

Ingredients:
- 1 c. milk, scalded
- 1 tbsp. sugar or molasses
- 1 tbsp. butter
- 1 ½ tsp. salt
- 1 yeast packet dissolved in ¼ c. boiling water, cooled until lukewarm
- 1 ¼ c. water; add a bit more to reach desired consistency
- 3 ¼ c. to 4 c. flour to make a firm dough
- 2 tbsp. organic wheatgrass powder

Instructions:
Dough:
1. Pour hot liquid over sugar, salt, and butter.
2. Cool until lukewarm.
3. Add yeast, and then beat in sufficient flour to make a dough that can be lifted in a mass on the spoon leaving the bowl free of small amount of flour on board. Beat until loaf is smooth, elastic to

the touch, and stiff enough that it will not stick to a clean board when kneading. This will average about ten minutes.

4. To knead bread properly, fold dough from the back toward the center with fingertips, and then press down and away from the kneader with palms of hands.
5. Do this twice, and then give dough a quarter turn on board and repeat process. Always turn in same direction.
6. Do not use more flour than necessary.
7. Put in oiled bowl or one mixed with cold water.
8. Oil top or cover lightly to prevent formation of a crust.
9. Let rise in warm place until doubled in bulk. It will then feel tender, and a touch of the finger will leave an impression.
10. Work bread down and let rise a second time until doubled in bulk.

Loaf

1. Knead light dough on an unfloured board (to prevent streaks) just enough to distribute gas bubbles evenly.
2. Shape into a ball.
3. Then, make into a roll longer than the pan handling as lightly and quickly as possible.
4. Flatten and fold ends to center. Press firmly and seal. Fold sides to center and seal.
5. Shape into a loaf, place in an oiled pan, smooth side up. The pan should not be more than half full.
6. Let rise in a warm place until doubled in bulk.

Baking

1. Bake at 400° Fahrenheit for ten minutes.
2. Reduce heat to 350° Fahrenheit, and bake for 20 additional minutes.
3. If browned sufficiently after the first ten minutes, place paper over loaves to prevent crust from becoming too brown.

Wheatgrass muffins

Muffins are quick, easy breads that are baked in small portions. The word is derived from the French word *moufflet,* which means soft. In most cases, the word applies to either American-style muffins (similar to cupcakes) or English yeast muffins (circular in shape). Muffins are often eaten for breakfast, but they can be enjoyed any time. They were popular at tea time in 19th century England. Muffin recipes were as prevalent in 19th century cookbooks as they are in cookbooks today. You can find hundreds of recipes online, and it is easy to create your own. Use the following muffin recipes as a basis for creating your own wheatgrass muffins.

Apricot-wheatgrass muffins

Apricots are rich in beta-carotene, vitamin C, and lycopene, a cancer-fighting nutrient. They are also a good source of potassium, manganese, and copper. Dried apricots have a higher nutritional content than fresh ones because the nutrients are concentrated. This recipe calls for apricots, but you can substitute acai berries or cranberries for a different taste and texture but similar nutritional composition.

Ingredients:
- ¾ c. dried apricots, chopped
- 1 c. whole wheat flour
- ¾ c. all-purpose flour
- ¾ c. plus 1 tbsp. toasted wheat germ, divided
- 1 c. buttermilk
- ½ c. orange juice, divided
- 2 large eggs
- ½ c. packed light brown sugar
- ¼ c. canola oil
- 2 tbsp. freshly grated orange zest
- 1 ½ tsp. baking powder
- 1 ½ tsp. organic wheatgrass powder
- 1 tsp. vanilla extract
- ½ tsp. baking soda
- ¼ tsp. salt

Instructions:

1. Preheat oven to 400° Fahrenheit. Coat 12 muffin cups with cooking spray.

2. Combine apricots and ¼ cup of orange juice in a small saucepan. Bring to a simmer, and then remove from heat. Set aside to cool.

3. Whisk whole wheat flour, all-purpose flour, ¾ cup wheat germ, baking powder, baking soda, and salt in a large bowl.

4. Whisk eggs and brown sugar in a medium bowl until smooth. Whisk in buttermilk, oil, orange zest, vanilla, and remaining ¼ cup orange juice. Add to the dry ingredients and mix with a rubber spatula just until moistened. Add apricots and juice and mix just until blended. Scoop the batter into the prepared muffin cups. Sprinkle with remaining 1 tablespoon wheat germ.

5. Bake the 15 to 25 minutes or until lightly browned. Let cool in the pan for five minutes. Loosen the edges and turn the muffins out onto a wire rack to cool slightly before serving.

Poppy seed wheatgrass muffins

Use of poppy seeds as a culinary spice dates back to the Middle Ages and is still popular today in kitchens across the world. It is used in a number of foods, such as confectionaries, bagels, gravies, and vegetables. Poppy seeds provide the diet with vital nutrients such as zinc, magnesium, and calcium.

Ingredients:

- ⅓ c. skim milk
- ¼ c. vegetable oil
- 1 container non-fat lemon yogurt, 6 oz.
- ¼ c. egg substitute
- 1 ¾ c. all-purpose flour
- ¼ c. organic wheatgrass powder
- ¼ c. sugar
- 2 tbsp. poppy seeds
- 1 tbsp. grated lemon peel
- 2 ½ tsp. baking powder
- ½ tsp. baking soda
- ½ tsp. salt

Instructions:
1. Heat oven to 400° Fahrenheit.
2. Line 12 medium muffin cups with paper baking cups.
3. Beat milk, oil, yogurt, and egg substitute in large bowl.
4. Stir in remaining ingredients just until moistened.
5. Divide batter evenly among muffin cups (should be about ¾ full).
6. Bake 16 to 18 minutes or until golden brown.
7. Immediately remove from pan and cool on a wire rack.

Candies, chews, and other sweet treats

Sweet tooth anyone? Many of us enjoy a tasty treat or delicious dessert — some more than others. Even though we do indulge at times, we know that constantly snacking on sugar-laden treats is not beneficial to the body. The following recipes have been chosen with this in mind, using healthy alternatives for many high-calorie, high-fat ingredients. In the mix, you are sure to find a treasure,

Carob-wheatgrass truffles

Try this tasty dessert that contains a mixture of ingredients that are beneficial to your body. Rich in phosphorous and calcium, carob is often used to fight against osteoporosis. Carob pods contain neither caffeine nor oxalates, but still have a chocolate-like flavor.

Ingredients:
- ½ c. almonds soaked 12 to 48 hours and dehydrated eight hours
- ½ c. pecans soaked six to eight hours and dehydrated eight hours
- ½ c. pine nuts
- 1 c. Medjool dates
- 2 tbsp. raw carob powder
- 1 tsp. vanilla
- 1 c. shredded coconut

Instructions:
1. Process almonds, pecans, and pine nuts in a food processor using the "S" blade.

2. Slowly add dates and continue processing until the mixture forms a ball.
3. Add carob and vanilla; mix well.
4. Form mixture into ½-inch balls, and roll in coconut.
5. Refrigerate for two hours.
6. Serve and enjoy.

Wheatgrass turtles

A variation of the famous chocolate turtles, this recipe is healthier and has fewer calories.

Ingredients:
- 1 c. slivered almonds
- 1 c. coconut oil (melted in bowl)
- 2 tsp. vanilla
- 2 tbsp. organic wheatgrass powder
- ¾ c. ground cacao nibs (peeled cacao beans)
- ¼ c. almond butter
- Dash agave nectar

Instructions:
1. Mix all ingredients.
2. Spread on wax paper.
3. Chill for at least two hours.
4. Break and serve.

Wheatgrass-almond energy balls

This recipe is great for parties. It is also beneficial to the body as it contains almonds, bananas, and coconut. These ingredients are amazing energy sources and, as a bonus, also promote healthiness of the heart.

Ingredients:
- 4 mashed ripe bananas
- 1 c. almond butter
- 1 ½ c. shredded coconut
- ¾ c. coarsely chopped almonds

- ½ c. ground sunflower and pumpkin seeds
- ½ c. pre-soaked dried tropical fruit mix
- 6 tbsp. skim milk
- 2 tbsp. flax meal
- 1 tbsp. organic wheatgrass powder
- 2 tsp. vanilla essence

Instructions:
1. Mix all ingredients, except ½ cup of coconut, in large bowl.
2. Roll into small balls.
3. Roll balls into coconut.
4. Chill in refrigerator for two hours before serving.

Crispy wheatgrass chews

Kids will like this variation of the well-known crispy rice treats. Let them enjoy preparing this treat as well as eating it.

Ingredients:
- 1 c. organic brown rice syrup
- ¼ c. organic peanut butter
- ¼ c. organic almond butter
- 3 c. organic crispy brown rice cereal
- 4 tbsp. organic wheatgrass powder

Instructions:
1. In a large sauce pan, heat brown rice syrup and nut butters over low heat until creamy.
2. Remove from heat and add crispy rice cereal and stir until well coated.
3. Press into a square brownie pan and cut.

Green energy chews

Raw cashews, Medjool dates, wheatgrass, and hemp seed provide the energy. You only need to supply the appetite.

Ingredients:
- 2 tsp. organic wheatgrass powder

- ¼ c. hemp seeds
- 1 c. raw cashews
- 1 c. pitted Medjool dates (about 8 large)

Instructions:

1. Mix the cashews, dates, and wheatgrass powder together in a food processor just until a rough dough has formed, allowing some cashews to remain coarsely chopped.
2. Add the hemp seeds and pulse several times until combined.
3. Place a sheet of plastic wrap on a cutting board and spill the dough out on top.
4. Use your hands to press and form into a 1-inch thick rectangle, and then cut into eight pieces.
5. Wrap and keep in the freezer for long-term storage.

Super food treats

Peanut butter and super berries make this a nutritional delight. Add some wheatgrass powder and you have an extra high nutritional treat.

Ingredients:

- 1 c. brown rice syrup
- 1 c. extra-crunchy peanut butter
- 3 tbsp. organic wheatgrass powder
- 3 c. puffed wheat cereal
- ¼ c. chopped dried acai berries
- ¼ c. raw almond slivers

Instructions:

1. Mix together and press into a pan.

Coconut lemon pats

Known for its therapeutic properties, lemon has been used for generations in all types of home remedies, while coconut is rich in protein and an excellent body builder. Lemon and coconut are both recommended by experts for healthy skin and hair.

Ingredients:

- 2 c. to 3 c. soaked cashews
- Zest from 2 lemons (just the outer yellow rind, not the white)
- Juice from 3 lemons
- 2 c. shredded coconut
- About ½ c. or more agave nectar or honey, to taste
- Any leftover almond pulp from making almond milk can be added

Instructions:

1. Process until mixture is smooth in food processor.
2. Roll into small balls and flatten thin onto cookie sheets.
3. Allow to dehydrate for at least a day.

Cocoa brownies

Cocoa powder is a wonderful antioxidant. When consumed in moderate proportions, cocoa will elevate your mood and have positive effects on your immune system and circulation.

Ingredients:

- 1 c. all-purpose flour or rice flour
- 1 ½ c. sugar
- ¾ tsp. baking soda
- ¾ c. cocoa powder
- ½ c. organic wheatgrass powder
- 1 tsp. cinnamon, optional
- 1 ½ c. boiling water
- 1 c. mayonnaise
- 1 tbsp. vanilla extract

Instructions:

1. Preheat oven to 325° Fahrenheit.
2. Lightly coat an 8-inch square pan with vegetable cooking spray.
3. Whisk the flour, sugar, and baking soda together in a bowl. Set aside.
4. In another bowl, whisk together the cocoa, wheatgrass powder, and cinnamon.
5. Add boiling water and/or hot coffee and whisk vigorously to

dissolve lumps in cocoa and allow the spices to bloom.

6. Add mayonnaise and vanilla and whisk until smooth.

7. Combine wet chocolate mixture with flour mixture and pour into pan.

8. Bake until toothpick inserted comes out clean or about 30 to 40 minutes.

Raw fudge

At one point in history, Medjool dates were consumed only by Moroccan royalty and their guests, as they were a gourmet delicacy and remain so today. This "diamond of dates" is prized for its large size, luscious softness, and extraordinary sweetness.

Ingredients:

- 1 c. Medjool dates and 1 vanilla bean cut into pieces, soaked overnight in just enough water to cover
- ¾ c. raw cashew butter
- 1 c. raw cacao powder (peel and dehydrate cacao beans then grind up to a powder)
- ¾ c. raw carob
- ½ c. raw mesquite powder
- 1 tsp. organic wheatgrass powder
- 1 tbsp. coconut oil
- Splash of agave nectar
- Pinch of salt

Instructions:

1. Blend all the ingredients in a powerful blender until it is a smooth batter.

2. Line a glass baking dish with wax or parchment paper and pour on the batter.

3. Freeze for a few hours.

4. Take out of freezer to cut into squares and put back into freezer overnight.

Oatmeal-pecan chocolate chip cookies

These cookies are a combination of oatmeal, chocolate chips, and wheatgrass. They are very rich, but very tasty, and wheatgrass healthy. You can omit the nuts if you are not a nut lover. This recipe yields about 60 cookies.

Ingredients:
- 4 c. flour (sift before measuring)
- ½ c. dehydrated wheatgrass powder
- 5 c. oatmeal
- 4 large eggs
- 2 tsp. vanilla extract
- 2 c. butter
- 2 c. raw turbinado sugar
- 2 c. dark brown sugar
- 1 tsp. salt
- 2 tsp. baking soda
- 2 tsp. baking powder
- 24 oz. organic chocolate chunks
- 3 c. chopped pecans

Instructions:
1. Preheat oven to 375° Fahrenheit.
2. Cream together the butter and the sugars.
3. Sift together flour, wheatgrass, oatmeal, salt, baking soda, baking powder, and chocolate.
4. Add eggs and vanilla to creamed sugar and butter, and then mix all ingredients together.
5. Mix chocolate chips and nuts into mixture.
6. Drop by onto ungreased cookie sheet in small drops.
7. Bake six minutes or until done.

Key lime pie

Considered the official pie of the Florida Keys, key lime pie is one of America's favorite regional dishes. It can also be made in a variety of ways. This one uses a variety of super foods for a super healthy treat.

Ingredients:
Crust:

- 1 c. almonds
- 2 c. walnuts
- 1 c. dates
- ⅓ c. raisins
- 2 tsp. wheatgrass powder
- 2 tbsp. orange juice

Filling:

- 1 large avocado or two small ones
- Juice of 4 limes or 7 key limes
- Zest of the limes
- ½ c. cashew nuts

Frosting:

- ½ c. almond milk or water
- 1 c. macadamia nuts
- ¼ c. cashews
- 1 vanilla bean, scraped, optional
- 3 tbsp. honey *or* 7 to 10 dates

Garnish:

- Crushed pistachios
- Lemon wedges

Instructions:
Preparing crust:

1. Process all ingredients until crumbly and soft.
2. Press into a 10-inch springform pan and chill.

Preparing filling:

1. Either blend ingredients in blender until thick and creamy or put through a champion or green power juicer.

Preparing frosting:

1. Put ingredients in a clean blender.
2. Whip it until extremely smooth.

Assembly:

1. Remove the chilled crust.
2. Spoon the filling on top.
3. Smooth it out with a spatula or spoon.
4. Let chill for one hour.
5. Remove and then pipe or spoon frosting on top.
6. Garnish with lemon/lime wedges and chopped pistachios.
7. Put in the refrigerator or freezer for another hour to set.
8. Enjoy.

Wheatgrass-lime granita

Granitas hail from Italy and are similar to sorbets. The addition of wheatgrass and agave nectar makes this granita more than a sugar-water dessert.

Ingredients:

- 2 tsp. organic wheatgrass powder
- 3 tbsp. fresh squeezed lime juice
- 2 tbsp. fresh squeezed lemon juice
- $\frac{1}{3}$ c. agave nectar
- 2 c. water

Instructions:

1. Mix all the ingredients together in a shaker cup or stir well in a glass.
2. Pour into a large bowl or plastic container.
3. Cover, and place in the freezer.
4. After about two hours, remove from the freezer and use the prongs of a fork to scrape the mixture and separate the ice crystals.
5. Place back in the freezer and repeat twice more over the course of three hours.
6. Serve when fully icy and fluffy.

Green power pop

For a refreshing summer treat, try this recipe. In fact, try all juices and smoothies in frozen form for a delightful change of pace.

Ingredients:
- 4 apples, peeled
- 1 ¼ fresh pineapple slices
- 2 lemons, peeled
- 1 lime, peeled
- 1 tbsp. agave nectar
- 2 oz. fresh wheatgrass juice

Instructions:
1. Blend all ingredients in blender or vitamix.
2. Pour into Popsicle molds.
3. Freeze for eight hours.

Other wheatgrass products

The use of herbs in cosmetic products dates back to the ancient civilizations. The Greeks, Romans, and Chinese recognized the value of plant substances for body care. They used the fruit, flowers, leaves, bark, and the roots of a variety of herbs to create tinctures, teas, and poultices to alleviate ailments and beautify the skin. Among the cereal grasses, wheat was a common medicinal and cosmetic aide. Today, wheat is still a popular ingredient for many cosmetic houses based on its vitamin E and antioxidant properties. The following recipes incorporate wheatgrass as a cosmetic and/or medicinal enhancer.

Wheatgrass soothing cream

Wheatgrass soothing cream can be used for sore muscles, rashes, insect bites, and open wounds. Soothing cream can be only be prepared for a single application, as the wheatgrass begins to lose its potency once it is exposed to the air.

Ingredients:
- One packet dried wheatgrass or crushed wheatgrass tablets
- 2 tsp. (10 ml) raw honey

Instructions:
1. Briskly stir the wheatgrass and the honey until well mixed.

2. Immediately apply to the skin.

Healthy face glow

Ordinary soaps tend to dry out the skin when used regularly, especially the face. Yet, the face can benefit from a gentle cleansing. Use this easy recipe to cleanse the face and create a natural glow.

Ingredients:
- 4 leaves fresh mint
- 1 large cucumber
- 1 egg white
- ½ tsp. wheatgrass powder

Instructions:
1. Mix a thick paste of oatmeal, yogurt, and wheatgrass.
2. Spread the mixture over face and allow to dry for 15 to 20 minutes.
3. Rinse face with warm water and pat dry with soft towel.

Lavender-mint body rejuvenator

This skin treatment combines wheatgrass with lavender and mint for a therapeutic skin rub and internal cleanse. It will rejuvenate the skin while cleansing and improve blood circulation.

Ingredients:
- 1 tray harvested wheatgrass
- 3 c. filtered water
- 1 tbsp. raw honey
- Petals from one lavender flower
- 2 to 3 sprigs fresh mint

Instructions:
1. Liquefy all ingredients in blender for one to two minutes.
2. Strain mixture through a fine mesh strainer.
3. Liquid can be consumed as a detoxifying drink (in 2- to 4-ounce dosages), used as a mouth and throat rinse, or as an enema.
4. Break off small pieces of the wheatgrass pulp and dab over the skin.

5. Leave on the skin for 20 minutes, and then anoint the skin with wheatgrass oil.
6. Leave the oil on the skin for five to ten minutes before removing with a soft cloth.

Wheatgrass oil

Wheatgrass oil can be used as a topical first aid treatment as well as a skin conditioner. It is good for treating scars and other skin blemishes.

Ingredients:

- One large, clear glass jar
- 2-inch round fresh wheatgrass
- Cold-pressed wheat germ oil
- Cold-pressed carrot oil
- 2 tsp. lavender oil
- Muslin cloth or cheesecloth

Instructions:

1. Place wheatgrass in jar.
2. Cover with oils.
3. Cover jar and let stand in a warm area for ten to 14 days, shaking gently every day.
4. Strain oil through muslin or cheesecloth.
5. Store in clear jar or bottle and use as needed.

Fungal foot powder

Feet tend to develop athlete's foot and other funguses when not properly cared for. These feet ailments cause itchy, burning dry skin that can be quite uncomfortable. Use this remedy after showering to get feet back into shape or prevent fungus from developing.

Ingredients:

- 2 tbsp. corn flour or unscented talc
- 2 tsp. wheatgrass powder
- 15 drops lavender
- 5 drops peppermint

Instructions:

1. Put corn flour or talc and wheatgrass powder into a small plastic bag.
2. Add the essential oils.
3. Tie or zip close the bag securely and let sit for 24 hours.
4. Shake well before each use.
5. Make sure feet are thoroughly dry before applying.

Dandruff shampoo

Potash is a compound that contains potassium and other plant nutrients. Potassium is beneficial for strengthening the hair and encouraging hair growth. Wheatgrass also contains potassium and other nutrients beneficial for the hair and scalp.

Ingredients:

- 2 c. distilled water
- 1 ¾ oz. white soft soap
- ⅓ oz. potash
- 1 tsp. wheatgrass powder
- 14 drops rosemary oil
- 6 drops eucalyptus oil

Instructions:

1. Bring the distilled water to a boil in a tall pot.
2. Add soap and let it dissolve.
3. Add the potash and stir thoroughly until smooth.
4. Simmer for about 30 minutes.
5. Cool the mixture and add essential oils and wheatgrass powder.
6. Stir thoroughly.
7. Pour it into a bottle and use regularly.

Simple cleansing rinse

Commercial shampoos tend to be alkaline, which can leave a film on your hair, depending on the pH balance of your water. This acidic rinse can be used after shampooing to help ensure a clean scalp.

Ingredients:

- 2 c. warm water
- 1 tsp. vinegar or freshly squeezed lemon juice or vinegar
- 1 oz. fresh wheatgrass juice

Instructions:

1. Place all ingredients in glass jar and shake well.
2. Apply after shampooing as a final rinse.

CASE STUDY: A STORY OF RECOVERY

Michelle Grubb Blackwood, RN, home educator
www.facebook.com/people/
Michelle-Grubb-Blackwood/1643454303
—maxoyd@aol.com

Michelle Blackwood is a registered nurse who decided to take charge of her health and the health of her family in a natural way. She is an avid believer in the power of juicing and eating a high percentage of raw foods. Blackwood resides in Virginia with her husband and two children.

Michelle Blackwood and husband Devon Blackwood.

I became interested in alternative health while working with telemetry patients at Monmouth Medical Center. These are patients that need cardiac monitoring but do not require intensive care unit placement. I noticed that the patients, although on drugs, were not getting better. Their diet consisted of fried, fatty, high-cholesterol foods. The hospital program to which they were prescribed was merely addressing the symptoms of their disease and not getting to the root of the problem. Some of these patients would be discharged, only to be readmitted later with a worsening of the same condition. We called them "frequent flyers." Upon re-admittance, we would stabilize them and, perhaps, change their medication. Yet, they got progressively worse. In some instances, they would not return. Not because they were better, but because they had died. It was very discouraging and depressing. I thought to myself, "There has got to be a better way."

Monitoring those patients day in and day out made me take a good look at my own lifestyle. Is that what the future held for me? I had always had a weight problem, and I began to seek ways to address this concern before it led to bigger problems. I started reading about nutrition and healthy living and came across a lot of information about raw food, juicing, and wheatgrass. I decided to give it a try. One of the first things I noticed with the juicing was an immediate loss of weight. I wanted to get my entire family involved and my husband decided to change his diet as well. So, we began our new lifestyle of eating raw foods, lots of fresh fruits and vegetables, and plenty of juice. I grew the wheatgrass myself on my back porch. It was easy, economical, and fresh.

I did not realize I had conceived my second child until I was about 20 weeks into the pregnancy. There was no morning sickness or other discomforts. At a pre-natal check-up, I was told that my hemoglobin was low due to my sickle-cell anemia trait. I increased the juicing and my hemoglobin stabilized — probably due to the iron content of the wheatgrass juice. I actually had a very good pregnancy. There were no problems, discomforts, or concerns. Also, I had no labor pains. I went to the hospital because I believed my water had broken.

Upon admittance to University of Virginia (UVA) Hospital, I was told that I was in full labor with contractions coming one to two minutes apart, but I was not fully dilated. The doctor wanted to dilate the cervix using the drug Cytotec, but I refused. He tried to convince me that the baby was in danger, and there was no time to dilate naturally. The only other alternative was a Caesarean section. I felt that I could deliver the baby naturally, but because my first child was delivered by Caesarean section, the doctor did not want to attempt a vaginal delivery. I was not happy, but the doctor performed the surgery. A baby boy was brought forth weighing 8 pounds, 5 ounces.

Recovery from Caesarean section can be slow and painful, but usually, the patient is released from the hospital in three to four days. On the fourth day, when I was about to be discharged, I began experiencing severe pain in the abdominal area. My vitals were checked and my heart rate was 170 beats per minute. A normal range is 60 – 100 beats per minute. Upon further examination, I was told that I was experiencing total septicemia (blood poisoning) due to a perforation of the bowels. The infection was due to fecal contamination of the abdominal cavity. I was placed under a medically induced coma for five days to undergo bowel re-section surgery. Out of that major operation came eight abscesses that needed to be drained of infected fluid. My lungs also were filled with fluid that needed to be drained. Instead of four days, I spent four weeks in the hospital; three weeks being in the intensive care unit in critical condition. Thankfully, I pulled through each of those life-threatening procedures. After being moved from ICU, I was placed on physical therapy that was to be continued at home upon discharge.

As soon as I was released from the hospital, I abandoned all drugs, prescriptions, and advice handed to me by the medical staff of UVA. I did not want to become dependent on those things. I went back to my family and my wheatgrass and other herbs. I resumed my juicing because that was my therapy and the source of my recovery.

I returned to the hospital for a four-week check-up and the staff was amazed. The recovery that should have taken four to six weeks had only taken two weeks. The wounds were completely healed, and there was no evidence of dead tissue in the intestinal area. Dead tissue would mean the placement of a colostomy bag to eliminate wastes.

I will continue with this lifestyle of eating raw food. I will continue to grow organic vegetables in my garden and pick dandelion leaves from my backyard. I will continue to grow and juice wheatgrass for myself and my family, and I will continue to share this testimony in hopes of encouraging someone else.

Please note: *The previous account is the personal story of Michelle Blackwood. In no way is this book or its publisher endorsing or advising the use of wheatgrass remedies over the medical advice, orders, or treatments of any physician.*

CHAPTER 8

Wheatgrass, Children, and Pets

"Children are our most valuable natural resource."

~ Herbert Hoover

Generally, children do not like to eat what is good for them. The sight of a large plate of spinach, broccoli, or kale placed before them will cause most children to turn up their noses in disgust. Greens, especially, are unpopular because of their stringy texture and bitter taste. Children are especially sensitive to bitter flavors because they have more taste buds, and these buds are closer together on the tongue than in adults. Yet, even children must consume a certain amount of green, leafy vegetables to nourish their bodies and keep them strong. According to several health organizations, including the National Institutes of Health, children and teens in the United States do not meet national recommendations for nutrition and need to be educated in this area. Their intake of fruits and deep yellow and/or dark green vegetables, especially, is low. According to a 1996 study by Archives of Pediatrics and Adolescent Medicine, "Nearly one-quarter of all vegetables consumed by children and adolescents were French fries." One large serving of french fries — 169 grams — contains

539 calories, 28.8 grams of fat, 328 mg of sugar, and 6.4 grams of protein. According to the study, only 1 percent of the group met all nutritional recommendations. Childhood obesity is also on the rise. According to the 2007-2008 National Health and Nutrition Examination Survey, about 17 percent of children and adolescents ages 2 to 19 years old are obese. Obese children and teenagers will more likely than not become obese adults and suffer from health problems.

The Problem with the Traditional Food Pyramid

In recent years, the federal government has placed fruit and vegetables at the base of the food pyramid, as these foods are key to combating several major diseases in the United States, including diabetes and cancer. The food pyramid was first developed in 1992 by the USDA. It was a visual presentation of the basic food groups and their relative proportion to a healthy diet. It served as the basis for federal food and nutrition education programs, including school lunch programs. The base of the pyramid, the bread and cereal group, represented the foundation of a healthy diet. The bread and cereal food group contains grains, breads, cereals, potatoes, and pasta. An abundance of these carbohydrate-rich foods was once thought to be the foundation of a healthy diet. According to Dr. Walter Willet of the Harvard School of Public Health and other notable medical researchers, however, the traditional food pyramid is misleading as its concept is based on out-of-date scientific data, and it is strongly influenced by corporations mainly interested in promoting their own wares.

It is also believed to be a contributor to the growing epidemic of childhood obesity. Specific problems with the food pyramid, according to Willet, include the following:

- The food pyramid offers no guidance on weight control and exercise.

- The pyramid insinuates that all fats are unhealthy when in reality it is only saturated and transaturated fats that are so. Monosaturated and polyunsaturated fats — found in fish, nuts, olive oil, and whole grains — are actually beneficial to the heart.

- The food pyramid's recommendation of six to 11 servings of carbohydrates a day is too great. Also, all carbohydrates are not good for you. Complex carbohydrates from whole grains and natural simple carbohydrates from fruits are healthier than refined carbohydrates from crackers and chips.

- The food pyramid does not specify which proteins are good for you and which are not. Fish, turkey, chicken, nuts, and beans are good sources of protein that are low in saturated fats. Red meat, such as beef, is high in cholesterol and saturated fat, which is not healthy for the heart.

- The claim that dairy products are essential to the diet is untrue. According to a 2005 review published in *Pediatrics*, dairy products have little to no contribution to building bones in growing children. On the contrary, dairy products pose certain health risks for children as well as promote the development of heart disease and diabetes. Consuming too much dairy can also lead to cancer of the reproductive organs. Calcium and potassium, important minerals, especially for children, as well as vitamin D can be obtained from legumes, vegetables, grains, fruits, and juices.

- According to the traditional food pyramid, potatoes are placed in the vegetable group when, in fact, they are starches. The sugar content of potatoes is very high, and they should be avoided by diabetics and individuals trying to lose weight.

In an attempt to reflect a healthier lifestyle and offer nutritional advice that corresponds to the latest scientific research, the USDA changed the traditional pyramid in 2005 to a new design called MyPyramid (**www. mypyramid.gov**). The new symbol was built by a variety of individuals, some professional food scientists and some not, and includes the following improvements:

- The importance of weight control is emphasized as well as the importance of exercise.

- The recognition of the potential health benefits of monounsaturated and polyunsaturated fats is included. It is recommended that 20 to 30 calories daily be obtained from them. A limited intake of transaturated and saturated fats is suggested.

- The benefit of whole grains is emphasized and Americans are encouraged to limit sugar intake through complex carbohydrates. The intake of fruits and vegetables is also emphasized.

The 2005 recommended daily allowances for fruits and vegetables for children, according to the *Report of the Dietary Guidelines Advisory Committee on Dietary Guidelines for Americans*, are as follows:

- Based on a recommended 1,200 calorie intake, all children ages 1 to 3 and girls ages 4 to 8 should consume 2½ cups of fruits and vegetables daily.

- Based on a recommended 1,400 calorie intake, boys ages 4 to 8 should consume 3 cups of fruits and vegetables daily.

- Based on a recommended 1,600 calorie intake, girls ages 9 to 13 should consume 3½ cups of fruit and vegetables daily.

- Based on a recommended 1,800 calorie intake, boys ages 9 to 13 and girls ages 14 to 18 should consume 4 cups of fruit and vegetables daily.

- Based on a recommended 2,200 calorie intake, boys 14 to 18 should include 5 cups of fruits and vegetables daily.

The Healthy Eating Pyramid

According to Willet, the new USDA MyPyramid falls short of its aim to educate the public on better health choices, as it is simply a revised edition of the old pyramid. It does not fully point the way to better health, and furthermore, it is ambiguous in its design. By law, the guidelines must be revised every five years. Instead of waiting to see what the 2010 USDA dietary changes would reveal, the Harvard School of Public Health created the Healthy Eating Pyramid, based on current scientific data linking heath to nutrition. The 2009 Healthy Eating Pyramid emphasizes weight control and daily exercise as the foundation of good health. It then builds a structure based on whole grains, healthy fats, and an abundance of fruits and vegetables. The pyramid emphasizes quality over quantity. Plant foods such as seeds, nuts, tofu, and beans are placed alongside such protein-rich foods as fish, poultry, and eggs. Dairy is limited to one to two servings of fat-free or low-fat products daily — or better yet, a vitamin D and calcium supplement daily. Red meats, refined grains (white rice, white bread, potatoes, pasta), sweets, and salt are placed at the top of the pyramid to use sparingly, if at all.

Incorporating Wheatgrass into a Living Food Pyramid for Children

The largest portion of a living foods pyramid would be the fruit and vegetable food group with leafy, green vegetables at the base. These are foundational foods that should be consumed generously. Leafy greens such as spinach and watercress deliver iron, while vitamins C and E are supplied by fruits and vegetables such as citrus fruits, tomatoes, cauliflower, and broccoli. The next important group would be sprouts (sprouted seeds) followed by nuts and seeds. These two groups supply protein and an abundance of amino acids to the body. Sprouts have a high concentration of RNA and DNA as well as protein and other essential nutrients. They are particularly high in vitamin C. Seeds offer unsaturated fatty acids to the body which are essential to good health. They supply protein and are one of the best natural sources of vitamin E, the B-complex vitamins, and lecithin, fatty substances found in animals and plant tissues. Seeds also provide the diet with fiber, which is important for proper elimination of the bowels. Nuts are also high in carbohydrates, fats, and protein and supply important minerals such as calcium, potassium, phosphorous, and sodium. Raw nuts have an abundant supply of vitamin F (essential fatty acids) as well as the B vitamins. Vitamin F is important for all-around body development while the B vitamins are essential for the nervous system and healthy brain growth. Some nuts (pecans, pistachios, cashews, hazelnuts) also contain vitamins A and K. Chestnuts are a significant source of vitamin C. Nuts and seeds should be eaten moderately and should always be eaten raw or sprouted, not roasted, toasted, or baked.

Herbs and cereal grasses are important elements of a living foods pyramid. These are considered medicinal foods. Herbs have been used in the diet for medicinal and culinary purposes since ancient times. A small amount of herbs eaten daily can contribute greatly to your child's health and general well-being. Herbs can also be used to enhance the flavor of food. Some herbs when used together, such as celery, thyme, and marjoram, can replace the need for salt. Other herbs, such as savory, nasturtium, and basil, can be used to replace pepper. Cereal grasses are juiced and can enhance the diet tremendously with their abundant supply of vitamins, minerals, and enzymes. Wheatgrass juice, in particular, can be used as a cleanser and rejuvenator. It is claimed that a small amount of wheatgrass in the diet can be helpful in preventing tooth decay. Concentrated amounts are often used to treat illnesses. Seaweed and algae top the living foods pyramid and provide growing bodies with a large range of essential minerals in colloidal form. Collodial form allows the minerals to absorb better into the bloodstream because the particles are small.

Example of a living foods pyramid.

As with all healthy diets, exercise and proper rest are essential for the building of the child's body. Plenty of water is also necessary to keep the body's cells hydrated and help flush toxins and waste products from the body. The standard recommendation of water intake for school-aged children is 1.5 to 2 liters a day — about six to eight glasses. According to the Institute of Medicine of the National Academies, teenage boys over 14 should consume

2.6 liters — about 11 large glasses — daily. As a reminder, school-aged children 5 to 10 years old need ten to 11 hours of sleep each night. Ten- to 17-year-old children benefit from 8.5 to 9.25 hours of sleep.

Introducing Children to Wheatgrass

Children can benefit from consuming wheatgrass as long as it is from a reputable source. They should be introduced to the product as early as possible to cultivate a taste for it. Foundations for healthy eating are generally established when we are young, but forcing children to eat well can cause rebellion. One solution to this dilemma is to allow children to help with meals. They are more likely to eat when they have a hand in the cooking.

In most cases, children will practice in adulthood what they have learned in childhood. It is not only important to serve children healthy foods but to educate and inspire them on how to make healthy food selections.

Another way to get children to eat more vegetables is to make juices or smoothies that blend fruit with vegetables. When fruit and vegetables are blended, the fruit dominates the flavor. Wheatgrass and other green vegetables can be added to fruit juices, and most children will be none the wiser. Of course, if you are educating your children in healthy eating practices, they should know how you have created this delicious beverage. Get them to try it first, and then show them how it was made. Also, children learn by example. If you want them to eat healthy and develop a healthy lifestyle, you must be a firsthand example. You cannot expect your children to desire carrots and greens for meals when you are devouring steak and fries next to them. Wheatgrass juice can be diluted with fruit juice when children first begin consuming it. Remember wheatgrass is an acquired taste. Start children young, and it will be easier to incorporate wheatgrass into their daily diet.

By drinking juiced produce, children can have direct access to every enzyme, vitamin, and mineral their body needs. The body can also assimilate these vital nutrients effortlessly into the bloodstream, nourishing all cells of the body. Fresh vegetable juice is especially helpful for children on a weight-loss diet, as fresh juice before a meal acts as a natural and healthy appetite suppressant. According to raw foodists, consuming produce raw is the only way to get all of the nutrients into the body, as many nutrients are just under the skin of the product. Often the easiest way to consume raw produce is by juicing.

Wheatgrass can be given to children. Use small doses, such as 5 to 10 milliliters, diluted with 50 percent water. A maximum daily dosage for children ages 4 to 7 is 1 ounce. DynamicGreens Wheatgrass, a distributor of field-grown wheatgrass, recommends 0.5 ounces for infants and toddlers and 1 ounce for school-age children. You can also follow Young's rule, which is a general rule used by pediatricians for determining a child's dosage. This method was devised by the scientist Thomas Young and involves using the age of the child multiplied by the adult dose, divided by the child's age plus 12. Pam Nees of Optimum Health Institute suggests 1 teaspoon for young children. Babies, according to Nees, should be not given wheatgrass juice until they begin to eat solid food. Babies that are breastfed can benefit from the juice through the mother's milk. Fully breastfed babies should not be given wheatgrass juice directly until they are weaned from the breast. Wheatgrass is very potent and babies' stomachs are very sensitive. Breastfed babies already tend to have loose bowels, and giving them wheatgrass juice too early can result in diarrhea. Just as with adults, when starting children on wheatgrass, you should build up to the maximum dosage. Wheatgrass powder can also be sprinkled in fruit or vegetable juices or on cereal for starters. Wheatgrass is not generally recommended for babies under 6 months, although, some mothers have periodically dipped a finger into the green juice and placed in the baby's mouth so that the baby can start acquiring a taste for the substance. Babies, including newborns, can also be wiped down or bathed with the juice, as it will be absorbed into the skin and can benefit the body in that way. *For information on wheatgrass, pregnancy, and babies, refer to Chapter 3.*

Ann Wigmore claimed that routine immunization could possibly be obviated for children who regularly consumed wheatgrass. Health professional Dr. Chris Reynolds reported several child-related success stories related to wheatgrass in his report "The Demise of Chlorophyll and a Fresh Look at Wheatgrass Therapy," published in the journal of the Australian Integrative Medical Association in May 2004. He also reported positive results from wheatgrass usage on molluscum contagiosum, a common viral infection involving small, itchy spots on a child's skin. Dr. Reynolds states, "In these days of increasing medical fees and costs, wheatgrass offers many patients an effective, safe alternative that can be self-administered and used indefinitely" without a prescription. Doctors at the pediatrics division of the Postgraduate Institute of Medical Education & Research in Chandigarh, India, reported positive results from several therapy trials of wheatgrass usage on thalassaemia patients. Thalassaemia is a hereditary anemic condition characterized by abnormally small red blood cells. Generally, regular blood transfusions are the only option for these patients. Daily wheatgrass use reduced the need for transfusions in the patients. Parents of children diagnosed with attention deficit disorder (ADD) or attention deficit hyperactivity disorder (ADHD) might find that wheatgrass provides a good alternative solution to drugs for treating these ailments. This is due to the high amino acid and vitamin content of wheatgrass that helps repair the vitamin and mineral deficiency of the child, which is a main cause of the ailments.

Medical disclaimer

According to the CDC, vaccinations are one of the most important tools available for avoiding contamination and disease. Not only do vaccines protect the child, they protect the community in which the child resides. This is very important for preventing an epidemic.

Health Concerns for Children on a Living Foods Diet

The health of your children is in your hands, so it is essential that you educate yourself in the areas of diet and nutrition. While there are many diets and health programs from which to choose, getting to know your child and how his or her body responds to different foods and food groups is an important part of choosing a nutrition plan that is right for him or her. The Living Foods Diet incorporates an abundance of raw foods. This plan must be carefully monitored to ensure that a growing child gets the balanced nutrition that he or she needs. Adequate intakes of calcium and vitamin D, especially, can be easily neglected on this plan. Special care must also be taken to ensure that infections and illnesses do not arise from incorrectly prepared raw food. Outbreaks of foodborne illnesses in 1988 led the FDA to advise the public of the health effects of eating raw sprouts. Children were among the group that could be affected by food poisoning from the sprouts. In 1999, the FDA expanded the warning to include the entire public. This warning is still in effect today. There is also the concern brought about by a recent study concerning fruit smoothies and dental concerns. According to a 2008 report on BBC News, smoothies can damage your teeth. While they might encourage children to eat more fruits and vegetables, the constant sugars and acids on the teeth encourage tooth decay. "Every time you sip on a fruit smoothie, your teeth are placed under acid attack for up to an hour," said Dr. Nigel Carter of the British Dental Health Foundation. The use of wheatgrass for children is also a question under debate in health circles. Using wheatgrass, or any herbal medicine for that matter, should be considered carefully. Please seek the advice of your child's pediatrician before attempting to treat any serious illness with wheatgrass or other medicinal herbs.

Wheatgrass and Pets

Before Ann Wigmore introduced the idea of juicing wheatgrass in the 1950s, she was experimenting with wheatgrass and animals. She claimed her pets preferred wheatgrass to the other grasses that she offered them, and so began a concentrated study on wheatgrass. She found that wheatgrass benefited the animals in several ways. Open sores were healed, mange — a contagious skin disease caused by mites, a tick-like organism — was reversed, and behaviors improved. Sick pets were instinctively drawn to the grass. Healthy pets also nibbled the grass. Many veterinarians, pet owners, and animal lovers have yet to use the power of wheatgrass for animal health. The sweet taste of the grass is appealing to a variety of animals. Ann Wigmore had a menagerie — a collection of common and exotic animals kept in human captivity. Wheatgrass can be chopped up finely and placed in the animal's feeding dish along with pet food. The juice can be administered with a medicine dropper or mixed into the drinking water. Wheatgrass juice can also be rubbed onto the pet's fur for absorption through the skin.

All dogs eat grass

Dogs eat grass naturally. Some have been known to sit in a field of grass and graze like a cow. Some may only nibble every now and then. Dog experts do not have a scientific answer to this seemingly bizarre behavior. Some attribute it to their scavenger background. Dogs will eat anything, especially if they are hungry. Some attribute it to their ancestral background. Grass was once a part of a dog's regular diet. Pack animals in the wild ate every part of their captured prey, including the contents of the stomach, which probably contained grass. Some veterinarians believe that dogs eat grass due to a lack of fiber in their current diet. Veterinary medicine expert, Dr. Richard Orzeck, concludes that dogs might eat grass simply because they like the way it tastes.

Dogs are carnivores with carnivorous tendencies. They will also eat plant matter. Dogs with stomach ailments, especially, gravitate to a grassy patch and begin to munch. Many times, this action will induce vomiting in the dog, causing the dog to bring up the entire contents of the stomach, including what was ailing it in the first place. Dogs also have a natural tendency to regurgitate, which allows them to spit out food that has not been processed correctly, and then reswallow it. This is not what is meant by vomiting. A primary cause of vomiting could be an infection or disease of the stomach or esophagus area. It could also be the result of toxins accumulated in the blood from other diseased organs of the body.

Dogs benefit from wheatgrass

Wheatgrass added to a dog's diet can help purge the system from accumulated toxins. It can also benefit the dog in many other ways. Wheatgrass has been claimed to help dogs with the following issues:

- Cancer, kidney, and thyroid problems
- Skeletal problems and skin problems
- Fertility
- Pregnancy and nursing

- Longevity

Wheatgrass contains vitamins and minerals that are not generally found in processed dog food but are necessary for a dog's nutrition. The enzymes in wheatgrass are beneficial for digestion. Dogs do not chew their food very well. Their teeth are designed to rip food apart. There is nothing to rip apart in processed dog food, as it already comes in small pieces. This results in the dog gulping down the food without chewing. Dogs that are overly possessive about a possession also eat fast because they believe the food will be taken from them at any moment. Rapid consumption of food or water by a dog can cause bloat, or gastric dilatation-volvulus (GDV). Bloat is a gastrointestinal disease affecting primarily large and giant dog breeds. Gastric dilatation is the swelling of the stomach from gas. Volvulus refers to a twisting of the stomach on its axis (line of connection to the body). Bloat occurs when too much air is present in the stomach, which is caused by gulping of the food, and can be fatal to the dog. According to research, bloat is the leading cause of death in dogs after cancer. Dr. Lawrence T. Glickman and other researchers at Purdue University suggest several ways to prevent bloat in dogs, including placing dogs on a high-nutrition diet and keeping them relaxed and stress-free.

The high nutritional content of the wheatgrass will provide a high-nutrition diet for the dog. Wheatgrass is also a natural cleanser. The enzymes will work to detoxify the dog's organs, especially the intestines and liver. It will aid the dog's body in expelling waste matter, promoting a healthy, well-functioning digestive system. Ridding the body of excess wastes eliminates the problem of constipation. Relieving constipation relieves stress. Detoxification is also important to help prevent cancer, which is a major dog illness.

Wheatgrass can also help improve the condition of a dog's skin. Regular consumption can aid in the healing process of open wounds and sores. A common dosage for clearing up skin problems in a dog is 1 ounce of wheatgrass juice per 20 pounds of a dog's weight. The juice can also be rubbed onto the dog's skin.

A cat's diet – what is best?

When you decide to bring a cat into your home, you become responsible for that cat's health and well-being. This means providing the cat with attention, exercise, fresh air and sunshine, and a nutritious diet. The nutritious diet can be a little tricky, as there is some controversy in the cat world as to what is the best diet for domestic felines. Advocates of a raw food pet diet state that because cats are natural carnivores, they must get an adequate amount of raw meat in their daily diet. Supporters of home-cooked meals claim that raw eating can promote food poisoning and a host other health ailments. Then, there are those who wonder what is wrong with the myriad dry and canned prepared pet foods already on supermarket and pet store shelves. The conclusion of the matter? You must decide. Cats do eat meat in nature. Meat provides cats with the protein, fats, and amino acids needed for good food digestion and proper body functioning. Cats are naturally equipped for the task of eating meat, as they have very sharp teeth that are made for ripping and tearing meat and crunching through pliable bones. Their stomachs also have strong acids to aid digestion and short digestive tracts to quickly and effectively process raw meat and bone. Food does not stay in a cat's system for long, so there is not time for a case of food poisoning to occur from rotten meat. Eating meat not only nourishes and strengthens the cat's body, it also benefits teeth, gums, and jaws. Cats that have been fed commercial cat food all of their lives are lacking in gnawing skills and jaw strength. For information about transitioning a cat to a raw food diet, visit Raw Fed Cats (**www.rawfedcats.org/practicalguide.htm**).

Whichever meal you choose for your cat, monitoring the cat and being watchful for signs of discomfort and illness can alert you to a problem and possible need to change the diet. Also, monitor your cat's intake of food. Obesity in cats is a common problem and can lead to health ailments such as arthritis and diabetes. For most adult cats, a once- or twice-a-day feeding is sufficient. Kittens have small stomachs and expend a lot of energy in play; therefore, they can be fed four or more small meals a day. According to Linda Zurich in her book *Raw Fed Cats*, amounts and frequency of feedings will depend on the "cat's age, weight, activity level, metabolism, and overall appetite." One important thing to remember when feeding a cat, especially when transitioning to a new diet, is to never let the cat go without food for more than a day. This can result in the fatal hepatic lipidosis, a form of liver failure that is common to cats. For more information about hepatic lipidosis, go to The Pet Education website (**www.peteducation.com/ article.cfm?c=1+1327&aid=217**).

A prescription of wheatgrass for cats

Many cats love to nibble on fresh greens, and wheatgrass is one of their favorites. Fortunately, the wheatgrass is also good for them. According to Gail Colombo, contributing editor of the now defunct *Tiger Tribe* magazine, wheatgrass has the highest concentration of nutrients of all the grasses available. It provides vitamins, minerals, and a host of enzymes that can boost cat health. Wheatgrass can correct bad breath in cats through its high chlorophyll content. Wheatgrass also aids in digestion and helps with hairball control. Hairballs sometimes form in the cat's stomach from hair ingested while grooming. This hair irritates the cat's stomach and will eventually be expelled by vomiting. It is claimed that the addition of wheatgrass to the diet will help the hairballs pass through the digestive system as opposed to being expelled through the mouth. Cats are usually fed high-protein diets. Adding wheatgrass to the diet can help balance nutrients needed for good health. The fiber in the grass aids waste elimination. Staff members of the Hippocrates Health Institute reported fewer illnesses with their cats when they were provided with wheatgrass on a regular basis. These cats were more energetic, exhibited positive behavior, had stronger immune systems, and had beautiful fur. Many cat owners have reported improvements in their cat's health with the addition of wheatgrass to the diet. Some also give accolades to organic wheatgrass cat litter, which manufacturer's claim eliminates odors and minimizes litter being carried throughout the house from cat paws. Allowing a cat free access to its own supply of wheatgrass will deter it from chomping on your prized houseplants. Spritz the grass with water to entice those that are a little more particular about trying new things.

Other popular pets

Other popular pets in the United States include rabbits, guinea pigs, hamsters, birds, fish, and reptiles. They all can be benefit from wheatgrass usage. It enhances the diet and, therefore, the health of the pet. This can be seen many times in its physical structure as well as its disposition.

The concept of juicing wheatgrass for human consumption was introduced by Ann Wigmore in the 1950s, but it did not experience a tremendous surge in popularity for the general public until the 1980s. Likewise, although Wigmore was also feeding wheatgrass to her own pets, it was not until 1996 that pet owners considered giving their pets wheatgrass. Harley Matsil, CEO and owner of Perfect Foods, one of the largest retail grass distributors in the world, discovered that the Bronx Zoo in New York had an indoor area for growing its own wheatgrass.

In a therapeutic study initiated by Dr. Chris Reynolds of Australia, veterinary surgeons tested the topical effect of wheatgrass extract on open wounds and eczema/dermatitis conditions in horses, dogs, and cats. It determined that the extract was "very effective" in 92 percent of the cases. Eczema is a chronic skin disorder that produces itchy, scaly rashes. Dermatitis is an inflammation on the skin due to an allergic reaction. Eczema and dermatitis conditions were predominately found in dogs. Veterinary herbalist Robert McDowell also trialed the wheatgrass extract spray and noted positive results in dogs and horses.

Horses need high-quality, digestible forage, as they have a simple stomach structure, unlike ruminant animals like cows, goats, and sheep that have a complex stomach system with four compartments, allowing them to partially digest, regurgitate, and fully digest their food. Intermediate wheatgrass and other grass types cultivated for grazing should not be allowed to grow to maturity, as they will be less nutritious and unpalatable to the horse. Slender wheatgrass is an excellent nutrient source for wildlife and has intrinsic value for oxen and sheep. The Navajo and Thompson Indians used slender wheatgrass as fodder for their horses, but it was also given to their dogs as a veterinary aid. Farmers in the Midwest have successfully used wheatgrass to correct infertility problems in their oxen. Some cattle farms and city zoos make grow the grass indoors to benefit animals year round.

Birds use their beaks to extract the juice from wheatgrass blades, discarding the indigestible pulp. Wheatgrass also helps companion and breeding birds with liver conditions due to the detoxifying properties of the wheatgrass. Liver disease is a major problem in companion birds due to the high-fat, seed-based diet they are given.

Providing a purchased or homegrown tray of wheatgrass for your pet — especially dogs and cats, as they have more freedom than most other pets — will enable the animal to feast on a grassy meal without consuming fertilizer and other chemicals that might be accumulating on outdoor grass supplies. All garden plants and houseplants are not healthy, so it is important that your pet does not consume poisonous plants or mushrooms that can cause illness. Many animals will readily eat as much wheatgrass as you give them. Guinea pigs, hamsters, and other small animals should be fed wheatgrass in moderation. Provide a few clippings in the feed bowl or allow the animal to nibble a little on the ends and put the rest away. A tray of wheatgrass also provides a nice "meadow" for these animals to play in, as they should not be taken outdoors to romp in the grass. Many companies provide grass kits specifically for animals that include a mixture of grass seeds.

Disclaimer

The information in this chapter concerning pet health care is for educational purposes only. Please discuss your pet's health with a veterinarian. Furthermore, do not attempt to treat your ailing pet without the advice of a veterinarian. Illnesses such as bloat in dogs and hepatic lipidosis in cats can be fatal and should only be handled by a professional. Although numerous studies have been done concerning wheatgrass and animals, there is no concrete, scientific proof that cats and other animals can extract nutrients from ingested cereal grasses. As with any product or diet, either natural or synthetic, always seek the advice of a licensed veterinarian before applying it to your pet. To find a holistic veterinarian in your area, visit the American Holistic Veterinary Medical Association website (**www.ahvma.org**).

CASE STUDY: COMFORT AND CARE FOR COMPANION ANIMALS

Phil and Randy Klein, owners
Whiskers Holistic Petcare
235 East 9th Street
New York, NY 10003
http://1800whiskers.com
Phone: 212-979-2532
Fax: 212-979-0075

Phil and Randy Klein are a husband and wife team with a love and compassion for animals. They believe that good health for animals begins with good nutrition — just as with humans. They have dedicated their lives to producing healthy foods and other products for companion animals. They operate out of two pet stores and are in the process of opening a pet grooming business.

We opened Whiskers Holistic Petcare in 1988, prompted by the passing of a beloved companion. At that time, there were very few alternatives to traditional, chemically based animal care. We were amongst the early pioneers. We believe that holistic care is the most viable means of treating illnesses in pets in conjunction with traditional veterinary care on an integrated basis. We provide holistic nutrition and cater to dogs, cats, rabbits, and other small animals.

There has been a great increase in pet illnesses over the past decade. We attribute this to over-breeding, poor genetics, and garbage food. The best diet that you can offer your pet is a diet of raw food followed by a diet of high-quality canned food mixed with home-cooked foods. A good reason to change your pet's diet would be to increase health and decrease the costs of veterinary bills. If you decide to change your pet's diet, it should be done gradually.

At Whiskers, the health and well-being of your companion animal — and all animals for that matter — is our primary concern. Our model is based on how that animal lived and ate in the wild. Nature is the best teacher…and the best healer. We offer a variety of products so that you can choose what is best for you and your pet. We do create our products in-house, and, as we create, we have you and your pet in mind. We want the best for both of you and cost and convenience are a major concern.

One product that we do sell that seems to be quite popular is wheatgrass. Animals enjoy wheatgrass. They should be given as much of it as they want. They consume it instinctively to get at the nutrients it possesses. Wheatgrass is a wonderful blood cleanser and a good source of fiber. It can also be a good alternative for treating pet illnesses, depending on the illness and the pet. There are some risks to giving wheatgrass to animals that stem from different variables such as poor-quality grass. The source of the grass, soil quality, and seed quality all play important roles in the production of a high quality product. Many people don't give wheatgrass to their pets because they are ignorant to the benefits that can be gained.

There are three important things you can do to keep your pet healthy: feed them well, exercise them, and love them. This is what we do at Whiskers, and we love it.

CHAPTER 9

Wheatgrass and Its "Super" Family

"The longer I live the less confidence I have in drugs and the greater is my confidence in the regulation and administration of diet and regimen."

~ John Redman Coxe

*I*t is only recently that the study of nutritional and medicinal plants has resurfaced in the health and nutrition arena. Pharmaceutical companies, which had so diligently worked with these plants from the 1920s to the 1950s, had turned their energies from isolating vitamins and other substances in life-giving plants to producing synthetic chemicals. Botanists continued to study plants and their properties, but science placed emphasis on chemistry. According to the book *Chlorella: The sun-powered supernutrient and its beneficial properties* by Dr. William H. Lee and Dr. Michael Rosenbaum, this shift is attributed to the fact that "synthetic substances could be patented and earn the company big profits." Of the $8 billion dollars spent annually in the United States on prescription products, only 22 percent is allocated to products that are plant-based.

The study of plants is vital to science and medicine because plants are the fundamental basis of practically all food chains. All living things depend — whether directly or indirectly — on plants for their sustenance. Living, green plants (chlorophyll-filled plants) provide food, such as vegetables, fruit, and grains; metabolic energy, which is a chemical reaction in the body that converts food into usable energy; and plant products, such as wood, wood products, fibers, resins, coal, petroleum, and drugs. Well over 100 chemical substances that have been derived from plants are in use as drugs and medicines. According to World Health Organization (WHO), over 80 percent of the populations in some eastern countries rely on plant-based traditional medicine for their primary health care needs. Public disillusionment with modern medicine, a growing concern for the widespread side effects of medication, health care costs, and a search for new drug sources has prompted consumers, researchers, and scientists to take a second look at "folk remedies" and eastern medicinal foods. Inevitably, there arose a revival of herbal medicine amongst industrialized nations. With this revival has come a burgeoning of claims about the miraculous power of super foods, including wheatgrass.

Other Super Grasses in the Wheatgrass Family

Wheatgrass is only one of several greens and cereal grasses hailed among the acclaimed "super foods" of the world. These natural foods are considered nutritional powerhouses loaded with essential vitamins, minerals, enzymes, and antioxidants important for good health. Many of these foods are also low in calories and fat. Believers of these products claim that a variety of these foods added to the diet will place your health in a new dimension. These concentrated green foods aid in fighting against nutritional deficiencies of critical nutrients in the standard American diet and the diets of cultures not agriculturally based. These diets are generally sufficient in macronutrition, including protein, carbohydrates, proteins, and fat, but lack micronutrition, especially trace minerals and phytochemicals that are derived from plant nutrients. Health experts and nutritional scientists recognize a direct link between reduced intake of micronutrients and the rise of chronic and degenerative illness. Nutrient-dense super foods also work to guard against the harmful effects of environmental pollutions and toxins that pose an increasing danger to public health. Many health advocates use these foods to boost health, prevent and treat disease, and reverse the effects of aging. Most super foods are easy to find in your local supermarket. Some might be a bit difficult to find in your local store and must be ordered online.

Barley grass

Barley grass, one of the top green cereal grasses, rivals wheatgrass in nutritional content. Some barley users claim that it is actually superior to wheatgrass and is the only plant on the earth that can solely support the nutritional needs of the body. Barley is of the grass family Poaceae and has been used as a basic food staple for centuries in many countries. Early records of its cultivation date back to 7000 B. C. It is still used worldwide today, primarily as livestock feed. It has also been used in the production of malted products, such as beer, wine, and malted milk, and pearled barley is used as a food source for humans. Pearled barley is a form of barley where the hull and some of the bran is removed from the grain. It is easier to consume but less nutritious than hulled barely (whole-wheat barley). Pearled barely is used to make flour. Barley in its grass form is used to make hay.

Barley has adapted to a variety of environments and is considered the most adaptable of the cereal grasses. Its leaves are very nutritious, as they have the ability to draw nutrients from deep within the soil. The leaves can be juiced, providing the body with an abundance of vitamins, minerals, and proteins that are easily absorbed into the bloodstream. The fiber in barley grass is reported to reduce cholesterol levels. Properties in the roots have been reported to stimulate the blood, and the bran is claimed to be helpful in protection against cancer. Research on the medicinal value of barley can be attributed to the work of Dr. Yoshihide Hagiwara, President of the Hagiwara Institute of Health in Japan. Dr. Hagiwara, like Ann Wigmore, restored his own health in the 1950s by changing his diet to include fresh herbs and leaves. He then turned his focus to barley grass and developed and patented a drying machine that was able to transform barley grass juice into barley grass powder. Barley juice powder is still used today as a cell detoxifier and immune system booster. It is claimed that 100 grams of barley contain

11 times more calcium than cow's milk, seven times more vitamin C than oranges, and five times more iron than spinach.

According to some cereal grass drinkers, barley grass juice is milder and bitterer than wheatgrass juice. If you are still wary of the taste of cereal juices, you can find barley in capsule form online and in many health food stores. For seeds and sprouting instructions for barley and other cereal grasses, visit the Sprout People website (**www.sproutpeople.com/seeds**).

Kamut

Kamut is a versatile plant closely related to the wheat plant. It is an ancient relative of durum wheat, or desert wheat. Durum wheat is a tetraploid wheat type, meaning it has 28 chromosomes compared to the 42 chromosomes of hard red winter and hard red spring wheat. It is about the same shape as a grain of wheat, but twice as large. It has a sweet, nutty flavor and is preferred for making pasta because of its hardiness, gluten strength, and high protein content.

The origin and classification of Kamut is under dispute among scientists, but it is agreed that this golden-colored grain has high nutritional value. Kamut has about 30 percent more protein and 65 percent more amino acids than other wheat grains. It does have less fiber, however, due to its larger size. It is considered a high-energy grain because of its high fat content. Kamut also contains high levels of vitamin E, phosphorus, zinc, magnesium, pantothenic acid, riboflavin, copper, and complex carbohydrates. One cup of cooked Kamut contains 251 calories, 52 grams of carbohydrates, 11 grams of protein, and two grams of fat. It is generally believed that individuals with wheat allergies can safely consume Kamut, and it is often added to food products as a wheat alternative. Please be aware, however, that Kamut does contain gluten and those with wheat allergies might be affected if it is consumed. Individuals with celiac disease, a disease of the digestive organs in which the small intestine is damaged and the absorption of nutrients from food is hindered, should not consume Kamut.

Oat grass

Oats were cultivated as early as 2000 B.C. and are used in many countries of the world. Humans and animals alike have benefited from their usage. Livestock and other animals thrive on oat straw, the above-the-ground stem of the oat plant after the harvest of the grain. Oat straw was once widely used as a stuffing for mattresses. Today it has many medicinal uses, including:

- Alternative health practitioners in Europe have used oat straw extract for the treatment of multiple sclerosis.

- Europeans also used oat straw to treat shingles, herpes, and neurasthenia.

- Researchers noted the influence of oat straw on reproductive hormones in several studies concerning cigarette smoking.

Green oat grass, the grass before it has matured into oat straw, is recognized for its high nutrient content. It grows a little slower than other green cereal grasses, but like the others, it has an abundance of vitamins A, B, C, D, and K. It is also rich in pantothenic acid (vitamin B5) and a variety of minerals. There are 39 milligrams of iron per one gram of dry oat grass, 19.2 milligrams of zinc, and 8.5 milligrams of manganese. Oat grass is also rich in protein and antioxidants. Green oat grass juice can be used in the treatment of avitaminosis, a disease developed from chronic vitamin deficiency.

Rye

Rye is a member of the wheat family and closely resembles barley and oats. It is believed to have developed from a wild grass of Central Asia or from a wild plant of Armenia, Syria, and Iran and was once regarded as an inferior grain. The Roman philosopher and author Gaius Plinius Secundus, referred to rye in his writings as "a food only fit to avert starvation."

Since the Middle Ages, cultivation of the rye plant has taken place in Central and Eastern Europe, and it is a main grain of those areas. The grain can be used whole, cracked, or rolled. The grain is usually ground into flour or used for animal feed. It is good source of dietary fiber (75.86 grams per 100 grams), protein (10.43 grams per 100 grams), and thiamine (vitamin B1). It also has a high content of potassium (510 milligrams), phosphorus (332 milligrams), magnesium (110 milligrams), and manganese (2.57 milligrams). Rye has 24 milligrams of calcium.

Rye has been found beneficial in the following ways:

- Cholesterol reduction

- Cardiovascular disease prevention

- Cancer prevention

- Treatment for diabetes, menopause, and digestive disorders

Rye grass is generally grown and used for lawns, pastures, and as a fodder crop in the form of hay. The young grass can also be cultivated and juiced very similarly to wheatgrass. For more information on sprouting and juicing rye grains visit the Sprout People website (**www.sproutpeople.com/ seed/ryegrass**).

Spelt

Spelt is an ancient form of the common wheat grain and is sometimes referred to as the "grandfather of wheat." Its heritage dates back further than many contemporary wheat hybrids. Spelt served as a staple grain in ancient civilizations, such as Rome and Greece. It was so highly esteemed during this time period that it was used as a gift of appeal to the pagan gods of agriculture for fertility and an abundant harvest. Spelt became a popular grain in early European history when Hildegard von Bingen (Saint Hildegard), a spiritual healer of the time, used it as a panacea for a variety of illnesses. The grain was cultivated moderately in the United States until the 20th century when an agricultural shift placed wheat in the spotlight. Today, a renewed interest in spelt has allowed it to be used in a number of ways.

Spelt can be used similarly to wheat. The grain is often ground and made into flour and pasta. Some nutritionists say that spelt offers a wider range of nutrients than its relatives, including common wheat, and contains a larger amount of thiamine (vitamin B1) and riboflavin (vitamin B2). Other nutrients in spelt include manganese, copper, and niacin. Claimed health benefits include the following:

- Reduced risk of atherosclerosis, a build-up of cholesterol or other fatty substances along the walls of the arteries

- Reduced risk of heart disease and heart failure; cardiovascular support for menopausal women

- Reduced risk of type 2 diabetes

- Kidney support; prevention of gallstone formation

- Protection against cancer

- Protection against childhood asthma

Spelt has a mild, nutty flavor and can be sprouted and juiced. Like oats, however, it tends to grow slower than other grains. Consumers of spelt juice report that it is even sweeter than wheatgrass juice.

Alfalfa grass

Alfalfa, a perennial plant that grows 2 to 3 feet in height, has played an important role in overall body well-being for centuries. It was mostly used by the Arabs in ancient times who recognized an improvement in health when alfalfa was added to the diet. The Arabs translated the words alfalfa grass to mean "the father of all foods." Technically, alfalfa is not a cereal grass but a legume. It is often grouped with the cereal grasses because of similar nutritional content.

Alfalfa grass has been commercially grown in the United States and other countries since the late 1800s. It is mainly used as a high-protein food stock for animals, but it is also a healthy addition to the human diet. Alfalfa supplies the body with calcium, potassium, magnesium, phosphorous, zinc, iron, and several trace minerals. It is also a good source of vitamins A, E, K, B6, and D. Claimed benefits to the body include the following:

- Relief from chronic constipation

- Regulates the bowels and helps the kidneys eliminate fluids

- Provides enzymes to help with digestion

- Aids in the healing of ulcers

- Helps the body to fight off infection

- Helps lower cholesterol

- Helps alleviate discomforts of pregnancy, aids in postpartum distress, and increases and sustains milk supply

Alfalfa grass can be purchased as powder or tablets from pharmacies and health food stores. Alfalfa sprouts, a popular and nutritious addition to salads, are readily available in most supermarkets.

Other super greens

Cereal grasses, with wheatgrass in the forefront, have been in the nutrition spotlight for the past two decades. Laboratory research on the nutritional value of these grasses has disclosed a high level of a variety of vitamins, minerals, enzymes, amino acids, and antioxidants. Health nutritionists and naturalists are exploring the use of these potent plants as an alternative therapy for a number of chronic health ailments. These are not the only greens, however, that are hailed for high nutrition and excellent health benefits. There are several other greens that deserve accolades for their nutritional makeup.

Spinach

Spinach is one of the most nutrient-dense dark, leafy vegetables. It is believed that spinach originated in ancient Persia (now Iran) and was brought to Europe in the 11th century. It was a specialty dish of the historical

Catherine de Medici, who left her home in Florence to marry the king of France, bringing along her own cooks to prepare her favorite spinach dishes — hence the development of the name "a la Florentine," which is used in references to dishes made with a bed of spinach leaves. Spinach became a renowned vegetable again in 1933 with the introduction of the cartoon character Popeye the Sailor Man, who consumed an abundance of spinach when he needed extra strength. The influence of this character is still prevalent among children today. Professor Chutima Sirikulchayanonta and other researchers at Mahidol University in Bangkok, Thailand, report that children who regularly watch Popeye doubled their intake of spinach and other green vegetables. The United States is one of the top producers of spinach.

Spinach contains a wide variety of vitamins, minerals, and antioxidants. It is an excellent source of vitamin A, vitamin C, vitamin B2, vitamin B6, vitamin K, folate, iron, manganese, magnesium, calcium, and potassium. It offers a good source of protein, vitamin E, copper, phosphorus, dietary fiber, and zinc. It is also a good source of niacin, selenium, and omega-3 fatty acids. The health benefits of eating spinach include prostate and ovarian cancer prevention, cardiovascular protection, blood stabilization, gastrointestinal health, bone support, and increased mental health. Spinach also promotes better eyesight and provides energy.

Food tables generally show high calcium content in spinach, but according to physiologists at Children's Nutrition Research Center at Baylor College of Medicine, this calcium is not available in a form that can be easily absorbed by the body. Spinach can be purchased throughout the year, but it has the best flavor when obtained during its natural growing season, which is from March through May and September through October. Spinach tends to grow in sandy soil, so a thorough washing is needed before consumption.

Kale

Kale and other vegetables in its family, such as Brussels sprouts and cabbage, are rich in nutrients and compounds that can be beneficial in warding off sickness and disease. Studies suggest that these vegetables contain large amounts of phytonutrients that might be beneficial in neutralizing potentially cancerous substances in the liver. Kale is a good source of beta-carotene, which is an important nutrient for good vision. It is also a good source for vitamin C, which is important for warding off colds and influenza. Vitamin C also helps protect the colon from cancer and other diseases. There is also an abundance of protein and trace minerals such as calcium, iron, manganese, and potassium in kale. It contains a high level of folic acid, which is good for preventing anemia. The high fiber content improves digestive health.

Some individuals avoid kale because of its strong flavor. While this highly nutritious, versatile vegetable can be on the bitter side, it can also be paired with sweeter greens, such as collards, to create a milder flavor for those with sensitive taste buds. Also, different varieties of kale have different flavors. You can also choose a plant with smaller leaves, which might offer a milder, sweeter taste. Kale can be found year-round in most supermarkets.

Mustards

Mustard greens are the pungent, peppery leaves of the mustard plant. This nutritious plant originated in the Himalayan area of India and has been cultivated for over 5,000 years. Mustard greens were a notable vegetable in Southern America during slavery times and are still an integral part of American cuisine.

Mustard greens supply the body with a high level of vitamin A, vitamin C, and vitamin E. These flavorful greens are also an excellent source of folate, manganese, and dietary fiber. Benefits to the body include a decrease in menopausal symptoms, lung support, heart strengthening, protection against rheumatoid arthritis, support of women's health, and mental clarity.

Young leaves of the mustard plant are tender and mild-flavored. These can be eaten raw in a salad. Cooking of the outer leaves should be sparse to retain the nutrient level of the greens.

Super fruits

Nutritionists are encouraging the addition of antioxidants and fiber to the diet for good health and disease prevention. One of the easiest ways to get more antioxidants and fiber to is to eat more fruits. Fruits are also full of a wide range of vitamins, minerals, and enzymes. According to the CDC, people who eat generous amounts of fruits and vegetables are more likely to have reduced risks of such chronic diseases as stroke, cardiovascular disease, and certain types of cancer. Substituting fruits and vegetables for sugar-filled, high-fat foods can also be part of a weight-loss strategy. It is important to eat a wide range of fruits to best benefit from the variety of nutrients in each one. Some fruits have been labeled super fruits because they possess exceptionally high concentrations of certain nutrients.

Acai berries

The acai berry comes from the Brazilian palm tree of the Amazon rainforest. Also called the Cabbage Palm, the acai has a long history with the Amazon natives who used it for food and medicine. This history includes a bit of folklore. According to legend, an chief named Itaki had a daughter named Iaca. During a particularly harsh famine in the land, Chief Itaki ordered all newborns killed to prevent feeding extra people. Princess Iaca gave birth to a daughter, and the baby was killed as well, according to the chief's order. The princess, heartbroken, bewailed her daughter day and night. One night, while lamenting, Iaca heard the loud cries of a baby outside of her dwelling. She went outdoors to search for the sound but only found a palm tree laden with purple fruit. On the next morning, the Indian princess was found dead under the palm tree. Chief Itaki was very sorrowful, but even in his sorrow, he noticed that the fruit from the palm tree was good to eat. He fed the entire tribe with the purple fruit, and they were revived by its strength. Afterward, the chief named the tree in honor of his daughter. Iaca is acai spelled backward. The king lifted his death order, and the tribe never went hungry again.

The story of Iaca might be a myth, but the tale of the acai berry's rejuvenating strength has been passed from one nation to the next. Trial research is suggesting that there just might be something to all the claims. Former Harvard professor Dr. Jack F. Bukowski, director of the Nutritional Science Research Institute, reports, "While additional research is needed, pilot studies suggest that in otherwise healthy, overweight adults, daily consumption of pure organic sugar free acai reduces cholesterol significantly and several markers of metabolic syndrome associated with an increased risk of diabetes, cardiovascular disease, and stroke."

Acai berries are rich in antioxidants, having twice the concentration of the antioxidant-rich blueberry. Clinical studies reveal significant amounts of omega-3 and omega-6 in the berry, which have been linked to lowering cholesterol levels in the blood. The high amino acid content helps increase metabolism, promoting weight loss. There are several other beneficial nutrients in acai berries.

Combining acai with guarana, another fruit from the Amazon region, produces a highly potent drink that has been used in the past by Brazilian natives to increase energy and build stamina. It is said that this juice can be used as a powerful aphrodisiac. A standard dosage of this nutrient-rich formula is 100 grams, but doses as high as 500 grams have been taken. When shopping for products made with acai berries, be careful not to purchase products including the seed of the berry. Some companies are selling acai products that contain the seed, but it is the pulp and the skin of the berry that has undergone nutritional research — not the seed.

Goji berries

Another fruit that comes with a legend is the authentic goji berry of Mongolia, Thailand. It has been said that the medicinal use of this bright red berry, nicknamed the "red diamond fruit," was discovered by a doctor studying an ancient Himalayan society. Certain members of this society were well over 100 years old and were in excellent health. They had no signs of aging, such as a loss of teeth and gray hair. The doctor noticed that these youthful seniors lived near wells of water overgrown with goji berry vines. He soon realized that the water was filled with the nutrients from ripened berries that had fallen into the well. All who drank the nutrient-charged water were rejuvenated.

Some of the first people to test the legendary goji berry's purported healing properties were the Himalayans. They valued the sweet, red berries that flourished in the valleys of the great mountain range and used them to increase health and promote longevity. Traditionally, these prized fruits could not be touched before they were ripe enough to fall off the branches on their own accord. Touching the berries would cause them to oxidize and turn black, meriting them useless. The Himalayans did not keep their knowledge of the precious berry a secret, but broadcasted its nutritional properties throughout India, Tibet, and China.

Today, the Goji berry is receiving increased attention through the media and the teachings of prominent figures such as best-selling author and self-proclaimed vitamin guru, Dr. Earl Mindell. The berry is said to offer several health benefits including cholesterol and blood pressure control, organ maintenance, human growth hormone production, improved energy, and increased vision. It has been given a No. 1 rating on the Oxygen Radical Absorbance Capacity (ORAC) scale by the USDA. This scale measures the level of antioxidants in foods; the higher the rating, the more potent the food is at combating free radicals that damage cells.

It is important to note that the nutrient content of goji berries (as well as other berries) can vary according to the species, the method of production, the growing location, and the quality of the growing soil. Also, the authentic Lycium berry of the Tibetan and Mongolian people should not be confused with the common Chinese wolfberry (*Lycium barbarum*). The wolfberry is said to have an inferior genetic makeup reflecting climatic and toxic changes in its growing environment. The use of DDT and other toxic chemicals by private and commercial Chinese botanical farms make the Chinese wolfberry unsafe as a medicine or food source.

Amla fruit

Amla fruit, also known as Indian gooseberry, has been treasured by Indian and Tibetan herbal practitioners since ancient times. Today, it is cultivated in the plains and low mountainous regions of India. It is believed that this small, sweet/sour, green berry has 30 times the amount of vitamin C found in oranges (about 720 mg of vitamin C per 100 grams of fruit), making it one of the richest known sources of vitamin C. It is also a good source of pectin. Pectin is a fibrous structure found in plants that is useful in gelling foods and drinks. It is a source of dietary fiber in the human diet.

Several studies have revealed amla's possible role as an antioxidant in preventing ulcers for diabetics. This research was done on rodents and amla was found to be helpful in controlling cholesterol and blood sugar levels, delaying the development of diabetic cataracts, and eliminating problems with memory. Because of its fiber content, amla is very helpful for keeping the bowels regulated. Chinese researchers at the Nagasaki University School of Pharmaceutical Sciences, which is located in Japan, discovered that amla fruit contains a combination of several therapeutic chemicals that can be beneficial in the prevention of cancerous cell growth in the stomach, skin, and womb.

Noni fruit

Noni is an evergreen shrub related to the coffee tree. It was introduced to Hawaii by Polynesian colonizers who prized it for its dyes and medicinal potential. The shrub adapted naturally to this tropical region and spread throughout the Pacific coast. It was known by a variety of names such as noni, morinda, hog apple, canary wood, cheesefruit, and Indian mulberry. Its fruit is known to have an unpleasant smell and bitter taste.

Noni was used as a food source for centuries by the Polynesians who valued it in times of famine. The leaves, bark, and fruit of the tree have been used for therapeutic purposes in Polynesian folk medicine. The noni fruit and its juice were used to treat a number of illnesses including diabetes, high blood pressure, heart disease, cholesterol problems, rheumatism, and psoriasis. Soldiers stationed in the South Pacific during World War II used the fruit for sustenance. During the 1990s, noni juice was marketed as an herbal remedy, which piqued interest in it as a health drink. Today, noni juice (usually combined with other fruit juices) is promoted in the

United States and other countries as a general health tonic that can relieve stress, cleanse the face and body, and boost nutrition. Some individuals drink it as a preventative for diabetes and cardiovascular disease based on its chronic disease prevention claims. It has been recommended by medical practitioners for the removal of parasites and used topically to treat skin conditions and joint pain.

Noni juice was approved in 2003 by the European Commission as a novel food for human consumption. A novel food is a food product or ingredient that was not used significantly in the European Union before May 15, 1997. At different intervals from 1988 to 2006, the FDA warned pharmaceutical companies about broadcasting noni juice as a health remedy based on unfounded claims. Studies are currently underway to investigate such claims.

Noni juice and pulp powder has a high concentration of vitamins A and C. It also contains substantial amounts of niacin (vitamin B3), iron, and potassium. Other vitamins and minerals are present in more moderate amounts. Noni juice is not recommended for pregnant women and infants.

Other "super" berries

There are a number of other berries that possess an extraordinary amount of antioxidants and health-building nutrients. These berries, when consumed on a regular basis, can also strengthen the immune system and help the body to fight certain sickness and disease.

The maqui berry has an ORAC rating that surpasses both the acai and goji berries. This berry also has a long history with the Mapuche Indians in South America for increasing strength and stamina and treating disease. The maqui berry was believed to reduce inflammation and protect the cells from oxidation and aging. It was used in the treatment of sore throats, fever, ulcers, and diarrhea and aided in weight loss.

Acerola berries are native to the tropical regions of the Americas, but they are also grown in the Caribbean. The acerola berry is a rich source of vitamin C, with one berry containing 80 milligrams, which is 133 percent of the recommended daily dose. These berries are also good sources of vitamin

A, calcium, and iron. They are used for fighting infections, strengthening the immune system, and healing open wounds. Health and beauty manufacturers are using acerola extracts to enhance skin care products, as the vitamin C content is believed to combat cellular aging.

Blueberries are of Canadian origin and have been a known source of high antioxidant value for a number of years. Early American explorers discovered that the nutrient-laden berry was used in a number of ways by Native American tribes. Blueberry tonics were given to expectant mothers to aid in childbirth. Blueberry juice was consumed to cleanse the blood and increase longevity. This versatile berry has since gained recognition by researchers and health professionals for its anthocyanin (skin dye) and phytochemical (chemical compounds), which seem to be the source of its antioxidants. Blueberry consumption is believed to increase eye health, protect against cardiovascular disease and stroke, guard against aging, and reduce the risk of cancer. In recent USDA studies concerning free radical neutralization, blueberries have consistently ranked No. 1.

The cranberry hails from North America but was exported extensively to Europe in the 19th century. Early colonists named the fruit based on the shape of its flowers and flower buds, which resembled the great sandhill crane that nested in the area. The "craneberry," as it was initially called, was considered a symbol of peace by the Native Americans. The fruit was used for making dyes and medicinal salves. Colonial sailors used it to prevent scurvy, a disease caused by vitamin C deficiency. Today, the cranberry is an American tradition during Thanksgiving.

Cranberries are a rich source of vitamin C and a good source of dietary fiber, manganese, and vitamin K. They have been long valued in the treatment of urinary tract infections and are now being used to prevent the formation of kidney stones, control cholesterol levels, promote gastrointestinal and oral health, and prevent the risk of cancer. Cranberry juice is also useful in treatment of candida infections and can help prevent age-related macular degeneration (ARMD), a vision problem in older people.

Avocados

Avocados (*Persea Americana*) have been cultivated since the days of the Aztecs and are native to Central America. They qualify as a super fruit based on their extremely high monounsaturated oil content comparable only to olives. These fruits also possess high levels of fiber, potassium, magnesium, folate, and vitamin E.

Two types of avocados are available for purchase in the United States. The Hass avocado from California has graveled green-black skin, a nutty flavor, and buttery texture. It is rich in monounsaturated oil (about 18 to 30 percent in each avocado). It was named for the Wisconsin mailman, Rudolph Hass, who patented the Hass avocado tree in 1935. The West Indian avocado from Florida is smooth-skinned, light green in color, and larger and juicer than the Hass. It is less buttery and has a lower oil content.

Research done on the avocado has revealed its ability to aid the body to better absorb nutrients from other foods. Therefore, it is a powerful "nutrient booster," according to the California Avocado Commission. High levels of oleic acid (monounsaturated fat) in the fruit aid in cholesterol reduction. Potassium content works to regulate blood pressure and helps guard the body from heart disease, strokes, and indigestion. Potassium is also good for fighting fatigue. Avocados contain high amounts of carotenoid lutein. Recent research reveals that carotenoids and tocopherols effectively inhibit the growth of cancer cells in the prostrate. Research conducted at Tufts University in Medford, Massachusetts, suggests that avocados greatly aid in brain function and health. Avocados are high in calories (48 calories per ounce), but they can help curb appetite and aid in weight reduction if eaten in moderate amounts.

Super fruits or super fiction?

The term super fruit was first introduced in 2005 by the drug and beverage industry. According to Kerri Glass of the CBS's *The Early Show*, it was a marketing term given to fruits that were of an exceptional status, quality-wise or taste-wise. Scientists maintain that in order for a fruit to be elevated to the super fruit status, it must show scientific evidence of possessing high quantities of specific nutrients. Many fruits have found their way into the elite group based on their good taste, exotic background, or as a marketing tactic. Most of the research on these fruits, such as the amla fruit, has been conducted on animals.

Super algae and seaweed

The following sections describe the benefits of algae and seaweed to the overall health of one's body.

Chlorella

Chlorella, a dark-green, single-celled alga, has a two-billion-year history on this planet. Its long survival is due to its tough outer shell, which protects its inner genetic structure. Although man has selected the best strains of these algae to grow and harvest, the genetic structure has been left intact.

Chlorella has a high chlorophyll content. This and its rapid reproduction rate make it one of the most efficient whole foods on the earth. It is a natural food and has the ability to support life. Chlorella is also considered a pure food because it is grown in purified water, has no chemical additives, and is free of toxic residues.

Chlorella has been known to help the body in the following ways:

- Stimulate and protect the liver

- Stimulate and correct the bowels

- Cleanse the bloodstream; normalize blood pressure

- Normalize blood sugar; support and balance pancreatic functions

- Counteract colds and flus

- Heal wounds

- Build up the immune system

Experiments with chlorella have shown that it stimulates and protects the liver and regulates the bowels. The following studies have been performed with chlorella:

- In a German study, the liver was protected from damage caused by malnutrition through application of chlorella. Chlorella lowers blood cholesterol and triglycerides, which are associated with liver metabolism and fat intake. The cleansing effects of chlorella on the liver support the natural defenses of the entire body. Chlorella is resistant to damage by toxins such as ethionine.

- Dr. Motomichi Kobayashi, director of a hospital in Takamatsu, Japan, administered chlorella to all of his patients suffering from constipation. One of the first things he noticed was that chlorella stimulated and regulated the underactive bowels.

- A U.S. Army medical facility in Colorado discovered that when scenedesmus, an alga related to chlorella, was mixed with chlorella and given to volunteers, the quantity of waste expelled by the bowel increased.

- A 1857 study by Japanese physician Dr. Takechi found that chlorella promoted the rapid growth of lactobacillus, a bacterium that helps with colon health. The chlorophyll in the chlorella cleaned the bowel while the tough cellulose membrane attached to the heavy metals and carried them out of the body. The membrane of the chlorella alga cannot be digested, so it acts as a good broom for the intestinal system.

Spirulina

Spirulina, a fresh water, blue-green alga (and also a form of bacteria), has excellent muscle-building potential. Its high protein content combines with all the major vitamins and minerals such as calcium, iron, and magnesium. Like chlorella, it has a simple, one-cell form. It is related to the kelp algae, but it is not categorized as a sea plant.

Spirulina is also a pure food, able to remain so because of its ability to thrive in hot and alkaline environments. No other organism can survive under these conditions, so the waters — and the spirulina — remain pure. Spirulina is considered one of the cleanest and most naturally sterile foods in nature. Even in extreme conditions, spirulina is able to maintain its high nutritional value, which makes it valuable as a processed food. Spirulina has complete protein percentage of about 65 percent to 71 percent. It also has a perfect balance of essential amino acids. These factors all attribute to spirulina being developed as the "food of the future."

Kelp

Kelp is a type of seaweed that has high nutritional value. It belongs to the brown algae family and can grow as forests on the ocean floor. A variety of marine life, such as fish and sea otters, depend on kelp for their sustenance. Kelp is useful to humans as well. It produces soda ash when burned, which differentiates it from other sea vegetables. Soda ash is a white, powdery substance used to make glass and other products. Alginate is also produced from kelp, which is a carbohydrate used primarily to thicken toothpaste, ice cream, and other products. Kelp has been a staple of the Japanese diet for many years. Because it is becoming increasingly popular in the United States, it can now be found on local supermarket shelves. Kelp and other sea vegetables are nature's richest sources of iodine. Iodine is said to promote healthy function of the thyroid. Kelp also contains a high level of folic acid, useful for averting birth defects and cardiovascular disease. The magnesium in kelp is helpful for relieving menopausal symptoms.

Super nuts and seeds

There is no secret concerning the vast health benefits of nuts and seeds. Researchers have been exploring their nutritional value for years. In a 1996 women's health study conducted in Iowa, it was found that women who consumed nuts more than four times a week were 40 less likely to die of heart disease. In 1998, a study conducted by the Harvard School of Public Health discovered similar results in a separate group of women. The 2002 Physician's Health Study disclosed that men who consistently ate nuts two or more times weekly had a reduction in sudden heart failure. Many other recorded studies confirm the weight-reducing, cholesterol-lowering, brain-enhancing, immunity-building power of nuts and seeds.

Almonds and hazelnuts are the "top" super nuts because of their high fiber content and low saturated fat content. Almonds also have a high content of vitamin E, iron, calcium, and riboflavin. Hazelnuts are rich in vitamin C, iron, folate, and thiamin. Pistachios are the only nuts that contain significant amounts of lutein and zeaxanthin, which are necessary for good eye health.

The star list of nutritious seeds includes flax seeds, sunflower seeds, sesame seeds, and pumpkin seeds. Flax seeds are good for soothing stomach disorders or discomforts in the bowels. They contain lignans that have anti-fungal, anti-viral, anti-bacterial, and anti-cancer properties. Flax seeds help with digestion, aid in maintaining blood glucose levels, and fight against tumor formation as well as enhance cardiovascular health. Sunflower seeds contain all necessary nutrients except vitamin D. They are especially high in calcium, potassium, magnesium, and phosphorus. Sunflower seeds are good for the skin, brain, and digestive tract. Pumpkin seeds contain omega-3 and omega-6 fatty acids. They are a high source of vitamin A, iron, and calcium. Sesame seeds are small, but they are packed with protein and other nutrients. They are an excellent source of calcium and vitamin B.

With the many nutrients that nuts and seeds contain, it is important to note that they are most beneficial to the body when they are eaten in their raw state. Roasting, toasting, and baking nuts diminishes their nutritional value.

Comparing Wheatgrass with Other Super Foods

There is little difference in the nutritional value of barley grass, wheat grass, and rye grass. Wheat blades can be lighter in color, and wheatgrass juice can taste sweeter to some. Alfalfa is actually a legume, so although its macronutrients are similar to the cereal grasses, it has a different balance of micronutrients. Important points to consider when comparing the cereal grasses are how and where they are grown and method of production. Whereas wheatgrass and barley grass grown in the same field might be nutritionally the same, wheatgrass grown indoors and wheatgrass grown outdoors are nutritionally different. Also, wheatgrass grown organically and wheatgrass grown inorganically are nutritionally different. Dehydrated wheatgrass, including powders, capsules, and tablets, might be lower in nutritional value than fresh wheatgrass, but studies have shown that they are more nutritious than most green vegetables, including spinach and kale. Also, the nutrients from wheatgrass are more easily absorbed into the bloodstream than the nutrients of these fibrous vegetables. You also might need to eat more of these vegetables to fulfill the RDA requirement for vegetables.

All the super fruits and berries have a high concentration of one or two major nutrients. Many are high in antioxidants. The acai berry, in particular, is considered one of the richest sources of antioxidants in the world. It has a high calorie and fat content, however, compared to wheatgrass — 247 calories per 100 grams of berries compared to 21 calories per 100 grams of wheatgrass juice. Acai berries can also be expensive. As wheatgrass is a complete food containing practically all of the major vitamins and minerals (as opposed to one or two nutrients), it seems unjust to compare it to super fruits and berries.

While nuts and seeds are an excellent source of many good nutrients, some nuts are higher in some nutrients than others. Almonds are a high source of potassium, while walnuts are a good source of omega-3 fatty acids, which are good for the heart and diabetes. Cashews are very high in protein (17.2 grams per 100 grams of nuts). Wheatgrass is a balanced food, containing protein and all of the vitamins and minerals necessary for good body nutrition. The only super foods that compare to wheatgrass and the other cereal grass are nutrient-rich chlorella and spirulina, which are complete foods as well. Look at the following nutrition comparison chart of wheatgrass to other super foods.

Vitamin and Mineral Comparison of Wheatgrass and Other Super Foods						
Per 100 grams		Wheat-grass	Spinach	Blue-berry	Avocado	Chlorella
Calories	Cal	21	23	57	160	421
Carbohydrates	g	2	4	14.5	9	92.7
Chlorophyll	mg	42.2	—	n/a	n/a	1,469
Dietary Fiber	mg	10	2	2.4	7	0.3
Fat	g	06	.35	0.3	15	9.3
Moisture	g	95	91.4	84.2	73.2	4.6
Protein	g	7.49	2.86	0.7	2	58.4
Vitamins						
Biotin	mg					0.2
Choline	mg	92.4	18	6	14.2	2.3
Folic Acid/Folate	mcg	29	194.4	6	81	0.9
Vitamin A	IU	427	6715	54	146	51,300
Thiamine	mg	08	0.1	0	1	1.7
Riboflavin	mg	0.13	0.189	0	0.1	4.3
Niacin	mg	0.11	0.72	.4	1.7	23.8
Pantothenic Acid	mg	6	65	.1	1.4	1.1
Vitamin B6 (Pyridoxine HCl)	mg	0.2	0.195	.1	0.3	1.4
Vitamin C	mg	261	28.1	9.7	10	10.4
Vitamin E	mg	12.45	1.89	.6	2.1	<1.5
Minerals						
Calcium	mg	24.2	99	6	12	221

Vitamin and Mineral Comparison of Wheatgrass and Other Super Foods						
Per 100 grams		Wheatgrass	Spinach	Blueberry	Avocado	Chlorella
Iron	mg	.61	2.71	.3	0.5	130
Magnesium	mg	24	79	6	29	315
Phosphorus	mg	630	49	12	52	895
Potassium	mg	147	558	77	485	1360
Selenium	mcg	< 1 ppm	1	.1	.4	—
Sodium	mg	10.3	79	1	7	21.9
Zinc	mg	.33	.53	.2	.6	71
Amino Acids						
Alanine	g	.295	.142	31	.109	.43
Aspartic Acid	g	.453	.24	57	.236	.47
Cystine	g	.134	.35	8	.27	.7
Isoleucine	g	.287	.147	23	.84	.23
L-Arginine	g	.425	.162	37	.88	.33
L-Lysine	g	.245	.174	13	.132	.3
Leucine	g	.507	.223	44	.143	.47
Methionine	g	.116	.53	12	.38	.13
Phenylalanine	g	.35	.129	26	.232	.277
Proline	g	.674	.112	28	.98	.24
Threonine	g	.254	.122	20	.73	.24
Tyrosine	g	.674	.108	9	.49	.26
Valine	g	.361	.161	31	.107	.32

The nutrient content of foods can vary depending on location of production and methods of preparation. Laboratory reports also vary. This table is compiled from a variety of sources and should be considered an approximation. It is not meant for diagnosis but to give the reader a general comparison of various super foods.

Combining Wheatgrass with Other Super Foods

Wheatgrass can be combined with a number of food groups. This can be done to boost the nutritional value of other foods groups, create an ultra super food product, or balance the tastes of one or more of the food products. If you own a juicer, you might try juicing the steamed outer leaves of the kale plant in combination with other vegetables and fruit, such as carrots or apples. By doing so, you can recreate some of the enzymes that are lost when vegetables are cooked. Cereal grasses provide the same nutritional value, so mix and match freely. A barley and wheatgrass combination provides an interesting taste, as the bitter barley is balanced with the sweetness of the wheatgrass. When combining wheatgrass with other food remember that wheatgrass is an alkaline food and mixing it with too many citrus foods may lower the alkaline level. *Refer to Chapter 7 for nutritious recipes combining wheatgrass with other super foods.*

Spirulina and wheatgrass powder make a good combination for fortifying pets. It is recommended for strengthening the immune system of companion birds, especially during breeding. It also enhances the quality of their feathers.

Vitamin overload

You have heard that too much of a good thing can be bad for you. This is not just a cliché; it is a fact. While we are fortunate to have at our disposal an abundance of food choices, we must be temperate in all things. Just as it is important to obtain the right amount of nutrients for the body, so it is important to have the right balance of nutrients. Vitamin imbalance, deficiency, or overload can cause negative effects on the body. Take heed to the following conditions that are related to vitamin overload:

- Excessive protein can overload the kidneys; too many vitamins and minerals cause damage to the liver.

- Various forms of alfalfa can present some health risks. Alfalfa sprouts, alfalfa seeds, and alfalfa in powdered form contain L-cavanine, a substance that may cause spleen enlargement, abnormal blood cell counts, or recurrence of controlled lupus.

- Gluten in wheat and rye can cause allergies in some individuals.

- Kale contains goitrogen, a substance that occurs naturally and can interfere with thyroid function.

- Spinach contains purines, which are naturally occurring but can be harmful to some individuals with kidney problems. Oxalates in spinach can also contribute to calcium deficiency.

- Mustard greens contain oxalates, which can cause additional problems for individuals with kidney or gallbladder problems.

- Too much "amla," the Indian gooseberry, in the body may cause heart damage.

- The high concentration of potassium in the highly prized noni fruit could cause problems for individuals with kidney difficulties.

- Noni juice manufacturers have been warned by the USDA for making unsubstantiated health claims.

- Liver damage has also been reported with the use of noni.

- Cranberry juice consumed in high quantities can cause diarrhea and upset stomach.

- According to the Hong Kong Dietitians Association, high levels of protein, vitamins, and minerals in spirulina can cause liver and kidney problems.

Please inform your health care providers of any complementary and alternative practices you might be using before they prescribe any drugs for you. This is a safety measure for both you and your practitioner.

CASE STUDY:
THE MILK OF THE EARTH

Michael Morales, ND, board certified
naturopathic physician
150-07 78th Avenue
Kew Gardens Hills, NY 11367
Phone: 718-969-1469

Dr. Michael Morales is a 30-year board-certified naturopath. He spends his time between the continental United States and Puerto Rico, teaching others about the benefits of nutrition and the importance of taking care of the body.

I have been practicing natural medicine for 30 years. I work with degenerative diseases. I believe that a combination of faith and super foods — foods that have a high nutritional content — are the best hope for a cure for treating incurable diseases such as diabetes and cancer. I believe natural medicine is a viable alternative for treating and preventing such diseases. All illnesses stem from an imbalance of the body's biochemistry. A re-nourishing and rebalancing of the biochemistry is needed so that the body can heal itself as it was meant to do.

Super foods are great. I would say the top super foods include wheatgrass, miso, seaweed, whole grains and beans, nuts and seeds, green and orange vegetables, garlic, ginger, olive oil, sesame oil, and sea salt. Fruits are also good — berries, in particular. Of course, everyone's body chemistry is different and the sugar content of berries might be too high for some individuals to consume regularly. The important thing to remember is that these foods must be used in conjunction with a nutritious diet. No one thing gets us ill. No one thing will cure us. It takes the right combination of foods to benefit the body.

Wheatgrass is the milk of the earth. As the young child is nourished by its mother, so Mother Earth nourishes its children. Wheatgrass benefits the body in many ways. It is a great detoxifier. It is especially good for cleansing and strengthening the kidneys and liver. I have had patients who were able to forego kidney dialysis because they chose to incorporate wheatgrass into their diet. It is a blood cleanser. Because of its chlorophyll content, it acts as a natural detergent, cleansing the blood and the body. It is an alkalizer. It helps neutralize acids in the body, which is important for good health. We can look around us at nature and see the importance of wheatgrass and other green foods to the diet. Consider the apes and monkeys, very similar in chemistry and body structure to humans. Their diet consists of an abundance of green matter, which should tell us that our diets, too, should consist mostly of green foods. The earth itself is filled with forests and other green vegetation. Surely, this also is an indication of the importance of living, green matter.

It is important not to overdo wheatgrass usage. It must be taken at the proper time and in the right amounts. And, once again, it must be used in conjunction with a nutritionally balanced diet. Three important things to remember concerning wheatgrass and other super foods is quality, balance, and method of preparation. We are complex beings, and we need an abundance of different foods in our diet to maintain good health.

CHAPTER 10

Growing Wheatgrass for Profit

"No one knows what he can do until he tries."

~ Publilius Syrus

Now that you know what wheatgrass is, how to use it, and how to grow it, you might be interested in learning how to sell it for profit. Many wheatgrass businesses began as an extension of personal wheatgrass usage. Users began growing for themselves and their families and realized that they could probably grow for others as well. Wheatgrass has increased in popularity in recent years and many health-conscious individuals are purchasing juicers and trays of wheatgrass to prepare their own fresh drinks at home. Health food stores across the nation are selling tray after tray of the green, slender blades. But, someone needs to *grow* the wheatgrass. Could it be you?

With a little ingenuity, perseverance, and some basic business skills, it *can* be you. You can be a supplier of fresh-grown wheatgrass. You might not have been born a businessperson, but business skills can be acquired. Often, they are acquired through experience. This is not to say that owning your own business will be easy. There are sure to be a few challenges along the way.

You must also ask yourself some pertinent questions. Do you have a desire to make this idea work? Are you a hard worker? Are you self-motivated? Can you focus? *Do you enjoy growing wheatgrass?* The idea of owning a business might be glamorous, but to achieve success, it takes desire, planning, discipline, organization, dedication, marketing, and a positive attitude.

Setting Up a Home-based Business

Driven by the desire to be financially self-sufficient, thousands of individuals have taken up the challenge of starting a business at home. In fact, the easiest and fastest way to financial independence is by having your own business. But, unless you inherit that business, it is going to take some time and effort to build and establish your brand, gain customer confidence, and obtain a respectable position amongst the competition. According to data by the Small Business Administration, 99.7 percent of all employer firms are represented by small businesses. You will not be the only one out there selling wheatgrass. It is also going to take much patience and careful planning to navigate through legal and tax issues, determine space allocations, and establish time management discipline.

A home-based business is a good business model for beginning entrepreneurs; it allows for the opportunity of owning a business but with limited responsibilities and risks. Home-based businesses are growing in popularity and are fast becoming the No. 1 way to operate a small business. One of the greatest advantages of a home-based business is reduced start-up costs, such as leasing space, phone and utility deposits, lease hold improvements, and major office equipment. Other benefits include personal freedom, control of capital, tax advantages, increased productivity and growth opportunities, and greater flexibility and creativity. The good thing is that you do not need to have all the major pieces in place to start. You do not have to have a large building, extensive staff, or abundant capital to begin your wheatgrass business. You can start by conducting business as a sole proprietor, following the rules and regulations of your city or state. Contact the local planning/zoning department of your county to make sure that your location is zoned for business activities. Once zoning is cleared — inquire about a conditional-use permit if zoning is a problem — you can begin planning.

Start with a plan

A business plan is a document that outlines the key functional areas of a business, including operations, management, finance, and marketing. It does not have to be complicated, but it does need to be complete. In most cases, it should have the following in place:

- **Executive summary:** Key points detailed in the plan; should be able to stand independently

- **Company analysis or business overview:** Describes type and history of the business, location, business model, legal entity (structure), key assets, and method of operation

- **Industry or market analysis:** Market overview; plans for catering to target market

- **Customer analysis:** Identifies target customers; identifies customer need; plans for catering to target customer

- **Competitive analysis:** Outlines the strengths and weaknesses of competitions; states competitive edge strategy

- **Sales and marketing plan:** Pricing and sales information; product attractions; methods of reaching audience

- **Operations plan:** How the business will function; physical set-up; explanation of tasks

- **Management plan:** Descriptions, backgrounds, and working relationships of all involved in operation of business

- **Financial plan:** All financial information; start-up costs; maintenance costs; projection costs

- **Appendix:** Sales forecasts; performance sheets; balance sheets

Having a business plan equates to having a road map. Any good driver understands how important it is to have the travel plans mapped out *before* the journey begins.

The plan: A twofold purpose

The reason for the business plan is twofold: 1) to help you, the entrepreneur with the planning and development of the business; and 2) to demonstrate the feasibility and potential profitability to potential investors, lenders, and other outside audiences. The length of the plan generally depends on the size and scope of the business. According to author and business planner Tim Berry of BPlans.com, plan length should not be measured by pages, but by readability and summarization. According to Berry, the proper length should be according to the purpose and nature of the plan. The purpose and nature of a home-based wheatgrass business plan should be to describe the business and how it will be managed and to identify a customer base. The market — people with possible interest in the product — is already identified: wheatgrass buyers.

The business plan can be used for management purposes, to help identify workable partners and staff, to serve as a feasibility study for the business (allows the identification of a business's strengths and weaknesses), and to help you stay focused. Most importantly, the plan can help you control the destiny of your business, including obtaining necessary funding for operating and growing the business. For a free reading of Tim Berry's book *Hurdle: The Book on Business Planning*, go to **www.hurdlebook.com**. A variety of free sample business plans can be found at the following sites:

- Bplans.com (**www.bplans.com/sample_business_plans.cfm**) offers free sample business plans for various industries and a software program for purchase that can edit these plans. This site also has a number of articles geared toward helping the beginning entrepreneur.

- MoreBusiness.com (**www.morebusiness.com/business-plans**) has sample business plans and a free business e-book available. Their Marketing Plan Pro software is ranked as the world's most popular marketing planning software program.

- PowerHomeBiz.com (**www.powerhomebiz.com/bplan sampleplans.htm**) lists all the free business plans that are available on the Web. It offers several articles about business start-ups as well as free expert advice.

Select a business structure

Within the company analysis of your business plan, you must declare a legal or business entity or structure. This means you must decide which type of business form you will operate under. The choices include: sole proprietorship, partnerships (general and limited), corporations (C and S), and limited liability company (LLC). These business forms are established by state law for legal and federal tax purposes.

A sole proprietor is someone who operates the business as an individual. Starting a sole proprietorship is fairly easy and not too expensive set up. It usually entails paying a small, one-time fee to the county or state to register your business. It is also just a matter of filing a "Schedule C" on your personal tax returns to report the business income. The problem with operating as a sole proprietor is that there is no legal protection for your business assets, including your business name. You also cannot take advantage of any tax breaks offered to corporate businesses, and you cannot sell your business or pass it down to any inheritors. To obtain any special business amenities, you must set up your business under one of the other corporate entities.

Partnerships are formed when two or more individuals decide to join together to operate the business. Each partner contributes money, labor, time, or property and expects to share the profits and losses of the operation. In a general partnership, each partner is personally responsible for the liability of the entire business. In a limited partnership, the limited partner is only responsible for his or her individual investment in the business. In a partnership, each individual is considered self-employed and must claim an individual share of the partnership's income of the tax return.

A corporation consists of an individual or a group of individuals owning shares in a company and who are protected by the company from legal liabilities. A share is a divided portion of the value of a company. A C Corporation can have any number of shareholders with various legal structures. A C Corporation pays tax as one unit and individuals of the corporation must claim dividends as taxable income individually, resulting in double-taxing for each corporation member. An S Corporation allows the investors to claim their individual portion of the corporation's income on their tax returns directly. S Corporations are more expensive to form and are generally limited to 75 shareholders, which is ideal if you are interested in a small business.

An LLC is a cross between a partnership and a corporation. It is not a corporation. It has the management structure of a partnership with the tax and liability benefits of a corporation. There are many advantages to forming an LLC, and it is becoming the most popular way to start a business. LLCs are easy to set up and maintain, and they have a flexible ownership structure. One person can form an LLC and is not considered a sole proprietor if an LLC is the elected business structure. LLCs, by default, are taxed as a sole proprietorship or partnership but have the option of corporation taxation. Other benefits of an LLC include:

- Ease of transfer
- No ownership restrictions
- Living trust flexibility
- Flexibility in fundraising
- Credibility

You do have the option of changing the business structure of your company, if the need or desire arises. However, you should really put some thought into how you wish to be classified, as switching gears down the road could cost you time and money.

Seek outside assistance

Starting a new business can be an exciting adventure, but it involves working through several technicalities. The very thought of writing a business plan can be daunting, and it can be easy to get discouraged before you have even begun. There is no rule that states a home-based business must be planned and organized by the owner alone. In fact, it would be wise to seek outside help, especially in the planning stage.

Free online counseling and training programs are offered by the SBA and other organizations that can help you with the start-up and expansion of your business. There are also several local in-person services, such as the Service Corps of Retired Executives (SCORE) Association, which can provide you with the help you need. SCORE (**www.score.org**) offers free mentoring, low-cost workshops, and business counseling. Other sources of business help include the following:

- Small Business Institute (SBI) (**www.smallbusinessinstitute. org**) is an organization dedicated to helping small businesses, entrepreneurial firms, and other organizations through field-based student consulting and outreach.

- Small Business Development Centers (SBDCs) (**www.sba.gov/about sba/sbaprograms/sbdc/index.html**) are designed to help the small business owner in all aspects of business start up and management.

- Cooperative Extension System (**www.csrees.usda.gov/Extension**) offers assistance in management to current and prospective business owners.

- Start Your Wheatgrass Business Today (**www.wheatgrassbusiness. com**) offers a variety of programs including online tools and training to help you launch a successful wheatgrass business.

It is advisable to seek the assistance of a lawyer and professional accountant to help you with the actual writing of the business plan. Their guidance can help you produce a concise plan that you can rely on to successfully build your business.

Licensing and registration

Operating a home-based business most likely will require some type of legal documentation. Seeking the help of a lawyer can be beneficial in securing the proper documents you need to become a legal, established business. Most businesses need a city or county license. There might also be county, state, and/or federal licensing requirements. If you plan to register your business under a fictitious name, or a name that is not your own, you might have to register that name with the county as required by the Trade Name Registration Act. Your local government will be able to help you determine if this needs to be done. If you have a particular idea or concept that needs protection, you might need to seek trademark, patent, or copyright protection. Once again, your state or local government can advise you. Call or visit your local city hall to find out where to purchase the various licenses. The fees that accompany these licenses are usually minimal. It is important that you get your business off to a good start by taking heed to all regulatory details. Negligence in this area could cause you some major obstacles down the road.

Registering your business name

The name of the business owner is the legal name of the business. If you are the sole proprietor of your business, then your full name becomes the legal business name. If the business is operating as a partnership, the business name is the last names of the partners or the agreed upon name in the partnership agreement. For corporations and LLCs, the legal name of the business is the name registered with the state government. The legal name of the business is required on all government forms and applications concerning the business. You can, however, conduct business under a fictitious name or "doing business as" (DBA) status, but this name might also need to be registered with a government agency, depending on where you reside.

Obtaining an EIN

A federal tax identification number or employer identification number (EIN) is assigned by the IRS to all businesses that offer products or services that are taxed. It is used to identify the business to federal offices responsible for regulatory practices. If you are not sure whether you need an EIN, call the IRS Business and Specialty Tax Hotline at 800-829-4933. Most businesses, however, must file an SS-4 Application to apply for this number even if they are not hiring employees. Businesses are also required to file a DR-1 Application for Certificate of Registration, which is a sales tax number. Certain items must be taxed, according to state law. Visit the IRS site at **www.irs.gov/businesses/small/article/0,,id=102767,00.html** to apply for an EIN online. You can also visit the SBA website (**www.sba. gov**) for a start-up guide and free online business planning training.

Also, the Internal Revenue Service (IRS) has a clear definitions as to what can and what cannot be considered a business deduction on tax returns. It is important to become familiar with this criteria, which can be done by visiting the IRS business site at **www.irs.gov/businesses/small/ article/0,,id=109807,00.html**. You can also find income tax rules outlined in the IRS publication #587, "Business Use of Your Home," which can be found at **www.irs.gov/pub/irs-pdf/p587.pdf**. Now is the time to learn as much as you can about operating a home-based business so that you can put all the pieces in place. Laying a solid foundation is key to building a strong, successful organization.

Laws and regulations for selling wheatgrass

Although most businesses must comply with a general set of rules and regulations, some laws might apply only to specific businesses. Wheatgrass production sites and facilities are regulated by the FDA because wheatgrass is a food and wheatgrass "sprouting" is considered food processing by the FDA. In 1998, due the large number of foodborne illness cases reported, the FDA issued an advisory against consuming raw sprouts. Therefore, government regulations concerning facilities and production processes are currently under examination. Keep up to date with FDA advisories for wheatgrass by visiting the FDA website at **www.fda.gov**.

Contact your state's Department of Health to learn about current regulations for food handling. The local sanitarian, an on-site inspector of restaurants and food preparation facilities, will also be able to assist you. Anyone in food services, even a home-based food processing service, must have their kitchen or area plans approved before establishing a business. The National Sustainable Agriculture Information Service (ATTRA) recommends learning what an inspector can and cannot require of commercial producers. Also, check federal and state code requirements for space, ventilation, lights, and heating.

To operate your wheatgrass business, you might be required to obtain a business license or reseller certificate. A reseller certificate allows you, as a business, to purchase tax-free goods from distributors and wholesalers that would normally require a valid tax ID. You will be required, however, to collect taxes from those living in your state who buy your goods. More information about starting a food products business can be obtained from your local Cooperative Extension. Virginia Tech and Virginia Cooperative Extension offer training, product development research assistance, and one-on-one consultation through their Food Products Assistance Program.

Financial logistics

One of the most important aspects of running a business concerns understanding the financial requirements for your business. Having a good handle on cash flow management will enable you to keep your business out of debt and into profits, which is the purpose of starting the business in the first place. Estimated start-up costs and operational costs, current and future, must be determined and placed in the business plan. At this point, you also need to determine how you will fund your business. In reality, you should have a certain amount of money set aside for business use before you begin your business. According to the Virginia Department of Business Assistance (VDBA), outside investors and lenders "like to know that the entrepreneur has some personal investment in the enterprise beyond their labor." Personal investments might include savings, credit cards, and gifts or investments from family and friends.

According to the VDBA, about 95 percent of new businesses are financed by personal funds and loans. To obtain a listing of financial resources, contact the Capital Resources Directory of the VDBA at **www.dba.virginia. gov/financing_business.shtml**. The Community Affairs: Small Business Resource Guide (**www.occ.treas.gov/cdd/sbrg09032003.htm**) and the Citizen's Guide to State Services (**www.sec.state.ma.us/cis/ciscig/a/a2a17. htm**) are also helpful resources. A solid business plan is required by most lenders and investors, so be sure to have this in place before seeking a commercial loan application. Preparing the financial portion of the business plan can be difficult if you do not have a background in accounting. Remember to seek assistance when necessary.

Business insurance

Liability insurance must be purchased for the operation of any type of food production business. This insurance will protect you and your business from unforeseen circumstances that could be financially devastating, such as a lawsuit pertaining to an illness or death traced to your facility. It is critically important that you keep a high standard of cleanliness in your facility to avoid contamination of your products. Also, maintain records of supply purchases, especially seedlots, which have been under much investigation since the mid 1900s. Consult with your attorney to discuss liability insurance and other types of business insurance that you might need such as health insurance, property insurance, or workers' compensation. *The Legal Guide For Direct Farm Marketing* by Neil Hamilton is a good book to have in your library.

Banking

Whether you have applied for a loan or not, you should research and choose a good banking system. As a small business owner, you will need to have a business checking account and a business credit card. You may even need a business referral or credit reference from your banker, so try to establish a good banking relationship as soon as you open your account. Remember to keep business finances and personal finances separate to simplify bookkeeping and tax issues. While you are opening your bank account and establishing your business line of credit, start thinking about how you will receive payment from your customers. The options include cash only, checks, credit cards/debit cards, credit loans and leases, and online payments. To learn about the pros and cons of each of these methods go to the Business.gov website at **www.business.gov/manage/finances**.

Create key business assets

Business assets are business purchases that have long-term value such as a truck or computer equipment. Office supplies and gardening tools are not considered assets but are deducted expenses. Business assets are categorized as tangible and intangible. Tangible assets have a physical existence such as real estate, equipment, and cash while intangible assets represent values that cannot be physically touched such as copyrights, patents, trade names, and franchises. Key business assets, both current and projected, should be purchased and/or created and included in the financial segment of the business plan.

Choose a theme or brand identity

One of the most important assets your business will own is its brand or identity. A company brand is much more than a log or tag line. It is the image that appeals to your target audience and sets you apart from the competition. Creating a strong brand will prove beneficial once customers build confidence in you and your product; it helps with the selling process. Brand expert and author of best-selling business book *Brain Tattoos: Creating Unique Brands That Stick in Your Customers' Minds* Karen Post points out that brands are built on a four-point platform: purpose, personality, point of difference, and promise. Steps for establishing a successful brand are:

1. Draft your brand, making it totally you
2. Learn your target audience and relate the brand to them
3. Choose a unique brand name
4. Create a compatible logo
5. Apply the brand to all aspects of your business
6. Create a demand for your brand

Patent or copyright any original ideas

Many times, opening a new business generates innovative ideas or concepts. If you have developed a unique theme or idea, you might want to get it patent protected or copyrighted. Ideas should be thought of as property. Patents, copyrights, trademarks, and business secrets are considered intellectual property, and it is a good idea to get all intellectual property protected. Many business owners have failed to quickly move forward with the protection of an idea only to find that someone with a similar idea has already taken advantage of copyright laws and moved that idea into the full marketing phase. Once this has happened, the idea legally belongs to the other party, and in most cases, they have full rights to it. Visit the SBA website at **www.sba.gov/smallbusinessplanner/start/protectyourideas** for information on copyright and patent laws. A confidentiality agreement is also good to have in place when discussing your business ideas with others. Confidentiality agreements are available as legal forms and can serve to protect both parties exchanging business information. Keep in mind that even if you do not wish to preserve an idea of your own, you are responsible as a business owner for not infringing on the rights of others.

Obtain a spot on the Web

You have probably heard it several times: "Every business needs a website." In today's environment of intensive internetworking, yes, it would be profitable to have a website. In fact, your domain name, or your website's URL, is one of the greatest assets of your business. It gives you an online identity, which is essential for promoting your brand. As soon as you settle on a company name, register it through a domain registration service. By doing so, your domain name can be secured, even if you do not build a site right away. Many business owners are capable of building a website themselves. "There's no reason not to do it yourself, particularly with the out-of-the-box solutions available nowadays," said author and marketing coach John Jantsch of the Duct Tape Marketing system for small businesses. Popular website building software includes Adobe Dreamweaver, retailing for about $399, and Microsoft's Frontpage, selling for $199. If you would rather not take up the challenge of building your own site, several low-cost Web services offer domain registration along with site building, web hosting, and e-mail and e-commerce set up. Web hosting is the space given to you for the publishing of your website. Having an e-commerce site allows you to take orders. Intuit Small Business (**www.intuit.com/website-building-software**) is a good example of an all-in-one hosting service. Of course, you can always hire a professional Web designer, ranging in cost from about $2,000 to $20,000.

Websites can serve several purposes. Before launching your site, you should determine the purpose of the site. What do you want it to do? The entire design and development of the site should relate back to its primary purpose. The following are some functions a website can perform:

- Provide general information about your company and its products

or services
- Generate sales leads and provide online customer support
- Sell products or services online
- Allow communications and transactions with suppliers

Having a website can help you promote your business. Keeping the site updated with relevant content is important. Promoting your business can be done through methods such as online display marketing by purchasing display space on relevant sites with a link back to your own site; search engine marketing by driving traffic from searchers of Yahoo!, Google, and other search engines to your site; and e-mail marketing by using e-mail to get the message out about you and your products or services. Visit Startup Nation (**www.startupnation.com/steps/66/3767/1/plan-web-presence**) for help with building a successful website. BizWeb2000 (**http://bizweb2000.com/freehelp.htm**) can help you with marketing strategies for your business. The Home Business Advantage (**www.home-business-advantage.com/website-marketing-strategies.html**) explains the different methods of online marketing and how they can work for you.

Develop a marketing strategy

Developing a marketing strategy is a very important aspect of the business plan because it helps to identify how you will reach your prospective audience. Production and distribution of goods largely depend on marketing, and marketing contributes to the success of the business. Marketing is the means of letting your audience know about you and your product or service. It helps boosts product sales and builds a reputation for the business. Marketing entails advertising, public relations, promotions, and sales. A marketing strategy works to increase the profit and revenue growth of the company by addressing the need of the customer and increasing the level of competitiveness against other businesses.

The marketing plan

What is the purpose of your business? The marketing plan should reveal this purpose, vision, or mission statement. It should also highlight the objectives you wish to achieve and produce the research that was done to develop your marketing strategy. The action plan for the marketing strategy should be outlined.

It is important that a business knows its product well and is also familiar with industry trends concerning the product. The marketing plan should detail the product and services. By reading this book, you have learned about the history of wheatgrass, the benefits of wheatgrass, and how to grow and use wheatgrass. Now, it is necessary to become familiar with the current happenings with wheatgrass. It is also time to identify your target audience. Who will you sell this wheatgrass to? Are there health food stores or juice bars in your area that can buy from you? Is there a farmer's market? Do you have neighbors who drink wheatgrass? How old are they? What are their lifestyles or beliefs? You might be able to gather information from the agricultural trade association in your area. Remember that you are marketing fresh produce, so do not consider markets too far out of your area. Also remember that, in reality, people are not seeking products; they are seeking solutions to problems. Your product or service should be able to provide the solutions that they seek. *Evaluating a Rural Enterprise* and *Organic Marketing Resources* published by ATTRA are two publications that can help you with your marketing endeavors.

By identifying your target audience, you will also identify your competition. Who else is selling around you? Are they selling by the tray or by the bag? Once your competition — and your competition's product — has been identified, it is time to establish your pricing, method of distribution, and product positioning in the market. If you have direct, local competition, you might wish to price your wheatgrass in the same price range of your competitor. Having the lowest price is not necessarily the smartest pricing strategy, as it keeps you from obtaining needed profit margin. Profit margin is the company's net profit, or the total earnings over a given period of time, divided by total sales. It is usually better to have average prices and focus on quality and service. Knowledge of the product and services of your business is not enough to effectively generate sells. Your business also needs a unique way of capturing the attention of the audience and introducing your product or service to them. What is the plan? Can you offer free delivery? Your marketing plan tells exactly what is offered by your company and outlines a plan for the future.

Marketing material

To implement your marketing strategy, you will need to invest in materials for marketing your services. Marketing materials should be informative and persuasive. You want to inform your audience that you have something to sell and persuade them to purchase from you. Your marketing material must stand out from that of your competition or you sales will suffer. Marketing material includes a logo, business cards, post cards, flyers, brochures, and other direct marketing devices. A logo is especially important because it gives both visibility and credibility to your business. You should have your material professionally designed to avoid amateurish or unpolished designs. If you are on a tight budget and would rather create these materials yourself, try Brandoozie (**www.branddoozie.com**), a do-it-yourself marketing tool that allows you to create a logo and match it with business cards, flyers, and brochures. Companies such as Vistaprint (**www.vistaprint.com**) offer professional-looking material at affordable prices. Marketing materials will increase business sales as well as your confidence, so complete this task as soon as possible.

Preparing for work

You have developed a business and marketing plan your new business. This is not enough to begin operations. You must plan again. This phase of planning entails setting up a workspace, creating a work schedule, and purchasing equipment and supplies. If these items are not in place *before* you actually begin working, you are bound to run into problems that will be a hindrance to business progress. To avoid confusion and disorganization, take the time to prepare for work.

Setting up workspace

It is important to have a designated area for operating your business, preferably separated from your regular living quarters. Business records must be kept separate from family papers. Prior to setting up space, make certain that you have obtained the necessary permits and licenses for the operation of the business. Investigate your method of getting the produce into your customer's hands. Will you offer delivery? Can the customer pick up the produce? While planning your workspace, be sure to allow for customer parking and entrance into the work area. Check with the local chamber of commerce to check if there are limitations as to the type and number of workers that can be used in your area. Check with city hall or the local zoning office to make certain you are following all of the codes and zoning restrictions related to your business. Consider your neighbors. How will they be affected by your decision to create a workspace at home?

Creating a work schedule

Operating a home-based business, no matter how small, takes discipline. Some people find it hard to make and keep work schedules, even within an organized corporate organization. It is essential, however, that you are focused and develop certain time-management skills to eliminate avoidable distractions and kill procrastination. Creating a daily list of responsibilities and checking them off as they are completed might be necessary in the beginning months of the business. Keep a planning and operating log to keep track of vital information. Consider the installation of a business phone line with an answering machine to eliminate phone distractions.

Purchasing equipment and supplies

Despite the Federal Seed Act, which was established in 1939, contaminated seeds are still found in growers' supplies. The Federal Seed Act serves as a protection for the farmer from the effects of purchasing seed that is defected, contaminated, or mislabeled. These restrictions can be enforced by the Secretary of the Department of Agriculture and action is taken against violators, but little remedies are offered to the purchaser. Therefore, it is important to inspect the labels and even test products before purchasing a seed lot that might be defective. *For pricing of materials and supplies, refer to Chapter 5.*

Operating your business

Once your business and marketing plans are in place and you have adequately prepared for work, you can feel comfortable with opening the doors of your business. This is an important time and one that can be marked with some type of momentous event. Many businesses have grand openings that include sales, giveaways, and much fanfare to highlight their existence in the community. Generally, however, this does not happen until the business has been in operation for a few weeks. A new business can have a "soft opening" to commemorate the first day or week of operations. A soft opening takes place without much fanfare, but it lets the public know that you are officially open for business. Sometimes, this can take place with word-of-mouth advertising or a sign over your door signifying that you are open. A soft opening can help you to ease into the routine of work, while working out problems that still need to be addressed before you become swamped with customers. Of course, if your business is in a remote location, your "soft opening" might have to entail more than just opening the door and waiting for customers.

Once you have become accustomed to operating the business and have a few customers, you just might want to have that "grand opening." The following online articles can help you out with this event:

- "Free Grand Opening Ideas for a Small Business" by Chris Wolsk (**http://smallbusiness.chron.com/grand-opening-ideas-small-business-3323.html**)

- "Grand Opening Ideas for a Business" by Miranda Brookins (**http://smallbusiness.chron.com/grand-opening-ideas-business-515.html**)

- "Making the Most of a Grand Opening" by Al Lautenslager (**www.entrepreneur.com/author/977**)

- Golden Openings (**www.goldenopenings.com/ProductPages/Guide/GrandOpeningGuide.htm**) has a guide book that walks you through the steps of the grand opening process.

Working toward a grand opening can be exciting. After the hoopla is over, however, you must settle down and carry on business with sobriety and purpose. There will be many days filled with challenges that you must overcome. When things get a bit difficult, remember to reflect back on your vision — the reason you wanted to start your own business in the first place. Also, remember to seek help when dealing with the unfamiliar. A business support group can also be beneficial. *The benefits of connecting with other growers is discussed in Chapter 11.* Many small businesses fail because they do not seek the help and support they need to get them through the hard times.

Exploring other business angles

Once you have been growing and selling wheatgrass for some time, you might want to consider a few things. Ask yourself some questions. Have you been successful growing and selling wheatgrass in your area? Do you want to continue in this direction? Do you want to change your method of growing? Expand your business to include other angles? Exploring other business angles might be profitable at this time. There are several possibilities as wheatgrass can be used in many ways.

Open a wheatgrass juice bar

Organic wheatgrass shot with tray of wheatgrass shoots, items typically sold in a juice bar..

You have your business license. You have been cleared by the health department to sell food products. You are convinced that wheatgrass is good for you. Why not open a juice bar featuring wheatgrass drinks? It might also be possible to buy into an existing juice bar franchise system. This means that you will have the rights to market the goods of a company that is already established. You might have to revisit your marketing plan, do some extended marketing research, consider a loan, and purchase some additional equipment, but opening a juice bar is a feasible angle to explore. Visit the following sites to get you started in this direction:

- Gaebler.com Resources for Entrepreneurs (**www.gaebler.com/ Opening-a-Juice-Bar.htm**) provides step-by-step instructions on how to get up and running.

- StartupBizHub.com (**www.startupbizhub.com/start-a-juice-bar-business.htm**) offers basic tips on starting a juice bar business including business structure, menu, location, start-up costs, and profits.

- Juice Gallery Multimedia (**www.juicegallery.com**) offers consulting, software, and recipes.

Sell other wheatgrass products

Individuals who consume wheatgrass are generally health conscious and interested in consuming healthy foods and using natural products. Therefore, selling other wheatgrass products might be an angle worth exploring. You do not necessarily need to make these products yourself. There are several companies that do sell products that contain wheatgrass such as wheatgrass capsules, powders, and tablets, other food products such as wheatgrass pasta, cosmetics, and medicinal products. You might even be able to purchase these products wholesale and resale them on a local level. Please make sure you have your resellers certificate if you decide to go this route. You can find products to sell for your business by searching online, using library sources, joining buying groups, attending trade shows, and asking other wheatgrass growers. The following websites can help you learn more about purchasing products wholesale:

- Love to Know (**http://buy. lovetoknow.com/wiki/How_to_ Buy_Wholesale_and_Sell_Retail**) explains the basics of buying wholesale and selling retail.

"Candle in Wineholder" centerpiece designed by Val Calpin for The Wheatgrass Grower. Photo used courtesy of The Wheatgrass Grower.

- AllBusiness.com (**www.allbusiness.com/specialty-businesses/ home-based-businesses/4554491-1.html**) speaks about wholesale pricing and how to determine pricing for resale.

If you are adventurous and up for the challenge, you can make and market your own wheatgrass products. *The recipes in Chapter 7 can help you get started with this.* Whether you make your own or purchase products for resale, selling other wheatgrass products could be a profitable venture.

"Topiary" centerpiece designed by Val Calpin for The Wheatgrass Grower. Photo used courtesy of The Wheatgrass Grower.

Start a floral wheatgrass business

In Chapter 5, it was mentioned that wheatgrass could be grown for decorative purposes. The floral wheatgrass business is a very unique business concept that is becoming trendy with some growers. These growers customize wheatgrass growing to meet the needs of a variety of customers. The wheatgrass is decked in an array of flowers, bows, or whatever else the customer requests. Some desire these floral wheatgrass pieces as centerpieces for weddings and other special events. Others, such as photographers, use them for props in photo shoots needing greenery. Decorators and florists are also requesting custom-designed grass. Expanding into a floral wheatgrass business might create a new position in the wheatgrass growing industry and is another angle worth exploring. For more information about how to get a floral wheatgrass business started, visit Dogwood Gardens Organic Farms (**www.wheatgrassman.com/site/1538595/page/871486**). This company offers DIY kits and other supplies. The e-book *Creating and Growing Wheatgrass Centerpieces* by Carolyn Gibson is also available, offering advice and tips from experienced growers. To purchase ready-made or customized floral wheatgrass pieces, visit The Wheatgrass Grower website (**www.wheatgrassgrower.blogspot.com**).

Acquiring a staff

You have now been in business for some time and have a growing customer base. You have even explored some other business angles and, perhaps, have taken on one or two. You might now realize that your one-man show can no longer continue. It is time to look for some hired help.

Finding employees for your wheatgrass business is a job in itself. Not only must you find someone with the skills you need to get the job done, you must find someone who can fit in with your business model. It would be ideal if he or she, too, were interested in health, gardening, or green living. If he or she has an interest in what he or she is doing, the employee will be more likely to put forth his or her best effort to help you succeed. Finding the right people to help you with your business might be a challenge. The following websites offer insights into acquiring a staff and can help you with the hiring process:

- Microsoft Startup Center (**www.microsoft.com/smallbusiness/ startup-toolkit/employee-management-system.aspx**) outlines all you need to know about acquiring employees, including how to find the best candidate, considerations for employee benefits, and dealing with employee tax responsibilities.

- Dun and Bradstreet Credibility Corp (**http://smallbusiness.dnb. com/human-resources/workforce-management-hiring/476-1. html**) points you in the right direction for finding recruiters and offers tips about hiring and managing a staff.

- U.S. Small Business Administration (**www.sba.gov/idc/groups/ public/.../serv_pubs_pm_pdf_pm1.pdf**) not only shows business owners how to hire workers but how to pay them as well.

Consider virtual assistance

With the rising costs of employee labor, many companies are turning to the Internet for "virtual" assistance. In many cases, hiring a virtual assistant (VA) can help offset employee costs. A VA is a professional online service provider. While an online assistant will be of very little use to you when it comes to monitoring sprouting seeds or preparing the soil for your wheatgrass trays, he or she might be very helpful in handling administrative tasks such as bookkeeping or managing your website. Hiring a VA is an important step in moving your business forward, as you can be relieved of time-consuming, although important, responsibilities and give yourself to other areas that need your attention. A good VA can also help you market your business. Hiring a virtual assistant might also be a consideration when dealing with space limitations. The following websites can give you more information about VAs and how to acquire one:

- Entrepreneur (**www.entrepreneur.com/humanresources/hiring/article70586.html**) points to sources for obtaining virtual assistance.

- Small Business Review (**http://smallbusinessreview.com/technology/get_help_virtually**) offers tips and advice for hiring VAs and where to find them.

- Ask Sunday (**www.asksunday.com/**) is a company that has trained VAs for hire.

CASE STUDY: THE BUSINESS OF GROWING AND SELLING WHEATGRASS

Ellen McGlynn, owner and grower
The Wheatgrass Grower
419 Carbondale Road
Clarks Summit, PA 18411
www.wheatgrassgrower.com
wheatgrassgrower@frontiernet.net
Phone: 570-587-5704
Fax: 570-587-5704

Ellen McGlynn, an Herbal Information Specialist through the American Botanical Council, has been the owner and proprietor of The Wheatgrass Grower, LLC since 2005. The Wheatgrass Grower is a private residential micro eco-farm and USDA-certified nursery dedicated to excellence in the production of nutritional greens. The company has been featured in several local newspapers as well as a national farming magazine.

I am a boutique grower of wheatgrass. By growing within a limited space (15x20 feet), I am not able to compete with larger growers on quantity or wholesale pricing, so I have chosen to concentrate on the quality of my product as its selling feature, including the quality of the grass itself, its attractive packaging in biodegradable plant-based plastics, and its shipping in thermal-lined boxes. My operation can only maximally produce

80 to 100 pounds of fresh-cut product per week year round. It is shipped via UPS mainly to the mid-Atlantic states (Pennsylvania, New York, New Jersey, Delaware, Maryland, and Washington, D.C.) and is also sold through local retailers in Northeastern Pennsylvania. We are part of the Buy Fresh Buy Local initiative and apply only organic and sustainable methods of growing. Because we are such a small business, we are not officially "Certified Organic" because of the expense and man-hours required to administratively tend to that certification.

Ellen McGlynn, The Wheatgrass Grower, in the growing room.

I have been using and growing wheatgrass since 2002 when my husband was diagnosed with a very late-stage terminal cancer. Wheatgrass had such a positive impact on his end-of-life quality that several neighbors asked me to continue growing it for them even after he passed away in 2003. I guess that is technically when I began selling wheatgrass out of the garage of our suburban Philadelphia home. At that point in my life, however, faced with the situation of having to sell my husband's restaurant and our home while raising our infant daughter, I decided to relocate back to my roots in Northeastern Pennsylvania. There, I purchased a home on agriculturally zoned land and established a micro eco-farm in the spirit of my late husband's environmentalism. With a strong enough local interest in my product by the spring of 2005, I was able to turn Wheatgrass Grower into an LLC. Online marketing of the product followed in 2007.

CONCERNING WHEATGRASS USAGE AND DOSAGE

I personally use wheatgrass juice several times a week, if I am lucky. I would juice more often, but I all too frequently give up my own share of

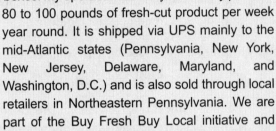

the crop to paying customers. I use wheatgrass for general detoxification and fatigue. I am in generally good health, so I do not drink wheatgrass on what I would consider a "therapeutic" level (several ounces a day). I do like to take at least an ounce a day when possible, and there are times when my body will actually crave more. I often just follow what my body tells me. Every day our bodies are pummeled with dietary and environmental toxins that build up in our systems and create chronic illnesses that often cannot be diagnosed through standard medical testing. It is this kind of constant pummeling that leads to more serious chronic illnesses like cancer. Wheatgrass juice with its high chlorophyll content has been shown to act as a chelator, a chemical that bonds with and removes toxins from substances, for damaging substances within the body, and it is my response to those types of physical stressors that cannot be individually controlled because they are so ubiquitous on a daily basis. I use wheatgrass in juice blends with things like pineapple juice, granny smith apples, orange juice, bananas, and berries. I also drink it straight. I also use wheatgrass as a base for floral arrangements.

My late husband used wheatgrass when he was diagnosed as terminally ill with melanoma. He was given two months to live. His hemoglobin levels were extremely low. He was so anemic that he required multiple blood transfusions, and he also took iron supplements in a pill form, but neither was particularly effective. Once he changed his diet and began using wheatgrass regularly as a juice and in enemas, there was a measurable difference in his hemoglobin count, and he generally felt better. He was able to snap back after a crippling round of chemotherapy pretty quickly. This level of empowerment had a huge impact on his psychological outlook and improved his quality of life during his illness. He survived ten months instead of two.

As a general dietary supplement, one ounce of wheatgrass juice can be used as a daily detox and to help combat fatigue. To treat an illness, one ounce three times a day before meals on an empty stomach is recommended. This is based on an observation I made speaking with customers who were referred to me by medical professionals.

The amount of grass that a tray yields varies from grower to grower, depending on the size of trays used and how densely the grass is grown. Generally speaking, a 10x20-inch tray can grow ¾ to 1 pound of grass. One pound of grass will produce about 10 to 12 ounces of juice.

An individual drinking only one ounce a day should only buy one tray and harvest it when the grass starts to split into its second shoot. They should then store the remaining grass in an airtight container and keep it in the crisper bin of the fridge to use as needed. Grass cut in this manner should retain its freshness for up to two weeks in the refrigerator. Based on this information, one can calculate how much a family might need to buy or grow to cover their juicing needs.

Wheatgrass can be taken during pregnancy. There are no known negative side effects to taking wheatgrass while pregnant other than those reported in the general population, such as nausea and darkened stools. A pregnant woman who is already suffering from classic morning sickness and heightened olfactory senses might want to steer clear of wheatgrass during the first trimester.

Wheatgrass juice has the capacity to build hemoglobin levels — that much exists in scientific literature — so I encourage anyone who has cancer or an anemia-related conditions to speak to their doctors about including wheatgrass juice in their diets. Wheatgrass juice, for reasons that are not entirely clear, is also effective at leaching environmental and dietary toxins from the body. In terms of antioxidants, its oxygen radical absorbance capacity (ORAC) rating is shown to be even higher than blueberries.

Some people are against wheatgrass usage because there is not enough scientific investigation and support from conventional doctors due to the lack of scientific investigation. It is a vicious cycle. Sadly, at this point in time, most of wheatgrass's good press comes from anecdotal reports. I do follow the scientific literature, however, and can tell you that universities (unfortunately, mostly overseas) have been producing more in the way of wheatgrass studies in the past several years. I am also dealing more directly now with medical doctors, especially in integrative medical fields, who support the use of wheatgrass and recommend it to their patients.

CONCERNING THE TASTE OF WHEATGRASS

Fresh wheatgrass juice tastes exactly as it smells — like a freshly mown lawn. Wheatgrass should be sweet, not bitter. If it is bitter, it has passed its optimal harvest date. Do I enjoy the taste? Yes; sometimes I even crave it. On the other hand, sometimes, I just cannot get it down, and I need to take a break from it. Frequent users of wheatgrass will often tell you they just cannot drink it anymore. It is a common phenomenon. It usually means it is time for a break or that you should try a little more variety by mixing it with other fruit or vegetable juices. It is better to take a break rather than ruining your relationship with wheatgrass juice forever by forcing it down.

It is acceptable to experiment with the wheatgrass juice. You might be surprised at what you are able to mix it with. I have mixed wheatgrass with simple orange or pineapple juice, and the combination is quite delicious. Wheatgrass with banana makes for a great shake. I also like my wheatgrass juice chilled, so whatever I mix it with, I shake it with ice before drinking. Have fun with it. Treat it like a fancy cocktail. Drink it in different glasses. Add a fruit chunk for garnish, like pineapple, and chase the wheatgrass by sucking on the chunk of fruit.

THREE TIPS FOR USING WHEATGRASS

1. **Wheatgrass is not a silver bullet.** Like all nutritional supplements, it has its beneficial properties, but it is meant to be used in conjunction with a healthy diet in order to reap its full benefits.

2. **Do not overdo it.** Daily regimens including more than two ounces of wheatgrass juice per day should be stretched out over the course of the day for maximum benefit (i.e., one ounce three times per day). Drinking more than two ounces at once will probably only result in a distaste for the product.

3. **Do not give up on wheatgrass juice if you cannot stomach drinking it straight.** Mix it with other juices to make it more palatable, such as pineapple, granny smith apple, or banana.

ON GROWING YOUR OWN WHEATGRASS — ADVANTAGES AND DISADVANTAGES

There are several benefits to growing your own wheatgrass. First and foremost would be cost. It is much cheaper to grow your own than to buy it. Most of the cost of wheatgrass is due to labor and packaging. It is also very therapeutic, almost magical, to watch your crop grow and know you have complete control over your end product. Growing your own also enables you to stagger your growing schedule in such a way that you can plant several trays each with different start dates and then cut it fresh every day if you like, which would be optimal.

I think this last point, however, has often been a point of confusion for those who believe it is *always* better to buy grass in the tray as opposed to the cut product in the bag. Unless you are able to consume 10 to 12 ounces of juice within a three-day period (tops!), it is better to just buy a pound of fresh-cut grass in the bag and store it in the refrigerator for use as needed over a one- to two-week period. Unless taking it therapeutically, it takes most people a week or more to drink the juice that could be harvested from a tray of wheatgrass. That being said, wheatgrass does have an optimal harvest time when the grass starts to split and form its second shoot, generally around day ten, after which it begins to turn bitter and decline in nutritional value. It also starts turning yellow and keeling over and harboring mold. So, on one hand, if you start cutting before the grass splits, you get less than the optimal amount of juice from your tray because it is not fully grown or at its nutritional peak. But, on the other hand, if you cut after the grass splits, you get a bitter-tasting, less nutritional product. Fresh-cut product in the bag is cut at its optimal harvest time so that you get the most nutritious product for the most reasonable price.

Harvesting determination can vary depending on the seed and the climate. Because I grow in a climate-controlled room, I am able to work on a more predictable harvesting schedule.

Some of the drawbacks of growing your own grass include having the space, time, and interest in growing your own grass. Often, growing grass is just not practical for the fast-paced professional who spends most of his or her time at work or who has limited living space such as an apartment dwelling. It might also not be a practical option for those who are very sick and barely getting by rushing from one medical appointment to another.

I grow my wheatgrass indoors and do not have any significant experience growing wheatgrass outdoors. When growing indoors, it is a good idea to have a separate room with a water source for growing wheatgrass. Soil prep and harvesting can be messy jobs, leaving soil and grass stains behind. Consider areas outdoors where you will be able to compost your wheatgrass mats so that you can either reuse the soil for growing more wheatgrass or use it in your outdoor gardens. Consider investing in large trash bins for storing things like soil and soil amendments indoors, especially if you live in the north where soil can freeze outdoors in the winter. Seed should always be kept in tightly lidded storage containers so that you do not attract mice. Indoor areas are best because temperature and humidity are able to be controlled. Unbelievably, the fear of high temperatures and humidity can be extremely stressful for the wheatgrass grower who does not have the proper climate-control measures in place. If sufficient ambient lighting is not available, invest in full-spectrum grow lights. Metal growing racks are prone to rust, so it might be best to go the plastic route. Always aim to work with racks on wheels so that they can be easily moved for cleaning and mopping.

I would encourage anyone who has the interest and the time to grow wheatgrass themselves to do that rather than buy from a grower for two reasons: 1) It is cheaper to grow your own because you are not paying someone else for the labor; and 2) It is therapeutic. It is very emotionally uplifting and empowering to raise a productive garden.

THE INFAMOUS MOLD

Mold is a very tricky subject. Because there are several ways mold can develop in your wheatgrass, there is no one definitive answer on how to combat it. Mold can develop from your soil, your seed, your water, or the air. If you are composting your own soil, particularly from wheatgrass mats that might have been moldy at the outset, you might find that you will need to find another soil source and just use your compost for outdoor use where the UV rays can deal with the mold and bacteria issues. If you are watering without a filter, you might be susceptible to molds that have collected in pipes, wells, or storage tanks. You can test your water for mold using kits available at larger hardware stores or online and should definitely consider using a water filter. Airborne molds are a larger problem. Be sure to clean growing-area surfaces regularly and consider using an air purifier.

Most often, however, I find that the mold is a result of the seed — even Certified Organic seed. I have experimented with several all-natural additives to my rinse water on moldy seed, but I have never experienced significant improvement with regard to mold. While I do rinse seeds with a food-grade hydrogen peroxide for sanitation purposes with regard to sprout-related pathogens and have even used a UV wand for same purpose, this does not seem to reduce the potential for mold. It is best to rinse often with plain water throughout the sprouting process (several times over the course of 12 hours) and do a final thorough rinse on the seed immediately before it goes into the tray.

Mold grows where it is wet and the air is stagnant, of course, so do not overwater your trays. Also, keep room humidity between 40 percent and 60 percent (a dehumidifier might be necessary) and use a fan, if necessary, to keep air circulating. Mold does not flourish in cooler temperatures, so keeping your room temperature around 70 degrees Fahrenheit (just enough for the grass to still grow at a normal rate) can help. In spite of doing everything right, there is no escaping the mold created by an ungerminated seed, and you will find ungerminated seeds in *every* batch of seed you buy. If you find that you have a lot of ungerminated seed, it is time for a new supplier. Generally speaking, molds that remain contained within the base area of the grass are safe, and cutting an inch above the root will help reduce your chances of ingesting it. Discard trays with molds that travel up the grass and create grass discoloration or slime.

THREE TIPS FOR GROWING WHEATGRASS

1. Mold is the bane of all wheatgrass growers. Keep humidity between 40 percent and 60 percent, temperature between 70 and 75 degrees Fahrenheit, air circulating, and growing areas clean.

2. If growing commercially, always order new shipments of seed *weeks* before your old shipment runs out so that you have time to test the new seed — even if you have a reliable supplier. If the new seed does not produce grass to your expectation, you will at least have time to order elsewhere.

3. Dirty growing trays rinse off quickly indoors using a deep utility sink and the jet feature on a garden hose. An inline fertilizer tank filled with a food-grade sanitizer can also be connected between your water source and hose connection to kill two birds with one stone.

THE BUSINESS OF SELLING WHEATGRASS

If you are interested in a wheatgrass-growing business, you must first check with your local township to see if your home or property is zoned for agricultural or business use. While certain office-related businesses are allowed to operate from residentially zoned properties, agricultural businesses are generally not. If not, you will need to apply for changes to your current zoning. I operate a home-based agricultural business on a property that is zoned for agricultural use, which makes anything I produce as an agricultural product fair game for sale. The USDA inspects my scales every year. This is mandatory when selling agricultural products by weight. However, the FDA oversees the regulations regarding wheatgrass and sprout production. As such, I operate my business in a manner that is compatible with FDA's published guidelines on sprouting and sanitation (2) and food labeling (3).

The following websites can be used as references:

1. **www.fda.gov/Food/GuidanceComplianceRegulatory Information/GuidanceDocuments/FoodDefenseand EmergencyResponse/ucm121288.htm#intro**

2. **www.fda.gov/Food/GuidanceComplianceRegulatory Information/GuidanceDocuments/ProduceandPlanProducts/ ucm120244.htm**

3. **www.fda.gov/Food/LabelingNutrition/default.htm**

The return on investment time frame for a wheatgrass business depends on how large your investment is. I have found that my overhead — the costs required to run the business, not including payroll — generally account for 40 percent to 50 percent of my sales. So, if you are selling wheatgrass at $15 per pound, you can roughly estimate that $7.50 to $9 per pound goes back to you in the form of wages, profit, or return on investment. A person just looking to make an extra $100 or more a week selling a dozen pounds of wheatgrass can do so with just an initial investment of under $500 and a few hours of labor per week. If you want to consider payment for labor as part of your return on investment, return can be had in less than a month if you have already established a client base. Two steel growing racks ($80 each at Lowe's), eight full-spectrum grow lights ($20 each at Lowe's), and 32 10x20-inch growing trays (about $1.50 each at Lowe's or online) are needed to get started. After that, expect to use three bags of top soil per week (about $6) and 15 pounds of wheatberries per week (about $30). You will also want to factor in the cost of packaging, utilities, and possibly automobile expenses to get a true estimate of your weekly expenses, and a portable conditioner/dehumidifier, if necessary, can run you several hundred dollars.

THREE TIPS FOR SELLING WHEATGRASS

1. Always answer the phone whenever possible and return calls promptly. Customers do not always understand that you might not be a larger organization with multiple employees, regular operating hours, or an office staff and will feel annoyed if they have to leave a message or wait longer than a couple hours for a return call. A cordless phone or business cell phone is a good idea in this profession.

2. Get a website even if you do not have an online store.

3. Make friends with your local grocers, health food stores, and food or farming organizations.

IN CONCLUSION

My favorite wheatgrass story is more a marketing story of happenstance. It was at a time when I had just developed my website to accommodate online ordering and had not quite tested my shipping strategy. I happened to be attending the Philadelphia Flower Show and was enjoying a lunchtime break over at Philadelphia's Reading Terminal Market when I stumbled upon the Fair Food Farmstand. I was not even thinking about handing out any business cards, but my brother-in-law insisted I give one to them. Within a week, they had placed an order for what I would consider my first "real" shipment. While they very much liked the product and the packaging, they informed me that the demand for wheatgrass was just not there. It was a disappointment, until a few weeks later when I received an online order from a woman who turned out to be a doctor from one of Philadelphia's leading medical universities. She happened to inquire about wheatgrass at the Fair Food Farmstand, and they immediately referred her to me based on that one shipment. She has not only been ordering from me ever since (and it has been years!), she opened the door for numerous referrals through her colleagues, and they have become my best clients. It is because of my business relationship with them I can confidently say that wheatgrass *has* become more accepted among members of the conventional medical community, and people ought not be afraid of discussing their interest in using wheatgrass with their physicians.

CHAPTER 11

Moving Beyond Home

"A quitter never wins and a winner never quits."

~ Napoleon Hill

Now that your business is up and running and you have made a name for yourself in your local community, you might feel the need to leave the comforts of home and venture into a world of greater opportunities. Now mind you, this does not necessarily mean a physical move. Whether you decide to move from home-based business to leasing a business space is not the discussion here. Rather, this chapter discusses making a move toward a more effective marketing strategy. Marketing is an important factor in business establishment and operation and plays a valuable role in business expansion. Improved marketing equals greater success. If you have decided that you have reached a plateau with your wheatgrass business and you want to move up higher and mingle with the big growers, it is time to make a marketing change, and just as you did when you first set up your business, you must plan.

Extending the Plan – An Addendum

When you decided to start a wheatgrass business you created a business plan and, within that plan, an outline of your marketing strategy. Now that you are expanding your business and tailoring your marketing strategy, it is necessary to create an addendum to the original plan. An addendum is an addition to a document that has already been created. In your marketing strategy addendum, you should do the following:

- Restate your business message and identify your new target market.
- Set objections or goals; define what you want to accomplish.
- Solidify your identity; re-evaluate the effectiveness of your logo; obtain a professionally produced one if you have not already.
- Review your marketing material; obtain business cards, stationery, and a business brochure using your logo; set up a website if you have not done so.
- Determine your visibility and decide which advertising channels you will use to emphasize visibility.
- Strengthen current customer relationships; consider a way to keep them informed about the business.
- Review your budget; determine which funds are available for new marketing strategies.
- Establish a schedule; set a time for accomplishing each of your new goals.

Integrated Marketing Communication

Communication has always been an important part of any thriving relationship, and it is still a vital strategy in the overall success of any business. However, today, communication must be implemented on a greater level. Gone are the days of mass marketing skills and business expertise through a singular medium to secure a solid customer base. This scattered marketing strategy is not effective today, in a time where media is no longer dominated by newspapers, television, and radio. A more focused approach is required to achieve long-term business success, and an increasing number of companies are adopting the principle of integrated marketing communication (IMC) as part of their corporate identification. IMC is a strategic marketing concept that uses two or more areas of marketing communications to establish a business brand through consistent interaction between the business and the target market. The concept emerged in the mid 1980s and has been used effectively by successful businesses to create and establish a visible brand or image of their business, product, and services in a competitive marketplace. "The shift toward the IMC perspective has been hailed as one of the most significant changes in the history of advertising and promotion … and as *the* major communications development of the last decade of the 20th century," wrote Dr. George Belch and Dr. Michael Belch in the study "Evaluating the Effectiveness of Elements of Integrated Marketing Communication: A Review of Research." During this evaluation, Belch and Belch explore the effectiveness of IMC campaigns through the traditional IMC tools of advertising, sales promotion, public relations/publicity, direct marketing, and interactive media. If you are going to forge ahead and integrate IMC strategy into your marketing plan, you will need to familiarize yourself with these tools and how they operate.

Advertising

Advertising is very important to the growth of your business. Effective advertising generates sales and increases public awareness of you, your products, and your services. Use traditional advertising methods to direct potential customers to your website for detailed information about your products and services. Traditional advertising includes campaigns that promote brand awareness and advertising in trade journals. As a small business owner, you might not have the budget for elaborate advertising campaigns, but there are free and affordable ways to advertise your business. Consider the following method of advertising:

- Put up a sign at your business location with the business name and website address.
- Place a bumper sticker or magnetic sign on your car advertising your business.
- Put your logo on T-shirts and distribute them among friends and neighbors.
- Create a flyer and post it on public bulletin boards.
- Always carry business cards and leave them behind in appropriate places.
- Place an ad about your business in all the local newspapers.
- List your business name in the telephone directory.
- Use e-zines (electronic magazines) and free classified on the Internet.
- Include your business Web address in your e-mail signature.

- Place a flyer or business card in all outgoing mail.

Sales promotion

Sales promotion is another tool of the IMC strategy. It entails employing media and non-media marketing strategies for a limited, predetermined period of time to promote the sales, usage, or trial of a company's products or services. The promotion could be directed at the consumer, staff, or local or wholesale distributors, but its purpose is to generate interest in the product. Sales promotion is particularly effective with the introduction of a new product or service. It can also be used, however, to revive interest in an old product. One of the challenges of sales promotion is differentiating yourself from other marketer promoting their products as well.

Popular sales promotion activities include the following:

- Discounted prices
- Product demonstrations and point-of-sale materials
- Contests and games
- Vouchers and coupons
- Free samples or give-away items
- Sweepstakes
- Buy-one-get-one-free (or half off)
- Refunds and rebates

Public relations

Any business interaction with the public, apart from customers, is considered public relations (PR). This includes vendors, local charities, journalists, and other public figures or groups. Business owners can get exposure for their products and services by building relationships with these individuals or organizations. PR differs from advertising in that it is basically free marketing that gets the media involved in what your company is doing. Somehow, they have learned about you and your product and are interesting in helping you promote it. Many times, PR is more effective than advertising. It reaches a wider audience than advertising and helps your company to be remembered for a longer period of time. It helps build credibility for your company, influencing customer decisions about you and your products. It might take some time and effort to establish your business through PR, but it is a worthwhile endeavor. Being known as an expert in your field is one of the rewards to PR marketing. To get the ball rolling in this direction, consider the following:

- Make sure you know everything there is to know about wheatgrass including wheatgrass growing, wheatgrass usage, and wheatgrass selling.

- Volunteer to speak at health functions, gardening shows, charity events, school programs, church affairs, or anywhere else where people might be interested in what you have to say.

- Contact trade publications in the health, gardening, or agricultural industry and volunteer information or offer to write an article about the benefits or wheatgrass or other pertinent subject.

- Offer free health seminars or workshops or participate in a job fair. Give out samples of wheatgrass or wheatgrass products.

- Become familiar with the local radio and television stations and try to appear as a guest on one of their talk shows.

- Learn how to write press releases and how to present them to different media outlets.

A public relations campaign is something you might want to add to your business plan. As with the marketing plan, identifying your target market is key. It is also important to identify your target media. Which newspapers or radio stations would be the best outlet for what you have to offer? Develop story ideas that you can pitch to them concerning your business and product. Create a positioning statement that differentiates you from other wheatgrass growers and include it with all correspondence to the press. Do not get discouraged if your story idea is rejected.

Direct marketing

Direct marketing pertains to the distribution of marketing material directly to the public. It is a vital aspect of a company's promotional plan. A direct marketing campaign includes methods such as database marketing, direct mail, and mailing list options. For each of these options, you will need to have a mailing list. You can compile a mailing list yourself, starting with your current customers. Match your list with a list from a professional database business and compare customer and prospective customer demographics. It is important that your list is made up of people who might have an interest in your product. It is also important to mail your material to the right person in the right department. Do some research and find out the name of the decision maker. Otherwise, your material will go unheeded and become junk mail. Follow up all mailings with a phone call.

Doing a test mailing to a select audience can help you determine whether your direct marketing strategies are effective. Consider these points when marketing directly:

- Learn how to write a direct mail piece.
- Obtain testimonials from current customers that you can use in the piece.
- Determine whether you will use postcards, traditional letters, or a sales brochure.
- Distribute business cards, brochures, and flyers throughout the community.
- Make your mailing stand out from other direct mail pieces by using bright-colored post cards or handwritten envelopes and applying third-class stamps instead of metered postage.
- Use first and last names of recipients and correct spelling.
- Keep your look consistent.
- Join your local chamber of commerce to connect with other business owners who may be interested in your product and services and distribute your literature among them.

Visit eSmallOffice (**www.esmalloffice.com/SBR_template.cfm?DocNumber=PL12_1400.htm**) for instructions on writing a direct mail piece.

The advent of social media

In recent years, the interaction between society and the Internet has brought about interesting data. There is a great buzz in the online world today concerning social interaction. According to a December 2008 research study from 16 industrialized nations, it was reported that adults spent "a third of their leisure time online, belong to two social networking sites and have regular contact with 16 people who they have 'virtually' met on the Internet." Citizens of the United States and most European countries make up 30 percent of those who spend one-third of their time online. Asia (China, Japan, and Korea) represented 40 percent.

"The immense popularity of social media enabled by today's Web 2.0 has opened many promising new conference marketing opportunities," observed Gary Rottman, principal and creative director of The Rottman Group. "Gradually, sole computing will impact almost every role, at every kind of company, in all parts of the world." The six basic types of social media include social networks, wikis, blogs, podcasts, forums, content communities, and microblogging. As a growing business, you could get involved with any of these media types and find a connection with someone, but we want to focus on connecting through social networking.

Social networking

The Internet is the most popular form of social networking today. There are hundreds of active social networking sites worldwide, supporting a variety of interests and practices. Some sites cater to a diverse audience, while others focus on a particular nationality, language, or religion. The *Journal of Computer-Mediated Communication* defines social network sites as "Web-based services that allow individuals to (1) construct a public or semi-public profile within a bounded system, (2) articulate a list of other users with whom they share a connection, and (3) view and traverse their list of connections and those made by others within the system." The journal also distinguishes between the term "social network sites" and "social networking sites," the former being characterized by individuals reaching out to those they already know and the latter involving individuals making new connections. With the understanding that social network sites can sponsor networking opportunities, academic and industry researchers are increasingly "intrigued by [the sites] affordances and reach."

You can make use of any social networking site to promote your business. Networking sites can be used as free business tools that can help you maximize the exposure and interaction of your business. They allow you to share your products and services with people all over the world. The key to effective marketing with these tools is knowing which tool is most useful for your business. In her article "Your Guide to Social Media Tools and Uses," Maisha Walker, president and founder of Message Media, presents these tools in several categories. They include directories, social bookmarking, video sharing, photo sharing, and blogging. The most popular sites are found in the categories of directories and blogging. The most popular social networking sites worldwide are Facebook (directory), Bebo (blogging), and Twitter (blogging); MySpace and LinkedIn (directories) are most widely used in North America. As society becomes increasingly "entangled in the Web," it can be difficult to ignore social media tools and how they can work within your relations communication strategy. You certainly do not have to embrace all or any of these prevailing media tools, but it might be beneficial to the growth of your business to choose a source that you can merge into your marketing strategy based on how you and those that work with you choose to communicate. If you own a business, it would be profitable to use social media tools to advance your business.

Making social media work for you

Social media sites can be used to share expertise, establish a brand, hire workers, and/or build business communities. You should choose your media site based on your target audience and the site that is most specific to your industry. Who are you selling to and what sites are they using? What is the most used site for a health and/or gardening business? You also need to set goals in order to market to your targeted audience. Specifically, what is it that you want to achieve? Are you looking to drive more traffic to your website? Do you want to solidify your brand and set yourself apart as an expert in the wheatgrass growing field? Do you want to generate more leads for sales of wheatgrass or wheatgrass products? You might want to revisit your business plan and integrate these new goals with those already established in the early days of your business.

You also need to become familiar with the different tools surrounding social media. Viral video, blogging, and RSS feeds are all important aspects of the media system. Even if you do not incorporate them into your marketing strategy, you should at least know what they are and what they do.

Once you have chosen your media site, set a few new goals in place, and become familiar with the various tools of the social media system, you can create your profile and begin marketing. Make certain you understand the site policies or terms and conditions before joining and actively promoting. Also, it is very important to remain active once you join the site. Consistency and determination are key factors in accomplishing the goals you have to grow your business. Building and maintaining relationships with customers is also key.

Building your brand using social media sites

Name branding through social media is a great way to grow your business. Media sites such as LikedIn, Facebook, and Twitter allow you to create a business presence before your current customers as well as reach a vast number of potential clients. Engage in conversations via the sites, join chatrooms and forums, and always be willing to share your expertise. Your customers get to know and trust you through your presence, so be professional, straightforward, and sincere. You want to appear as a leader in your field and your audience wants know that you are. They will be more willing to purchase your products or services once they are sure who you are. Your wheatgrass business is sure to prosper once you have established your brand using social media sites. Refer to Mashable (**www.mashable.com**) for the latest in social media news and step-by-step guides for getting started using such tools as Facebook and Twitter.

Generating leads through social media sites

One of the main goals of a business is to acquire more sales. This also can be done through social media sites by generating leads online. It was mentioned in the previous section how important it is to share your knowledge through the various communication channels online. Another important aspect in media marketing is getting in tune with your audience and listening to what they have to say. You do not want to appear as a know-it-all or a boastful business owner. Listening is an important skill and if you can hear what your audience is saying, you can serve them better by tailoring your products and services to their needs. Read the forum posts and carefully analyze what is being said before posting a reply. Search for viable conversations in your field via Twitter and pertinent keywords through indexing sites such as Reddit or StumbleUpon. Once a general conversation is established through the media, you can zero in on prospective clients and avail yourself to them for further conversations. If you effectively generate leads through social media sites, you might find that your audience will do a great deal of the marketing for you by word-of-mouth and link sharing.

For help on getting started with Twitter, visit Web Strategy (**www.web-strategist.com/blog/2009/02/08/for-the-professional-how-to-get-started-on-twitter**), a site that discusses how to get started on Twitter and making Twitter work for you.

Creating more traffic with social media sites

As a business owner, you should really put your website to work for you through social media marketing. Social media marketing is a great way to build your Web presence and attract website traffic from a variety of sources. Increased traffic means an increase in sales. A social media campaign can increase your popularity and build your reputation. It will also increase awareness of your product, service, and brand. Social bookmarketing techniques can alert individuals, businesses, and search engines about announcements, new content, or other relevant information placed on your site. It is also helpful in creating backlinks and inbound links that will increase confidence in your brand. If you would like to be more active on the social networking scene and do not have the time or personality to "get connected," consider having a social media company such as Search Engine Optimization (**www.searchengineoptimisation.com/social-media.html**) set up and monitor the entire process for you.

Connecting with other wheatgrass growers

As with any individual that forges out on a mission, having a support group to challenge and encourage you is important. Being a new business owner and building a fledgling business is no different. The process can be lonely and even frustrating at times. You might suffer even more if you have left a big company of office parties, health benefits, and a steady income to forge out on your own. Do not despair. Also, do not think that you are alone in this situation. As mentioned in Chapter 10, thousands of individuals have taken up the challenge of starting a business at home. Many have succeeded and are more than willing to share their experiences with you. The Internet makes it possible to connect with wheatgrass growers all over the world. It is only a matter of finding them, and social media, once again, can help.

You can also meet other wheatgrass growers at trade shows and other events. Be sure to exchange contact information so that you can keep in touch and "follow" each other online. Most importantly, reach out through your own online profiles. Make your expertise available to others, and keep your business approachable. There might be someone out there in cyberspace who needs to get connected with you.

Quick tips for making social media work for professional interests

- Set up a Facebook page for business networking. Post updates about products and services and get customer feedback on products and services.

- Evaluate and join an appropriate group on Facebook. Post your interest in the group and join in discussions to become recognized as an expert in your field.

- Create a profile on Twitter, emphasizing your expertise. Link to your business site or an online CV.

- Use Twitter to announce new products, services, or events pertaining to your business.

- Use LinkedIn to build relationships with other professionals, find helpful advice from industry experts, find employees, and connect with past and present colleagues and classmates for possible business opportunities.

- Use YouTube to share business expertise and market products and services.

- Choose a blogging platform and create a blog based on your product and services.

Establishing your own virtual community

Following the purpose and structure of these popular sites, a number of smaller community sites have developed offering a more personalized experience to users by focusing more tightly on a specific interest of the membership. These specialty sites, or "niche" sites, have prompted a move from large and small businesses alike to set up their own site to stay connected with employees and customers. There are many avenues to be explored with the decision to develop a social media site. What is the purpose of the site? Who will develop and host it? What legalities are involved? Who will work out the logistics? Who will manage the site? A professional programmer or designer can help you answer these questions and work with you on the building of the site. You can also subscribe to Ning (**www.ning.com**), which is a program that allows you to create your own social network site. Ning sites are a good way to stay in touch with a specific group you are working with, be it your employees, customers, or others in the industry.

Marketing and communications is key to moving your business from one level to the next. Although advertising, public relations, sales promotions, and direct sales are great tools for creating this elevation, today's businesses have broadened their marketing strategies to include a more interactive approach to growing a business. Social media is the latest in the history of communication tools. Social media strategy incorporated into the marketing and communications plan completes the communications puzzle.

Forging ahead

Once you have gotten your new marketing and communications plan underway, there is little more you can really do but forge ahead. You are bound to face many challenges, but remember there are others who have started where you have started and have gone on to become quite successful with their business endeavors. In several of the case studies presented in this book, you can find prime examples of business success — from growers of wheatgrass to distributors of wheatgrass products or tools to health services utilizing wheatgrass. And yet, there are many others across the globe who have created headlines with their wheatgrass endeavors.

CONCLUSION

"The only thing that stands between a person and their own perfect health is information."

~ Mike Adams, The Health Ranger

Wheat has a history of over 9,000 years and is one of the world's most important food crops. It is believed to have originated in the Middle East and was one of the first plants to be cultivated during that time. Wheat cultivation resulted in great changes in the lives of the people in that area. They no longer had to wander across the land in search of food and were able to plant wheat seeds and grow wheat in designated locations. This resulted in the establishment of permanent settlements due to the abundant production of the wheat crop. Wheat became a staple food supply and was so plentiful that it was able to be shared with other lands. This sharing initiated trade between various cultures. By 4000 B.C., wheat farming became so popular it spread into Europe, Asia, and North Africa. Several new varieties of wheat were developed as selected kernels were passed down by farmers from one year's crop to the next. By the year 2000, the world's wheat production was recorded at about 21 billion bushels.

Wheat is a national food staple in many countries. Its per capita consumption in the United States surpasses that of any other single food staple. In the United States, it is also the main cereal grain used for export and domestic consumption. Various types of wheat are used for various purposes. Of the five major classes of wheat grown in the United States, hard red spring and hard red winter are the prevalent classes. It is the hard red winter grain that is sprouted for the production of wheatgrass.

Wheatgrass, like the parent wheat grain, has made, and is still currently making, changes in the lives of people.

In the words of Ann Wigmore, "Health is what one makes of it." She goes on to say that it takes discipline and a mature attitude to rebuild failing health. In the words of Mary Kay Ash, founder of Mary Kay Products, Inc., "You can go as far as your mind lets you. What you believe, remember, you can achieve."

So, what is the conclusion to this entire matter of growing, using, and selling wheatgrass? The conclusion is that wheatgrass, a simple gift of nature in the cereal grass family gramineae, has the power to significantly change your life, be it physical, mental, social, or economical. No wonder it is called "green gold."

Suppliers of Wheatgrass and Wheatgrass-related Paraphernalia

U.S. Growers and Manufacturers

Amazing Grass
San Francisco, California
415-722-5710
Grower and processor of whole-leaf wheatgrass
www.amazinggrass.com

Catalog for Healthy Eating
Summertown, Tennessee
800-695-2241
Wheatgrass kits, automatic sprouters, sprouting seeds, fertilizer, and literature
www.healthy-eating.com/ sproutseeds.html

Dogwood Gardens Organic Farms
Wheeler, Texas
903-833-1024
Supplier of fresh Genesis wheatgrass, wheatgrass kits, and wheatgrass powder blends
www.wheatgrassman.com

Dynamic Nutraceuticals
Sebastopol, California
877-396-2473
Suppliers of freeze-dried wheatgrass juice — regular and mint-flavored
www.dyna-green.com

Gourmet Greens
Chester, Vermont
802-875-3820, Ext. 4; 866-616-8698

Supplier of certified organic wheatgrass and sprouts, seeds, and other supplies, and wheatgrass juicers
www.gourmetgreens.com

Grow Wheatgrass
Carpinteria, California
805-684-4071
Seller of wheatgrass kits, multi-tiered sprouters, juicers, and instructional DVD
www.growwheatgrass.com

Perfect Foods
Monroe, New York
800-933-3288; fax 845-651-2262
Major supplier of fresh wheatgrass, frozen grass juice, and wheatgrass juicers
www.800wheatgrass.com

Pines International, Inc.
Lawrence, Kansas
800-MY-PINES (800-697-4637); fax 785-841-1252
A full-line carrier of cereal products such as wheat, barley, alfalfa, and oats. Products are 100 percent whole-leaf, dried grasses of wheat and barley in powder or tablet form.
www.wheatgrass.com

Shasta View Wheatgrass
Ashland, Oregon
541-708-0248
A western supplier of fresh-grown trays of various sizes, a wheatgrass-barley combo, and wheatgrass for pets
www.shastaviewwheatgrass.com

Sheldon Farm, LLC
Chaplin, Connecticut
866-974-3375; fax 860-974-2836
A supplier of greenhouse-grown, freeze-dried wheatgrass juice in powder or capsule form

Sproutman.com
Great Barrington, Massachusetts
413-528-5200; fax 413-528-5201
Supplier of fresh organic wheatgrass, sprouting paraphernalia, literature, consultations, and wheatgrass juice powders, creams, sprays, and extracts
www.sproutman.com

Sproutpeople
San Francisco, California
877-777-6887
Supplier of wheatgrass seeds and growing kits
http://sproutpeople.org

Sun Grown Organics Distributors, Inc.
San Diego, California
800-995-7776
Distributor of fresh wheatgrass and sprouts
www.sungrownorganics.com

The Sprout House
Saugerties, New York
800-777-6887
Large supplier of wheatgrass kits, EasyGreen sprouter, seeds, and other supplies
www.sprouthouse.com

The Wheatgrass Grower, LLC
Clarks Summit, Pennsylvania
570-587-5704
Supplier of fresh-cut wheatgrass,
sunflower greens, and wheatgrass
floral pieces
www.wheatgrassgrower.com

Wheatgrass Express
Gainesville, Florida
800-859-4779; fax 386-462-7398
Sells certified organic wheatgrass
grown with Ocean Grown mineral
fertilizer and wheatgrass kits
www.wheat-grass.com

WheatgrassKits.com
West Springville, Utah
801-491-8700; fax 801-491-8728
Major manufacturer of wheatgrass
kits and supplier of a full-line of
wheatgrass supplies
www.wheatgrasskits.com

International Suppliers

Aquilahealth
South Africa
+2711 704-4949; fax +2711 704-6262
Supplier of wheatgrass juicers
and sprouters
www.aquilahealth.co.za

Bondi Wheatgrass Juice Company
Australia
02 9694 1100; fax 02 9694 1177
Offers a full line of products and
services pertaining to wheatgrass
and barley
www.bondiwheatgrass.com.au

DynamicGreens
Canada
877-843-9452; 905-910-0467
Major supplier of frozen field-grown
wheatgrass juice
www.dynamicgreens.com

Evergreen Juices, Inc.
Canada
1-877-91JUICE (877-915-8423)
Supplies frozen wheatgrass juice cubes
to health food stores across America
www.evergreenjuices.com

InnerGarden Wheatgrass
Canada
780-432-3424; 888-299-3807
Supplier of fresh and frozen
wheatgrass, wheatgrass kits, and juicers
www.innergardenwheatgrass.com

Keimling Naturkost GmbH
Germany
+49(0)4161-5116-12;
fax +49(0)4161-5116-16
Supplier of wheatgrass juice powders
and juicers
www.keimling.de

Mumm's Sprouting Seeds
Canada
306-747-2935; fax 306-747-3618
Supplier of organic wheatgrass seed
for sprouting
www.sprouting.com

NatureSource Organics Ltd.
New Zealand
1-866-838-3336 (free in U.S.); 0800-
400-900; fax 64-9-270 0291

Major distributor of bottled
wheatgrass and barley juice
www.naturesgreenz.com

Sprout Organic Wheatgrass
Australia
1300-79-30-70
Supplier of wheatgrass growing kits
and wheatgrass juicers
www.sprout.net.au

Wheatgrass Pty. Ltd.
Australia
+61 2 8579 0000; 1300 73 11 55; fax
61-3-9827-6293
Supplier of wheatgrass drink,
therapeutic sprays, extracts, and creams
www.drwheatgrass.com

Wheatgrass
Health Centers

Ann Wigmore Foundation
San Fidel, New Mexico
505-552-0595
www.wigmore.org

Ann Wigmore Institute
Rincon, Puerto Rico
787-868-6307; fax 787-868-2430
www.annwigmore.org

Assembly of Yahweh Living Foods
Eaton Rapids, Michigan
517-663-1637
http://assemblyofyahweh
.rawfoods.htm

Bastyr Center for Natural Health
Seattle, Washington
206-834-4100; fax 206-834-4107

http://bastyrcenter.org

Creative Health Institute
Union City, Michigan
866-426-1213; 517-278-6260
www.creativehealthinstitute.com

Hallelujah Acres
Shelby, North Carolina/Plant City,
Florida/Branson, Missouri
800-651-7622; 704-481-1700 (NC)
www.hacres.com
www.halifestylecenters.com

Hippocrates Health Institute
West Palm Beach, Florida
561-471-8876; 800-842-2125
www.hippocratesinst.com

Living Foods Institute
Atlanta, Georgia
800-844-9876; 404-524-4488
www.livingfoodsinstitute.com

Optimum Health Institute
San Diego, California/Austin, Texas
800-993-4325; 619-464-3346 (CA);
fax 619-589-4098 (CA)
512-303-4817 (TX); fax 512-303-
1239 (TX)
www.optimumhealth.org
www.optimumhealth.com

Tree of Life Center
Patagonia, Arizona
866-394-2520; 520-394-2520
www.treeoflife.nu

The UK Centre for Living Foods
Ludlow, England
+44(0)1584-875308
www.livingfoods.co.uk

Abscisic acid: A plant hormone related to vitamin A

Acetylcholine: An essential neuro-transmitter in the nervous system

Acai berry: *Euterpe oleracea,* comes from the Brazilian palm tree of the Amazon rainforest

Alfalfa: *Medicago sativa,* a perennial plant

Alopecia areata: A skin condition resulting in patchy and sometimes complete hair loss

Alphatocopherol: The most active of the eight forms of vitamin E

Amla fruit: *Emblica officinalis gaertn,* also known as Indian gooseberry

Ames Bacterial Mutagenicity Test: A test for determining if a chemical is mutagenic and potentially cancer-causing

Amino acids: Part of the enzyme and hormonal system, essential for proper nutrition

Amygdalin: A water-soluble compound naturally found in whole foods, fruit seeds, beans, and grass

Amylase: A digestive enzyme

Anticarcinogenic: Substances that work against the formation of cancer

Antimutagenic: An agent that hinders mutations or changes to a cell's DNA structure

Antioxidant: A collection of vitamins, minerals, amino acids, essential fatty acids, and enzymes

Antiseptic: A disinfectant

Arginine: An amino acid necessary for infants

Atherosclerosis: A build-up of cholesterol or other fatty substances along the walls of the arteries

Autoimmunity: A condition where the body's immune system attacks and damages normal body tissue

Autointoxication: An ancient belief that undigested foods accumulate in the colon causing toxic-producing mucus that, when absorbed into the bloodstream, poisons the body

Autolyzing: When the body processes its own fats and protein for energy because it has been deprived of foods for an extended period of time

Auxin: A substance found in the roots of wheatgrass that encourages cell repair

Avitaminosis: A disease developed from chronic vitamin deficiency

Barley: A cereal grass similar to wheatgrass

Beta-carotene: A processor of vitamin A, an antioxidant compound in plants

Biochemistry: The study of chemical substances and how they work within the body

Bioflavonoid: A group of antioxidants found naturally in plants

Biosolids: Sewage sludge

Biotin: A member of the vitamin B complex that is needed for the metabolism of protein, fats, and carbohydrates

Bloat: *See gastric dilation-vovulus (GDV)*

Boron: A trace mineral that plays an important role in brain activity

Bran: The outer coating of a grain kernel

Business assets: Business purchases that have long-term value

Business plan: A document that outlines the key functional areas of a business

Calcium: A mineral that works in the body to aid enzyme activity; helps build bones and teeth

Candida yeast: A fungus that causes an infection in the body often referred to as a yeast infection

Carcinoma: A malignant tumor

Celiac: A disease of the digestive organs in which the small intestine is damaged and the absorption of nutrients from food is hindered

Cereal grasses: Grasses that produce a starchy, edible grain

Chelator: A chemical that bonds with and removes toxins from substances

Chlorella: A dark-green micro-algae

Chlorophyll: A pigment in plants that gives them their rich, green color; absorbs sunlight into the plant to create energy

Chromium: A metallic substance that works with insulin in the metabolism of blood sugar

Choline: Lecithin, a nutrient in the B vitamin family, which is responsible for the manufacturing of acetylcholine

Cobalt: An essential mineral that helps the body to produce vitamin B12

Colon hydrotherapy: Also known as colon irrigation; eliminates toxins from the colon by flushing the waste matter out with water

Company brand: Personal image that appeals to the target audience and sets the business apart from the competition

Competition: Other businesses with the same product group

Composting: The biological breakdown of organic wastes by microorganisms and earthworms

Conjugated linoleic acid (CLA): A polyunsaturated fatty acid with close chemical make-up to linoleic acid

Copper: Helps with iron absorption, increasing energy levels in the body

Corporation: Consists of an individual or a group of individuals who own shares in a company and are protected by the company from legal liabilities

Cortisol: A hormone manufactured by the adrenal gland in response to stress

Crop residues: Materials left in the field after a crop has been harvested; the material left after a product has been processed for use

Cyanuric acid: A water-soluble compound formed by heating urea

Dental fluorosis: A condition caused by too much fluoride

Dermatitis: An inflammation of the skin due to an allergic reaction

Detoxify: The process of ridding the body of toxins or pollutants

Dextromethorphan (DXM): A drug found in medicines and suppressants

DHA: A form of omega-3 that is more readily assimilated by the body

Distillation: The process of boiling water to produce steam

Domain name: The designated, registered name of your website

Drug iatrogenesis: Adverse effects of prescription drugs

Dulse: A sea vegetable

Durum wheat: A tetraploid wheat type

E-commerce site: A website that allows you to sell merchandise or information

Einkorn: A type of ancient wheat

Embryo: The part of a seed that grows into a new plant if germinated

Emmer: A type of ancient wheat

Emulsified cosmetics: Cosmetics that include ingredients that do not blend with one another

Endosperm: The main part of the seed from which white flour is processed

Enema: The process of introducing liquids into the colon or rectum by way of the anus for the purpose of elimination

Entrepreneur: A person who organizes a business and assumes risk for it

Enzymes: Help control the metabolic processes of the body

Essential fatty acids: Fats or organic acids that the body needs but cannot produce itself

Ethionine: A toxin that can damage the liver

Ethylene gas: An odorless hormone that causes fruit to ripen and decay

Exfoliation: The process of removing dead skin cells from the surface of the skin

Fasting: Temporarily abstaining or resting from all or some food and/or beverages

Fermented food: Food produced or preserved by microorganisms

Fermenting: The chemical decomposition (breaking down) of organic substances

Filler: An ingredient added to fill a space or add weight or size to a substance

Fluoride: A form of the chemical element fluorine

Folate: Helps produce and maintain body cells and helps protects against cancer

Folic acid: Vitamin B9 folic acid and folate are paired together; folic acid (along with vitamin B12) helps with the manufacturing of nerve transmitters and the formation and division of all body cells

Free radicals: The by-products of metabolism; unbalanced molecules that can damage healthy cells by altering them and causing them to malfunction

Gallstone: Solid particles from bile components in the gallbladder

Gastric dilation: The swelling of the stomach from gas

Gastric dilatation-volvulus (GDV): A gastrointestinal disease affecting primarily large and giant dog breeds; also called bloat

Germ: *See embryo*

Germination: Takes place when a plant emerges from a seed and begins to grow

Ginseng: An immune stimulant

Globin: A blood protein

Guarana: A nutritious fruit from the Amazon rainforest

Gluten: Nutritional protein found in some cereal grains

Goitrogen: A naturally occurring substance that can interfere with the functioning of the thyroid gland

Goji plant: A woody perennial classified in the nightshade family of plants; nightshade is the common name for the *Solanaceae* plant family, some of which are edible while some are poisonous

Grains: The seeds of cereal grasses

Granulocyte colony-stimulating factors (GCSF): A hormone used to help the blood marrow produce stem cells and white blood cells

Grass Juice Factor: The nutrient found in all cereal grasses

Green blood: *See wheatgrass*

Green gold: *See wheatgrass*

Groats: Oat straw

Growth factors: Natural substances that promote cell growth

Healing crisis: A reaction of the body to the detoxification process

Hematological toxicity: A blood disorder, such as anemia, which can be potentially life-threatening

Hemolytic: An agent that opens red blood cells and releases hemoglobin

Hemorrhoid: Portions of the anal canal that help control bowel movements; can become inflamed and infected

Herbicides: Chemical weed killers

Hernia: The expulsion of an internal organ through a damaged portion of the abdominal cavity

Histidine: An amino acid necessary for infants

Holistic: Alternative health practice for the treatment of ailments

Homocysteine: An amino acid; excessive amounts of

homocysteine in the blood can increase the risk of stroke and coronary heart disease

Homeopathy: A form of alternative medicine

Homeostatic agent: An agent that controls balance

Hormones: Chemical substances produced in the body to regulate the activity of cells or organs

Hydrogen peroxide: A natural by-product of oxygen metabolism

Hydroponically: A method of growing plants without soil

Hypoglycemia: A condition where blood sugar levels are too low

Induction period: The time for contracting a disease after exposure to infecting agent

Inorganic: When plants are grown using chemicals or synthetic fertilizers

Insoluble fiber: Fiber that is not water-soluble

Intangible assets: Business assets that represent values that cannot be physically touched

In vitro: Tests done in a controlled environment outside of the organism, such as a test tube

In vivo: Tests conducted within a cell or an organism

Iodine: Important for healthy reproduction

Iron: Essential for the metabolism of the B group vitamins

Isoleucine: An amino acid

Jointing theory: A concept patented by Charles Schabel to determine the maturity of the wheat plant; the precise timing of wheatgrass sprout growth

Kamut: A versatile plant closely related to the wheat plant

Kelp: A sea vegetable

Kernel: Large cereal seeds

Ketone toxins: Pollutants in the bloodstream

Ketosis: A toxic condition in the body that can cause organs to fail

Lactobacillus: One of the bacteria that promotes colon health

Laetrile: The trade name for a substance allegedly synthesized and patented by Dr. Ernest Krebs, Jr., a California biochemist, for treating "disorders of intestinal fermentation;" chemically related to amygdalin, a naturally occurring substance found in some fruit seeds

Latrogenic injuries: Injuries resulting from medical treatment or advice

L-cavanine: A substance that can cause abnormal blood cell counts, spleen enlargement, or recurrence of lupus in patients with a controlled disease

Lecithin: Fatty substances found in animals and plant tissues

Leucine: An amino acid

Liability insurance: Protects you and your business from unseen circumstances that could be financially devastating

Linolenic acid (ALA): An omega-3 fatty acid, an essential fatty acid vital to human health

Lipase: A digestive enzyme

Limited liability company (LLC): A cross between a partnership and a corporation

Lysine: A genetically coded amino acid, vital for good nutrition

Living food: Food that is still growing

Macronutrition: Nutrition, or caloric intake based on protein, carbohydrates, and fat, the three main components of food

Mange: A contagious skin disease caused by mites, a tick-like organism

Magnesium: Essential for the conversion of stored blood sugar into energy

Manganese: Helps with the building of bone and is needed to manufacture thyroxine

Marketing: The means of letting your audience know about your business and its product or service

Marketing strategy: Helps to identify how you will reach your prospective audience

Melamine: A chemical compound used in cleaning

products, plastic, foam, and fertilizer

Melanoma: A skin tumor

Menagerie: A collection of common and exotic animals kept in human captivity

Methionine: An amino acid

Micronutrition: Includes trace minerals and phytochemicals

Microorganisms: Organisms that cannot be seen with the naked eye

Miso: A flavorful Japanese condiment made from aged soybean

Molluscum contagiosum: A common viral infection of school-aged children involving small, itchy spots that appear on the child's skin

Molybdenum: An essential trace element in plant metabolism that helps with the assimilation of iron

Mustard greens: The pungent, peppery leaves of the mustard plant

Myelin sheath: The membrane surrounding a nerve fiber

Myelotoxicity: A potentially life-threatening bone marrow disease caused by chemotherapy

Myoglobin: The red pigment in muscle and blood cells

Naturopathy: A form of alternative health

Naturopathic: Pertaining to alternative health; a physician that works with natural medicines

Nephron: The filter in the kidneys

Niacin: Vitamin B3; plays a key role in cell restoration

Ning: A program that allows you to create your own social network

Nitrogen: A major plant nutrient benefitting plant growth

Nonpathogenic: A term referring to substances, such as bacteria that do not cause harm to the human body

Non-emulsified cosmetics: Cosmetics that include blend ingredients

Noni: An evergreen shrub related to the coffee tree

Nonpathogenic: Does not cause harm to the human body

Novel food: A food product or ingredient that was not used significantly in the European Union before May 15, 1997

Oat grass: A pasture grass that grows from oat grain seeds

Omega-3: Essential fatty acids needed by the body

Organic: Plants grown without using chemicals or synthetic fertilizers

Organic soil: Soil that is nutritionally balanced

Osteoarthritis: Joint arthritis

Overhead: The costs required to run the business

Over-the-counter (OTC) drugs: Medicines that can be purchased by the consumer without a doctor's prescription

Oxalates: Naturally occurring substances found in plants, animals, and humans

Oxidation: A chemical reaction that occurs when a substance interacts with oxygen; turns food dark

Partnership: Formed when two or more individuals decide to join together to operate a business

Pantothenic acid: Vitamin B5; works with the enzymes responsible for the metabolism of proteins, fat, and carbohydrates and the synthesis of fatty acids and amino acids

Pasteurization: A process that uses high temperatures to destroy bacteria in foods

Pathogens: Organisms that cause disease

Pectin: A fibrous structure found in plants that is useful in gelling foods and drinks

Penicillin: An antibiotic derived from mold

Peptic ulcers: Open sores in the lining of the stomach

Performance status: Time period between blood transfusions

Perlite: Mineral formed from volcanic glass used in gardening

Peroxidase: An antioxidant that detoxifies the body by eliminating hydrogen peroxide

Phenylalanine: An amino acid

Phosphorus: Works along with the B group vitamins to help the body to use energy from starches and fats

Photosynthesis: The process of turning light energy into chemical energy

Plant mats: The intertwined root mats from the wheatgrass blades after they have been harvested

Phytochemicals: Micronutrition derived from plant nutrients

Potassium: Balances body acids and water and helps with the function of muscles and nerves

Poultice: A treatment for pain or inflammation

Predigested food: Food fermented outside the body

Profit margin: A company's net profit divided by total sales

Prophylactic: Preventive measure

Protein: Made up of amino acids; a part of every cell, muscle, tissue, and bone; builds and maintains tissues in the body

Protein blends: Products composed of more than one type of protein

Protease: A digestive enzyme

Purgative: Acts on the body as a cleanser, usually evacuating the bowels

Purines: Naturally occurring substances found in plants, animals, and humans

Pyridoxine: Vitamin B6; needed for proper food assimilation as well as the metabolism of protein and fat; also helps the body to absorb vitamin B12

P4D1: A compound found in young cereal grasses that works to repair DNA molecules and strips the protein sheath off cancer cells

Raw food: Food that is not cooked

Raw foodist: A person whose diet consists of 75 percent or more raw and living foods

Refined grains: Grains that have been significantly modified

Rejuvelac: A fermented wheatberry drink

Resource guarders: Dogs who are overly possessive about a possession

Rheumatoid arthritis: A disease that causes joint inflammation

Riboflavin: Vitamin B2; important for proper cell growth and general body health

Roughage: Fiber that helps with the elimination process

Rye: A member of the wheat family that resembles barley and oats

Sanitarian: An on-site inspector of restaurants and food preparation facilities

Scenedesmus: Algae similar to chlorella

Sea vegetables: Various types of sea plants, like seaweed, that grow in the ocean

Seborrheic: Relating to seborrhea, which is a skin disorder commonly known as dandruff

Sebum: An oily substance secreted by the skin

Seed: Consists of an embryonic plant, its food store, and a covering called the seed coat

Selenium: Works as an antioxidant enzyme in the body

Share: A divided portion of the value of a company

Sludge: Matter taken from sewage systems and industrial waste plants

Social networking sites: Social websites characterized by individuals reaching out to those they already know for the purpose of socializing or keeping in touch

Sodium: The major moderator of the body's water and mineral balance

Sole proprietor: Someone who operates the business as an individual

Spelt: An ancient form of the common wheat grain

Spina bifida: The incomplete development of the backbone and spinal cord

Spinach: A nutrient-dense, dark, leafy vegetable

Spirulina: Blue-green algae; a form of bacteria

Sprouts: Sprouted seeds

Sulfur: Helps regulate oxygen, which is important for proper brain function

Sulfured and pasteurized fruits: Contain sulfur dioxide as a preservative

Super food: A term given to food with an exceptionally high nutrient content

Superoxide dismutase (SOD): A powerful anti-aging enzyme that presents a high defense against the free radical damage of red blood cells and works to eliminate radiation damage in cells; also keeps the superoxide balance in check

Tamari: A flavorful Japanese condiment made from aged soybean

Tangible assets: Business purchases that have a physical existence

Thalassemia: An inherited blood disorder in which the patient has difficulty producing hemoglobin or produces defective hemoglobin; characterized by abnormally small red blood cells

Thiamine: Vitamin B1; encourages growth and strengthens the heart muscle

Threonine: An amino acid

Thrombin: Protein in the blood that acts as a coagulate, causing blood to clot

Thyroid hormones: Regulate metabolism, which affects a person's weight

Tryptophan: An amino acid

Thyroxine: The main hormone of the thyroid gland

Triglycerides: A major form of fat in the body used for energy

Ulcerative colitis: An inflammation of the large intestine and rectum

Urea: A substance in the urine

Vermiculite: Naturally occurring mineral; expands when heat is applied

Valine: An amino acid

Villi: Finger-like projections in the walls of the small intestine

Virtual assistant: A professional online service provider

Vitamins: Organic molecules that play various roles within the body

Vitamin B12: Water-soluble vitamin present in some foods

Vitamin B17: Laetrile, a chemically modified form of amygdalin, which is a substance found in seeds

Vitamin C: An essential antioxidant that aids wound healing and strengthens the body's resistance to infection

Vitamin E: Fat-soluble vitamin used as an antioxidant to protect the body from carcinogens; short name for tocopherols and tocotrienols

Vitamin F: Essential fatty acids in the form of omega-3 and omega-6; needed for tissue repair

Vitamin K: Produces thrombin and liver proteins responsible for blood clotting

Volvulus: Refers to a twisting of the stomach on its axis (line of connection to the body)

Water soluble: Able to be dissolved in water or another solvent

Weevils: Small beetles that sometimes attack wheat and other grain products

Web hosting: The space allowed to you for the publishing of your website

Wheat: A grain in the cereal grass family gramineae

Wheatberries: Wheat seeds for making flour or sprouting

Wheatgrass: The young blades of the common cereal wheat plant

Wheat grass: A variety of cereal grasses such as oats, barley, and rye that are grown in open fields

Wheatgrass juice: Dark, green liquid that is expressed from wheatgrass and converted into energy; a blood-cleansing agent

Yeast infection: *See Candida yeast*

Zinc: Helps the immune system to function properly

BIBLIOGRAPHY

Applied Ozone Systems <http://oxymega.com>.

Amazing Grass <http://www.amazinggrass.com/our-difference.html>.

DynamicGreens <http://dynamicgreens.com/>.

Green Life Foods <<http://www.greenlifefoods.co.uk/faq.htm>.

Organic Wheatgrass Plus <http://www.organicwheatgrassplus.com/winter_cultivation.htm>.

Store-it Foods <http://www.storeit foods.com/page/juicers-wheatgrass>.

The Wheatgrass Grower, <http://www.wheatgrassgrower.blogspot.com/>.

"100 Quick and Easy Recipes." *World's Healthiest Foods,* <http://www.whfoods.com/recipestoc.php>.

"Acai Reviews and What to Look for When Buying Acai." *Acai.org* <http://www.acai.org>.

"Alfalfa Grass." *Alfalfa Benefits* <http://www.alfalfabenefits.net>.

"Alkalize and Revitalize." *Health Before Beauty* <http://www.healthbeforebeauty.com/?q=alkalize-and-revitalize>.

"All About Acai." *World of Acai,* 2007: <http://www.worldofacai.com/PDFs/AllAboutAcai.pdf>.

Anderson, Jeff. "Digestive Enzymes." *The Daily PT,* June 10, 2009: <http://www.military-fitness.military.com/2009/06/digestive-enzymes.html>.

Anonymous. "How to Win at Social Networking." *The Futurist,* 2009.

Associated Press, "J & J Sales Plunge as New Drug Recall Announced." *North Jersey*, July 8, 2010: pp 1-2.

Avery, Robert W. "Enzyme Nutrition." *All Raw Times*, February 2006: <http://www.rawtimes.com/m2mEnzymeNutrtition.html>.

"Avocados, Raw, All commercial Types." *SelfNutrition Data* <http://www.nutritondataself.com/facts/fruits-and-fruit-juices/1843/2>.

Balch, James F., M.D., Phyllis A. Balch, C.N.C. *Prescription for Nutritional Healing*. Garden City Park, NY: Avery Publishing Group, 1997.

Beetz, Alice E. *Sprouts and Wheatgrass Production and Marketing*. Abstract, Fayetteville, AR: National Center for Appropriate Technology, 1999.

Beetz, Alice E. *Wheatgrass Production*. Abstract, Fayettteville, AR: National Center for Appropriate Technology, 2002.

Belch, George E., Michael A. Belch. "Evaluating the Effectiveness of Elements of Integrated Marketing Communications: A Review of Research." *College of Business Administration*, San Diego, CA.

Berry, Tim. "How Long Should a Business Plan Be?" <http://articles.bplans.com/writing-a-business-plan/how-long-should-a-business-plan-be/49>.

BizFilings. "An Abbreviate Guide to Starting a Business." *StartupNation* <http://www.startupnation.com/>.

"Blood Type FAQ." *Eat Right for Your Blood Type* <http://www.dadamo.com/faq/smartfaq/cgi?subject=988813483#988882645>.

Boutenko, Victoria. *12 Steps to Raw Foods: How to End Your Dog's Dependency of Cooked Foods*. Berkeley, CA: North Atlantic Books, 1007.

Brooks, Megan. "Obesity and Depression are a Two Way Street." *Reuters*, March 4 2010: <http://www.reuters.com/article/idUSTRE6234RF20100304>.

Brosco, Jeffrey P., M.D. "History of Modern Medicine." *Department of History*, University of Miami: 2005.

Burton, Alec. "Fasting and Rejuvenation." *AlecBurton*, December 2009: <http://www.alecburton.com/2009/12/fasting-rejuvenation/>.

Calloway, D. H., W. K. Calhoun, A. H. Munson. "Further Studies on the Reduction of x-irradiaton of Guinea Pigs by Plant Materials." *Quartermaster Food and Container Institute for the Armed Forces Report*, 1961.

Castrillo, C., F. Vicente, J. A. Guada. "Urinary Energy Losses in Dogs Fed Commercial Extruded Foods." *PubMed,* 2001: <**http://www.ncbi.nlm.nih.gov/pubmed/11686795**>.

"Carnivore vs. Omnivore." *Vet Balance* <**http://www.vetbalance.com/index.php?/carnivore-vs.-omnivore.html**>.

Carroll, Will. "Health Benefits of Fasting." *Serendip,* January 2008: <**http://serendip.brynmawr.edu/exchange/node/1834**>.

Carton, Robert J., Ph.D., Douglas W. Cross. "Flouridation: A Violation of Medical Ethics and Human Rights." *Occupation and Environmental Health,* Vol. 9 Jan/March, No. 1: 2003.

Centers for Disease Control and Prevention. "Safe and Healthier Foods." *Morbidity and Mortality Weekly Report,* October 1999.

"Chemical Cuisine." *Center for Science in the Public Interest,* <**http://www.cspinet.org/reports/chemcuisine.htm**>.

Cheri Calbom, Maureen Keane. *Juicing For Life.* Garden City Park, NY: Avery Publishing Group, 1992.

"Childhood Overweight and Obesity." *Centers for Disease Control and Prevention* <**http://www.cdc.gov/obesity/childhood/index/.html**>.

Cichoke, Anthony J. *The Complete Book of Enzyme Therapy.* Avery Publishing Group, 1999.

Clemons, R. M., D.V.M, Ph.D. "Intergrative Treatment of Cancer in Dogs." *Department of Small Animals Clinical Services University of Florida,* 1997: <**http://www.neurovetmed.ufl.edu/neuro/AltMed/Cancer/_AltMed.htm**>.

"Collodial Soil and Collodial Minerals." <**http://www.northupfamily.com/Farms/Collodials.htm**>.

Colombo, Gail. "Wheat Grass for Cats; Living Food for the Modern Cat." *Paws and Purrs, Inc.* <**http://www.sniksnak.com/cathealth/wheatgrass.html**>.

"Compost Use and Soil Fertility." *New England Vegetable Management Guide,* <**http://www.nevegetable.org/index.php/cultural/fertility**>.

Connett, Paul Ph.D. "50 Reasons to Oppose Flouridation." *Flouride Action Network,* April 12, 2004: <**http://www.fluoridealert.org/50-reasons.htm**>.

Cross, Douglas W., Robert J. Carton, Ph.D. "Flouridation: A Violation of Medical Ethics and Human Rights." *Flouridation and Human Rights*, Vol 9 No. 1, Jan/March 2003: <http://www.fluoridealert.org/50-reasons. htm>.

"Couple Grows Business with Healing Power of Wheatgrass." *Pacific Business News.* <http://www.bizjournals.com/pacific/stories/1998/09/28/smallb2.html>.

Dach, Jeffrey M.D. "Wheatgrass, the Path to Health." *Natural Solutions with Bio Identical Hormones*, <http://www.drdach.com/wheatgrass_8WDU.html>.

"Death Begins in the Colon." *Ohhira Mountain Fruits extract.* <http://omx2u.com>.

Dengate, Sue. "Dangers of Dried Fruits." *Food Intolerance Network*, <http://www.fedupwithfoodadditives.info/factsheets/Factdriedfruit.htm>.

DesJardins, Andrea. "Determining the 'Naturalness' of a Product." *Free Articles: Tutorial*, 2000: <http://www.errc.org/hercarticles/natural.htm>.

Dorje, Jigme. "Research Demystifies the Lycium Berry." *Tibetan Goji Berries* <http://www.gojiberry.com/research-1>.

Driscoll, Carlos A., Juliet Clutton-Brock, Andrew C. Kitchener, Stephen J. O'Brien. "The Evolution of House Cats." *Scientific American*, June 2009: <http://scientificamerican.com/article.cfm?id=the-taming-of-the-cat>.

Edwards, Jim. "Tylenol Ran Fewer Ads Before April Recall." *AdWeek*, Ma 31. 2010: <http://www.adweek.com/aw/content_display/news/media/3if3484cb6d538b8el e2893d9a5522a70a?pn=1>.

Eliasen, Mogen. "The Dog's Digestive System." In *Raw Food for Dogs - the Ultimate Guide for Dog Owners*, by Mogen Eliasen, <k9joy.com/RawFoodforDogs/DigestiveSystemExcerpt.pdf>. Novasol Judicare.

"Enzymes and Longevity." *Living and Raw Foods*, 1991: <http://www.living-foods.com/articles/enzymes.html>.

Fallon, Sally. "Vitamin B12: Vital Nutrient for Good Health." *Nourished Magazine*, December 2008.

"Fit the Social Media Puzzle Piece into Your Marketing Strategy." *The Center for Associate Leadership.* <http://www.asaecenter.org/PublicationsResources/eNewsletterArticleDetail.cfm?ItemNumber=5092>.

"Food for Brain Power." *Healthy Holistic Living*, <http://www.healthy-holistic-living.com/food-for-brain-power.html>.

Foods That Harm, Foods That Heal. Pleasantville, NY: The Reader's Digest Association, 1997.

"Fortify Your Knowledge About Vitamins." *FDA Consumer Health Information,* 2009: <**http://www.fda.gov/forconsumers/consumerupdates/ucm118079.htm**>.

Fowlkes, K. K. "The History of Wheatgrass." *Natural Health Web.*

Fellers, Carl R. Ph.D. "Pasteurized Dry Fruits." *Massachusetts Agricultural College and Experiment Station.*

Francis, F. J. "Seventy-Five Years of Food Science." *Department of Food Science,* University of Massachusetts, 1997: <**http://www.umass.edu/foodsci/about/history. pdf**>.

Freedman, B.J. "Sulphur Dioxide in Food and Beverages: Its Use as a Preservative and Its Effect on Asthma." *Pub Med,* 1980: <**http://www.ncbi.nlm.gov/ pubmed/7426352**>.

"Fruit Composition and Nutritive Value." *Chest of Books,* <**http://chestofbooks. com/food/household/Foods-And-Household-Management/Fruit-Composition-And-Nutritive-Value.html**>.

Fukuoka, Masanobu. *The One-straw Revolution.* Emmaeus, PA: Rodale Press, 1987.

Gach, Jerry. "Worm Composting Turns Green Waste Into Black soil Addendum." *Solutions for Green.* <**http://www.californiagreensolutions/com/cgi-bin/gt/ tpl.h,content=1449**>.

Gibson, Lance, Garren Benson. "Origin, History, and Uses of Oat (*Avina sativa*) and Wheat (*Triticum aestivum*)." *Iowa State University Department of Agronomy,* January 2002: <**http://www.agron.iastate.edu/courses/agron212/readings/oat_ wheat_history.htm**>.

Gil Bar-Sela, Medy Tsalic, Getta Fried, Hadassah Goldberg. "Wheat Grass Juice May Improve Hematological Toxicity Related to Chemotherapy in Breast Cancer Patients: A Pilot Study." *Nutrition and Cancer,* 2007.

"Goji Berry Nutrition Information." *Goji Juices* <**http://www.gojijuices.net/nutritioninformation.html**>.

Gowariker, Vasant, M. N. Krishnamurthy, Sudha Gowariker, Manik Dhanorkar, Kalyani Paranjape, Norman Borlaug. *The Fertilizer Encylopedia.* 2009.

Hamed, S. F., Mousa A. Allam. "Application of FTIR Spectroscopy in the Determinant of Antioxidation Efficiency on Surfaces." *Journal of the Applied Sciences,* 2006: pp 27-33.

Harrison, R., and M. Thomas. "Identity in Online Communications: Social Networking Sites and Language Learning." *International Journal of Emerging Technologies and Society.*

"Health Benefits of Rye." *Elements 4 Health*, June 10, 2008: <**http://www.elements4health.com/rye-health-benefits.html**>.

Henderson, Tom. "Popeye Propaganda: Kids Strong to the Finish Because They Eat Their Spinach." *Parent Dish*, August 9, 2010: <**htttp://www.parentdish.com/2010/08/09/kids-strong-to-the-finish-because-they-eat-their-spinach.html**>.

Henry-Socha, Nancy A. "Selecting Commercial Compost." *Sustainable Urban Landscape Information Series*, Department of Horticultural Science: University of Minnesota. <**http://www.sustland.umn.edu/implement/compost.html**>.

"High Protein, Low Carb Diets." *WebMD*, 2008: <**http://www.women.webmd.com/guide/high-protein-low-carbohydrate-diet**>.

"History of Pet Food." *Sojourner Farms*, 2006: <**http://www.sojos.com/historyofpetfood.html**>.

Hiti, Miranda. "Heart Disease, Colon Cancer Link?" *WebMD*, September 2007: <**http://www.webmd.com/colorectal-cancer/news/20070925/heart-disease-colon-cancer-link**>.

Hosford-Dunn Holly, PhD. "Strategic Messaging to Build Brand." *Integrated Marketing Communications.*

"How Much Sleep Do We Really Need?" *National Sleep Foundation* <**http://www.sleepfoundation.org/article/how-sleep-works/how-much-sleepdo-we-really-need**>.

Howlett, Greg. "Comparing Barley Grass, Wheatgrass, and Other Cereal Grasses." *HealthWisdom*, 2006: <**http://healthwisdom.com/barleygreen/compare.asp**>.

"How to Use Social Media to Connect with Other Entrepreneurs" *Mashable* <**http://mashable.com/2010/01/09/social-media-connect-entrepreneurs/**>.

Huston, Lucy M. "What are Free Radicals and How to they Contribute Cancer?" *Free Article: Tutorial*, August: 2006.

Hunt, Peggy, Stoney Wright. "Wainwright Germplasm Slender Wheatgrass." *Alaska Plant Materials Center*, January 9, 2008.

"Importance of Herbs with Diet." *Amazing Natural Herbs for Healthy Living*, August 3, 2005: **<http://natural-herbsblogspot.com/2005/08/importance-of-herbs-with-diet_03.html>**.

"Importance of Marketing." *Exforsys Inc.* **<http://sss.exforsys.com/career-center/marketing-management/importance-of-marketing.html>**.

"Importance of Nuts and Seeds." *Best Home Remedies*, **<http://www.best-home-remedies.com/articles/nuts&seeds.htm>**.

"Intermediate Wheatgrass." *Range Plants of Utah*, 2004: **<http://extension.usu.edu/range/Grasses/intermediatewheat.htm>**.

Jarvis, William T., Ph.D. "Fasting." *National Council Against Health Fraud*, February 1: 2002.

—. "Wheatgrass Therapy." *National Council Against Health Fraud*, January 15: 2001.

Johnson, Caitlin A. "The High Cost of Pet Care." *CBS Morning Show*, January 24, 2007: **<http://www.cbsnews.com/stories/2007/01/24/earlyshow/contributors/debbiereturner/main2393732.shtml>**.

Kessler, Karl. "Wheat 'Pasture' is for People, Too." *The Wheatgrass People*, 1997: **<http://www.wheatgrass.com/1997.05.15.as-seen-in-the-furrow-spring-1997/>**.

Kim, Ben. "Is Fasting One Day a Week Good for Your Health?" *Dr. Ben Kim*, June 2010: **<http://dr.benkim.com/fasting-fast-one-day-week.htm>**.

"Knowledge and Use of Folic Acid Among Women of Reproductive Age." *Centers for Disease Controls and Prevention*, 1998: **<http://www.cdc.gov/mmwr/preview/mmwrhtml/mm5010a2.htm>**.

Lagerquist, Ron. "How Long Should I Fast?" *FreedomYou*, **<http://www.freedomyou.com/fasting_book/length%20of%20fast.htm>**.

Lartique, M. "The Influence of Diet on the Biological Effects of Whole Body Radiation." *Quartermaster Food and Container Institute for the Armed Forces Report*, 1950.

"Leading Causes of Death." *Centers for Disease Control and Prevention*, 2006: **<http://www.cc.gov/nchs/fastats/lcod/htm>**.

Lee, William H R.P.H., Ph.D., Michael Rosembaum, M.D. *Chlorella — The Sun-powered Super Nutrient and Its Beneficial Properties.* **<http://www.chlorella-europe.com/literature.html>**.

LegalZoom. "Advantages and Benefits of Forming an LLC for Your Small Business." *NuWire Investor*, May 26, 2009: <htttp://www.nuwireinvestor.com/articles/advantages-and-benefits-of-forming-an-llc-for-your-small-53004.aspx>.

Levy, Juliette de Bairacli. *The Complete Herbal Book for the Dog.* Queens Square London: Faber and Faber, 1955.

"Livingston-Wheeler Therapy." *Memorial Sloan-Kettering Cancer Center*, December 11, 2009: <http://www.mskcc.org/mskcc/html/69283.cfm>.

"Method for Growing and Using Wheatgrass Nutrients and Products Thereof." *Patent Genius*, 1988: <http://www.patentgenius.com/patent/5820916.html>.

Meyerowitz, Steve. *Wheatgrass Nature's Finest Medicine.* Great Barrington, Mass: Sproutman Publications, 2006.

McClure, Joy, Kendall Layne. *Cooking for Consciousness.* Willow Springs, MO: NUCLEUS Publications, 1993.

"Miso." *Soya.be*, 2010: <http://www.soya.be/what-is-miso.php>.

Monastyrsky, Konstantin. "How Often Should I Move My Bowels?" <http://www.gutsense.org/constipation/frequency.html>.

Moore, Rusty. "High Insulin Levels Stop Fat Loss and Cause Weight Gain." *The Fitness Black Book*, May 2008: <http://fitnessblackbook.com/dieting_ for_ fat loss/high-insulin-levels-stop-fat-loss-and-cause-weight-gain/>.

"Myth About Raw Feeding." <http://www.rawfed.com/myths/omnivores.html>.

Nagel, Rami. "Tissue and Bowel Cleansing." *Your Return*, 2007: <http://www.yourreturn.org/Inertia/Bowel _Cleansing.htm>.

"Natural Garden Pest Control." *EarthEasy* <http://eartheasy.com/yard-garden/natural-pest-control>.

"Neglected Crops: 1492 From a Different Perspective." *FAO Corporate Document Repository; Plant Production and Protection Series*, 1995: <http://www.fao.org/docrep/t0646E0b.htm>.

Newman, Lisa B., N.D., Ph.D., Lee Veith, DVM. "Cautions Against Raw Food Diets." *Azmira Holistic Animal Care*, 2002: <http://www.azmira.com/StudyRawFoodDiets.htm>.

Nicholas, P. F., W. V. Cruess. "Sulfur Dioxide as Dried Fruit Preservative." *ACS Publications*, 1932: <http://pubs.acs.org/doi/abs/10.1021/ie50270a016>.

"Obesity and Depression May Be Linked." *ScienceDaily*, June 6 2008: **<http://www.sciencedaily.com/releases/2008/06/080602152913.htm>**.

"Obesity in Children." *Ann Collins* **<http://www.anncollins.com/obesity-in-children.htm>**.

"Organic Gardening: Importance of Balanced Soils." *Eco Walk the Talk*, June 14 2010: **<http://www.ecowalkthetalk.com/blog/2010/06/14/organic-gardening-importance-of-balanced-soils/>**.

Patenaude, Frederic. "What's Wrong With Wheatgrass." **<http://www.fredericpatenauds.com/blog/?p=253>**.

"Pet Food Recalls." *ASPCA* **<http://www.aspca.org/pet-care/pet-food-recall-overview.html>**.

"PH Scale, pH level, pH Balance." *Balance-pH-Diet*, **<http://www.balance-ph-diet.com/pH_scale.html>**.

PhysOrg.com. *Mediterranean diet is healthy for your heart: study.* PhysOrg.com, 2009.

Pico, Michael M.D. "Digestion: How Long Does It Take?" *Mayo Clinic*, 2010: **<http://www.mayoclinic.com/health/digetive-system00896>**.

"Protect Yourself from the Damaging Effects of Radiation." *Live Well Naturally Newsletter*, 2010: **<http://www.livewellnaturally.com/Health-and-Nutrition-Articles/Nutrition-Articles-2010/Protect-Yourself-from--Radiation-2-22-10-.html>**.

Question and Answer Guide for Starting and Growing Your Small Business. Virginia: College ofAgriculture and Life Sciences, Virginia Polytechnic Institute and State University, 2009.

Rabin, Roni Caryn. "Regimens: Eat Your Vegetables, but Not Too Many." *New York Times*, May 24, 2010.

Relfe, Stephanie. "Colon Cleanse: Natural Health for Your Intestines." *Health, Wealth, and Happiness*, **<http://www.relfe.com/colon_ cleansing.html>**.

Reynolds, Chris. "Efficacy of Wheatgrass Extract (WE) in the Treatment of a Variety of Conditions in Veterinary Practice." *Wheatgrass for Health Professionals*, July 2001: **<http://www.wheatgrassprofessionals.info/wound_healing_vet.htm>**.

Rutter, Diane Olson. "Gleanings-A Growing Concern: Hazardous Waste in Fertilizer." *Catalyst Magazine*, May 2003.

Sandoval, David. "Super Green foods: A Research Perspective." *Blender Culture.*

—. *The Green Foods Bible.* Topanga, CA: Freedom Press, 2008.

"Sea Vegetables." *World's Healthiest Foods,* <http://www.whfoods.com/genpage.php?tname-foodspice&dbid=135>.

Kevin Sedvec, Stephen Boyles. "Horse Pastures." *NDSU,* July 1993: <http://www.ag.ndsu.edu/pubs/plantsci/hay/r1062w.htm3#facts>.

Shelton, Herbert. "Fasting." *FalconBlanco,* <http://www.falconblanco.com/health/fasting.htm>.

Shermer, Michael. "Wheatgrass Juice and Folk Medicine." *Scientific American,* August: 2008.

Shetty, Priya. "Integrating Modern and Traditional Medicine: Facts and Figures." *Science and Development Network,* June 30, 2010: <http://www.scidev.net/en.features/integrating-modern-and-traditional-medicine-facts-and-figures.html>.

Singer, Natasha. "Children's Tylenol and Other Drugs Recalled." *New York Times,* May 2010: <http://www.nytimes.com/2010/05/02/business/02drug.html?_r=1>.

Smith, Li. *Wheatgrass Superfood for a New Millennium.* Danbury, CT: Vital Health Publishing, 2000.

"Smoothies, Lollipops, and the Myths of Wheatgrass." *Science-based Parenting,* May 2008: <http://sciencebasedparenting.com/2008/05/20/smoothies-lollipops-and-the-myths-of-wheatgrass/>.

"Spirulina's Nutritional Analysis." *Natural Ways to Health* <http://www.naturalways.com/spirulina-analysis.htm>.

"Sprouting Seed Info Center." *Sprout People* <http://www.sproutpeople.com/seeds.html>.

"Starting a Wheatgrass Farm." *StartupBizHub,* <http://www.startupbizhub.com/starting-a-wheatgrass-farm.htm>.

"Super Nuts Super Seeds." *Nature's Health Foods* <http://www.natureshealthfoods.com/nuts.html>.

Taylor, Leslie. "Differences and Similarities of Drugs and Medicinal Plants." *The Healing Power of Rainforest Herbs,* Chapter 2. Garden City Park, NY: Square One Publishers, Inc., 2005.

"The Amazing Acai Berry." *Supreme Health* <http://www.supremehealth.com/the-amazing-acai-berry.html>.

"The Dangers of Fasting." *Health Medical Articles,* December 2008: **<http://www.healthmedicalarticles.com/the-dangers-of-fasting/>**.

"The Healing Power of Juicing." *Journal of Applied Sciences,* Dr. Foster's Essentials: **<http://www.drfostersessentials.com/>**.

"The Healing Power of Juicing." *Dr. Foster's Essentials* **<http://www.drfostersessentials.com/store/forum_access.php>**.

"The Importance of Your Body's pH Balance." *The Wolfe Clinic,* 2007: **<http://www.thewolfeclinic.com/phbalancearticle.html>**.

The U.S. Department of Agriculture. **<http://www.mypyramid.gov/pyramid/kernal. html>**.

Tibbetts, Jim. "Parkinsons, Alzheimers." Six Sigma Nutrition, **<http://www.jimtibbetts.com/Parkinsons__Alzheimers_350U.html>**.

"Tips on Cooking Your Pet a Home-cooked Meal." *Medical News Today,* April 6, 2007: **<http://www.medicalnewstoday.com/articles/67288.php>**.

"Vanishing Civilization of the Maya." *Worldwide Story,* 2009: **<http://www. mahafatna.com/php/2009/11/maya-aztecs-inca-inuit-before-columbus/>**.

"Vitamin B9 (Folic Acid)." *University of Maryland Medical Center* **<http://www.umm.edu/altmed/articles/vitamin-b9-000338.htm>**.

Wagoner, Peggy, Anne Schauer. "Intermediate Wheatgrass as a Perennial Grain Crop." *Center for New Crops and Pant Products,* February 14, 1997: **<http://www.hort.purdue.edu/newcrop/proceedings1990/v1-143.html>**.

Wardrop, Murray. "Popeye Encourages Children to Eat More Vegetables, Claims Study." *Telegraph.co.uk,* August 8, 2010: **<http://www.telegraph.co.uk/science/ science-news/7933292/Popeye-encourages-children-to-eat-more-vegetables- claims-study.html>**.

"'Western Diet' increases Heart Attack Risk Globally." *Journal of the American Heart Association,* October 12: 2008.

"What Causes Overweight and Obesity." *National Heart, Lung, and Blood Institute* **<http://www.nhlbi.nih.gov/health/dci/Diseases/obe/obe_causes.html>**.

"What Exactly Are Carbohydrates?" *Help with Cooking,* 2010: **<http://www.helpwithcooking.com/nutrition-information/carbohydrates.html>**.

"What is Fasting?" Where God Builds Disciples, **<http://www.wgbd.org/fasting. html>**.

"What is Wheatgrass?" Mama Earth, <http://mammaearth.com/green-superfood/wheatgrass-powder-120g/prod_34.html>.

"What's Really in Pet Food." Born Free USA, May 2007: <http://www.bornfreeusa.org/facts.php?more=1&p=359>.

"Wheat." Baking Industry Research Trust <http://www.bakeinfo.co.nz/school/school_info/wheat.php#wheatgrain>.

"Wheat Grass." *GreenBarleyNZ.com*, <http://www.greenbarleynz.com/wheat_grass.htm>.

"Wheatgrass Healthy for the Body and the Bank Account" Landline <http://www.abc.net.au/landline/stories/s689970.htm>.

"Wheatgrass Madness." Skeptico, <http://skeptico.blogs.com/skeptico/2005/04/wheatgrass_ madn.html>: April 22, 2005.

"Whole Wheat." World's Healthiest Foods <http://www.whfoods.com/genpage/php?tname=foodspice&dbid=66>.

"Whole Wheat." World's Healthiest Foods, <http://whfoods.org/genpage.php?tname=dailytip&dbid=297&utm_source=bulletin_clic>.

"Why Do My Plants Need So Much Water?" Lansing State Journal, September 21, 1994: <http://www.pa.msu.edu/sciencet/ask_st/092194.html>.

Wigmore, Ann. "My Life Story." Dr. Ann Wigmore's Living Raw Living Foods Lifestyle, <http://annwigmore.com/dr-ann-autobiography.html>.

—. *The Hippocrates Diet.* Avery Publishing Group, 1984.

—. *The Wheatgrass Book.* Avery Publishing Group, 1985.

—. *Why Suffer?* Union City, MI: Creative Health Institute, 1985.

Woods, Marcia. "The Great Wheatgrass Bake-off — Used in bread, cookies and muffins." CBS Interactive Business Network, July <http://findarticles.com/p/articles/mi_m3741/is_n7_v39/ai_11183400/>, 1991.

Wylde, Bryce. "Wheat Grass." <http://www.alive.com/4906a12a2.php?subject bread cramb=7>.

*T*hough born in the United States, Loraine R. Dégraff considers herself "international" due to her military family background. Her father's assignments led the family through the states and overseas. She is a Duke University graduate and a recipient of a master's degree in graphic design from Pratt Institute. Pursuing a childhood dream of a writing career earned her an advanced diploma from the Institute of Children's Literature in West Redding, Connecticut. Dégraff currently lives in New York with her husband and five children, regularly augmenting her writing portfolio, which consists of several musical dramas, business and travel guides, children's stories, poems, and numerous articles.

Based on her interest in the human body and its ability to heal itself, Dégraff turned her writing focus to the area of alternative health. Her knowledge in this area, obtained through extensive research and hands-on experience growing and preparing organic herbs and produce beneficial to the body, laid a foundation for the writing of *The Complete Guide to Growing and Using Wheatgrass*. Dégraff believes individuals can make better decisions for their personal health if they are better informed of the choices available to them. For more information about Dégraff and her work, visit **www .lorainedegraff.com**.

"Natural forces within us are the true healers of disease."

~ Hippocrates

INDEX